Education, Identity and Women Religious, 1800–1950

This book brings together the work of eleven leading international scholars to map the contribution of teaching Sisters, who provided schooling to hundreds of thousands of children, globally, from 1800 to 1950. The volume represents research that draws on several theoretical approaches and methodologies. It engages with feminist discourses, social history, oral history, visual culture, post-colonial studies and the concept of transnationalism, to provide new insights into the work of Sisters in education.

Making a unique contribution to the field, chapters offer an interrogation of historical sources as well as fresh interpretations of findings, challenging assumptions. Compelling narratives from the USA, Canada, New Zealand, Africa, Australia, South East Asia, France, the UK, Italy and Ireland contribute to what is a most important exploration of the contribution of the women religious by mapping and contextualizing their work.

Education, Identity and Women Religious, 1800–1950: Convents, classrooms and colleges will appeal to academics, researchers and postgraduate students in the fields of social history, women's history, the history of education, Catholic education, gender studies and international education.

Deirdre Raftery is Chair of Research in the School of Education, University College Dublin, Ireland, and a Fellow of the Royal Historical Society, UK.

Elizabeth M. Smyth is Professor and Vice Dean in the School of Graduate Studies, University of Toronto, Canada.

Routledge Research in Education

For a complete list of titles in this series, please visit www.routledge.com.

127 **Refugee Women, Representation and Education**
Creating a discourse of self-authorship and potential
Melinda McPherson

128 **Organizational Citizenship Behavior in Schools**
Examining the impact and opportunities within educational systems
Anit Somech and Izhar Oplatka

129 **The Age of STEM**
Educational policy and practice across the world in Science, Technology, Engineering and Mathematics
Edited by Brigid Freeman, Simon Marginson and Russell Tytler

130 **Mainstreams, Margins and the Spaces In-between**
New possibilities for education research
Edited by Karen Trimmer, Ali Black and Stewart Riddle

131 **Arts-based and Contemplative Practices in Research and Teaching**
Honoring presence
Edited by Susan Walsh, Barbara Bickel and Carl Leggo

132 **Interrogating Critical Pedagogy**
The voices of educators of color in the movement
Edited by Pierre Wilbert Orelus and Rochelle Brock

133 **My School**
Listening to parents, teachers and students from a disadvantaged educational setting
Lesley Scanlon

134 **Education, Nature, and Society**
Stephen Gough

135 **Learning Technologies and the Body**
Integration and implementation in formal and informal learning environments
Edited by Victor Lee

136 **Landscapes of Specific Literacies in Contemporary Society**
Exploring a social model of literacy
Edited by Vicky Duckworth and Gordon Ade-Ojo

137 **The Education of Radical Democracy**
Sarah S. Amsler

138 **Aristotelian Character Education**
Kristján Kristjánsson

139 **Performing Kamishibai**
Tara McGowan

140 **Educating Adolescent Girls around the Globe**
Edited by Sandra L. Stacki and Supriya Baily

141 **Quality Teaching and the Capability Approach**
Evaluating the work and governance of women teachers in rural Sub-Saharan Africa
Alison Buckler

142 **Using Narrative Inquiry for Educational Research in the Asia Pacific**
Edited by Sheila Trahar and Wai Ming Yu

143 **The Hidden Role of Software in Educational Research**
Policy to practice
Tom Liam Lynch

144 **Education, Leadership and Islam**
Theories, discourses and practices from an Islamic perspective
Saeeda Shah

145 **English Language Teacher Education in Chile**
A cultural historical activity theory perspective
Malba Barahona

146 **Navigating Model Minority Stereotypes**
Asian Indian youth in South Asian diaspora
Rupam Saran

147 **Evidence-based Practice in Education**
Functions of evidence and causal presuppositions
Tone Kvernbekk

148 **A New Vision of Liberal Education**
The good of the unexamined life
Alistair Miller

149 **Transatlantic Reflections on the Practice-Based PhD in Fine Art**
Jessica B. Schwarzenbach and Paul M. W. Hackett

150 **Drama and Social Justice**
Theory, research and practice in international contexts
Edited by Kelly Freebody and Michael Finneran

151 **Education, Identity and Women Religious, 1800–1950**
Convents, classrooms and colleges
Edited by Deirdre Raftery and Elizabeth Smyth

152 **School Health Education in Changing Times**
Curriculum, pedagogies and partnerships
Deana Leahy, Lisette Burrows, Louise McCuaig, Jan Wright and Dawn Penney

Education, Identity and Women Religious, 1800–1950

Convents, classrooms and colleges

Edited by Deirdre Raftery and
Elizabeth M. Smyth

LONDON AND NEW YORK

First published 2016
by Routledge
2 Park Square, Milton Park, Abingdon, Oxon OX14 4RN

and by Routledge
711 Third Avenue, New York, NY 10017

Routledge is an imprint of the Taylor & Francis Group, an informa business

© 2016 Deirdre Raftery & Elizabeth M. Smyth

The right of the editors to be identified as the authors of the editorial material, and of the authors for their individual chapters, has been asserted in accordance with sections 77 and 78 of the Copyright, Designs and Patents Act 1988.

All rights reserved. No part of this book may be reprinted or reproduced or utilized in any form or by any electronic, mechanical or other means, now known or hereafter invented, including photocopying and recording, or in any information storage or retrieval system, without permission in writing from the publishers.

Trademark notice: Product or corporate names may be trademarks or registered trademarks, and are used only for identification and explanation without intent to infringe.

British Library Cataloguing in Publication Data
A catalogue record for this book is available from the British Library

Library of Congress Cataloging in Publication Data
Education, identity and women religious, 1800–1950 : convents, classrooms and colleges / edited by Deirdre Raftery and Elizabeth Smyth.
  pages cm
Includes bibliographical references and index.
1. Nuns as teachers–History–19th century. 2. Nuns as teachers–History–20th century. 3. Catholic Church–Education–History–19th century.
4. Catholic Church–Education–History–20th century. 5. Catholic schools–History–19th century. 6. Church schools–History–20th century.
I. Raftery, Deirdre. II. Smyth, Elizabeth M. (Elizabeth Marian), 1954–
LC490.E48 2016
371.071'2–dc23   2015016303

ISBN: 978-1-138-92354-6 (hbk)
ISBN: 978-1-315-68503-8 (ebk)

Typeset in Galliard
by Out of House Publishing

Printed and bound by CPI Group (UK) Ltd, Croydon, CR0 4YY

We dedicate this book to congregations of women religious everywhere, past and present, whose commitment to education has changed lives, especially the lives of girls and women.

Deirdre Raftery and Elizabeth M. Smyth

Contents

List of contributors   xi
Foreword by Carmen M. Mangion   xvi
List of abbreviations   xviii

Introduction   1
DEIRDRE RAFTERY AND ELIZABETH M. SMYTH

1   Coming to an edge in history: writing the history of women religious and the critique of feminism   6
PHIL KILROY

2   From Kerry to Katong: transnational influences in convent and novitiate life for the Sisters of the Infant Jesus, *c.* 1908–1950   31
DEIRDRE RAFTERY

3   Continuity and change within the Toronto Convent Academies of the Sisters of St Joseph and the Loretto Sisters, 1847–1950   43
ELIZABETH M. SMYTH

4   Sister-physicians, education, and mission in the mid-twentieth-century   60
BARBRA MANN WALL

5   Sisters as teachers in nineteenth-century Ireland: the Presentation Order   77
CATHERINE NOWLAN-ROEBUCK

6	Sisters and the creation of American Catholic identities MARGARET SUSAN THOMPSON	99
7	'Have your children got leave to speak?': the teacher training of New Zealand Dominican Sisters, 1871–1965 JENNY COLLINS	117
8	Great changes, increased demands: education, teacher training and the Irish Presentation Sisters LOUISE O'REILLY	135
9	The situational dimension of the educational apostolate and the configuration of the learner as a cultural and political subject: the case of the Sisters of Our Lady of the Missions in the Canadian Prairies ROSA BRUNO-JOFRÉ	160
10	A path to perfection: translations from French by Catholic women religious in nineteenth-century Ireland MICHÈLE MILAN	183
11	Loreto education in Australia: the pioneering influence of Mother Gonzaga Barry JANE KELLY	199
	Index	215

Contributors

Rosa Bruno-Jofré is Professor and former Dean (2000–10) of the Faculty of Education, cross-appointed to the Department of History, Faculty of Arts, Queen's University, Canada. She is the author of, among other books, *The Missionary Oblate Sisters: Vision and Vision* (Mc Gill-Queen's University Press). Her research is funded by the Social Sciences and Humanities Research Council of Canada. She is working on the history of the Canadian Province of the Religieuses de Notre Dame des Missions and on the Catholic dimension of processes of educationalization. She has published in major journals including *Educational Theory, Hispania sacra, Paedagogica historica, Catholic Historical Review, Bordon, Bildungsgeschichte: International Journal of Historiography* and others.

Jenny Collins is an Adjunct Professor at the Department of Education, Unitec Institute of Technology, Auckland, New Zealand where she teaches in postgraduate education programmes. She is the New Zealand editor for the online Dictionary of Educational History of Australia and New Zealand (DEHANZ). Her research interests include the academic and professional lives of women, international education, and the history of Catholic education. She has published widely in international journals in these areas. She has also coauthored a book, *Historic Portraits of Women Home Scientists: The University of New Zealand, 1911–1947* (2011), with Professor Tanya Fitzgerald. She is currently researching the educational contribution of Catholic Sisters in New Zealand.

Jane Kelly, having taught in secondary schools in Melbourne and Sydney, was appointed Principal of a Loreto Secondary College in Melbourne for six years, after which time she completed studies in theology at Heythrop College in London. Returning to Australia she was appointed Head of St Mary's College, University of Melbourne (1981–97), and since then has held a number of leadership roles in the Australian province. An historian by training, she was asked in 2004 to initiate and coordinate a process involving the commissioning of a narrative history of the order which resulted, in 2009, in the publication of *Loreto in Australia* by Mary Ryllis

Clark (University of New South Wales Press). In the following year, Jane was commissioned by the province to do further research on the founding Loreto Superior in Australia, Gonzaga Barry. Her interest is in exploring Gonzaga Barry through her writings – most particularly through her letters, concentrating on Barry's worldwide correspondence with some of her Sisters, and their shared desire to re-engage with their founding vision and to organize the structure and mission of all Mary Ward women differently.

Phil Kilroy is a Research Associate in Trinity College Dublin and is a member of the Society of the Sacred Heart. She received her doctorate in history in Trinity College Dublin. She published *Protestant Dissent and Controversy in Ireland 1660–1714* (Cork University Press, 1994) and continues to write on religious dissent and non-conformity in seventeenth-century Ireland. She also researches the history of women in Europe from 1600 to 1900, and in recent years has focussed on the life of Madeleine Sophie Barat (1779–1865), the founder of the Society of the Sacred Heart. In 2000 she published a biography of Barat, *Madeleine Sophie Barat: A Life* (Cork University Press, 2000), which has also appeared in French, Spanish, Polish, Japanese and Korean. Phil Kilroy has presented the biography in most parts of the world. In 2012 she published *The Society of the Sacred Heart in Nineteenth-Century France, 1800–1865* (Cork University Press), in response to the reflections and questions generated by the biography and posed by members of the Society of the Sacred Heart and the general public. Phil Kilroy is currently researching the biography of Marie de la Croix (1792–1879), a founding companion of Madeleine Sophie Barat. She also is completing a study of puritan women in seventeenth-century Ireland.

Carmen M. Mangion is Lecturer in Modern History in the Department of History, Classics and Archaeology, Birkbeck, University of London. She is the author of *Contested Identities: Catholic women religious in nineteenth-century England and Wales* (Manchester University Press, 2008) and the editor with Laurence Lux-Sterritt of *Gender, Catholicism and Spirituality: Women and the Roman Catholic Church in Britain and Europe, 1200–1900* (2010). Her articles on the history of women religious have appeared in many journals and edited collections including the *Women's History Review, History of Education and Continuity and Change*.

Michèle Milan's main area of research and publication is in translation history, with particular emphasis on the production, publishing and reception of translations in nineteenth-century Ireland. She also specializes in the compilation of bio-bibliographical data on translators. She holds a Ph.D. in translation history from Dublin City University. Supervised by Professor Michael Cronin, her doctoral thesis explored Franco-Irish translation relationships in nineteenth-century Ireland. Her current research topics include translation in the *Nation* newspaper, translation of poetry and song, travel and translation, religious translation, and Irish women translators.

Catherine Nowlan-Roebuck is a primary school teacher in a large Dublin school. At University College Dublin she completed a Ph.D. in the history of education, which examined the involvement of the Presentation Sisters in Irish education during the nineteenth-century. She has contributed articles to publications such as *History of Education*, and has a chapter in the recent book *Educating Ireland: Schooling and Social Change, 1700–2000*, edited by Deirdre Raftery and Karin Fischer (2014).

Louise O'Reilly received her Ph.D. in history in 2009 from the National University of Ireland, Maynooth, with a thesis titled 'The History of the Irish Presentation Sisters in the Twentieth Century, from Autonomy to Union'. As the first lay woman to carry out this type of study on the Presentation Congregation, she conducted extensive research in archives throughout Ireland, England and Rome. Her recently published book is *The Impact of Vatican II on Women Religious: Case Study of the Union of Irish Presentation Sisters* (Cambridge Scholars Press, 2013). Her research interests are in the area of the life of women religious in the twentieth-century, in particular in the post-Vatican period. She is a member of the Historians of Women Religious of Britain and Ireland (HWRBI). O'Reilly is currently working as archivist and researcher for religious congregations in Ireland, and she is researching and writing a history of Dom. Eugene Boylan, OCSO.

Deirdre Raftery is a historian of education at University College Dublin, and a Visiting Fellow, University of Southampton (2015–16). She has received a Fulbright award to continue her research on women religious at Boston College in 2016. Deirdre earned her Ph.D. at Trinity College Dublin, and she is an elected Fellow of the Royal Historical Society. She was Fellow at the University of Oxford in 2010, and a Visiting Research Associate at the University of Cambridge in 2005. Her current research on women religious has received awards from the Cushwa Centre (University of Notre Dame), the Canada Ireland Foundation and the Irish Research Council. She recently completed five years as joint Editor of *History of Education* (Routledge/Taylor & Francis). Publications include: *Women and Learning in English Writing, 1600–1900* (Four Courts Press, 1996) and, jointly, *Educating Ireland: Schooling and Society, 1700–2000* (Irish Academic Press, 2014); *History of Education: Themes and Perspectives* (Routledge, 2013); *Gender Balance and Gender Bias in Education: International Perspectives* (Routledge, 2011); *Infant Jesus Sisters Ireland, 1909–2009: The Voyage Out* (Infant Jesus Sisters Centenary Committee/Origin, 2009); *Female*

Education in Ireland, 1700–1900: Minerva or Madonna (Frank Cass and Irish Academic Press, 2009); and *Emily Davies: Collected Letters, 1861–1875* (University Press of Virginia, 2003).

Elizabeth M. Smyth is Professor of Curriculum Teaching and Learning (CTL) and Vice Dean at the School of Graduate Studies, University of Toronto. Her recent funded research projects include: *Leading Sisters, Changing Times: Women Religious in English Canada in the Post Vatican II World* (principal investigator); *Disciplining Academics: The Tenure Process in Social Science*; and *The State of the Consecrated Life in Contemporary Canada* (collaborating investigator). She is a member of the University of Toronto Governing Council, a Senior Fellow of Massey College and a Fellow of the University of St Michael's College. She was the recipient of the George Edward Clerk Award for outstanding contribution to Canadian religious history and the Lifetime Achievement Award from the History of Women Religious Network. With Tanya Fitzgerald, she is the coeditor of *Women Educators, Leaders and Activists: Educational Lives and Networks 1900–1960* (Palgrave Macmillan, 2014).

Margaret Susan Thompson is Associate Professor of History at Syracuse University, New York, where she is a Senior Research Fellow in the Campbell Institute of Public Affairs, and where she also holds appointments in political science, religion, and women's and gender studies. She received her A.B. from Smith College, and her M.A. and Ph.D. from the University of Wisconsin-Madison. She served as an American Political Science Association Congressional Fellow, and has written extensively on the history of US legislative behaviour (including 'The "Spider Web": Congress and Lobbying in the Age of Grant' [Cornell University Press]). Most of her recent work has been on the history of American Catholic women religious, on which she has spoken and published extensively. Recent publications include 'Adaptation and Professionalisation: Challenges for Teaching Sisters in a Pluralistic Nineteenth-Century America', *Paedagogica historica*, 49:4 (2013); 'The More Things Change, the More They Stay the Same: Historical Context for Current Tensions in US Women's Religious Life', *Magistra*, 19: 2 (2013); and 'Sisters' History Is Women's History: The American Context', *Journal of Women's History*, 26:4 (2014). She also has recorded an eighteen-lecture series on the history of women religious in the United States for NowYouKnowMedia. Her research has been supported by grants from, among others, the Rockefeller Foundation, the National Endowment for the Humanities, and the Cushwa Center for the Study of American Catholicism (University of Notre Dame).

Barbra Mann Wall is Thomas A. Saunders III Professor in Nursing at the University of Virginia School of Nursing. She received her B.S.N. from the University of Texas at Austin, her M.S. in nursing from Texas Woman's University, and a Ph.D. in history from the University of Notre Dame. She has published *Unlikely Entrepreneurs: Catholic Sisters and the Hospital Marketplace, 1865–1925* (Ohio State University Press, 2005); and *American Catholic Hospitals: A Century of Changing Markets and Missions* (Rutgers University Press, 2011). Her new book, published by Rutgers University Press in September 2015, is *Into Africa: A Transnational History of Catholic Medical Missions and Social Change*.

Foreword

Carmen M. Mangion
Birkbeck College, University of London

This edited collection is a most welcome outcome of the tenth annual conference on the History of Women Religious of Britain and Ireland (H-WRBI). This group, founded by Dr Caroline Bowden and myself in 2002 with the very first conference held at St Mary's University, Twickenham, aims at encouraging further research into the history of women religious. It is staffed by volunteers and operates virtually through a listserv of now over 250 worldwide members. The listserv harnesses the expertise of scholars, archivists, religious Sisters, students and others through their willingness to share their knowledge (both personal and academic) of this growing historiography. The annual conference brings some list members and newcomers together to hear the latest in new scholarship.

Deirdre Raftery and Elizabeth M. Smyth have had the laborious task of shepherding and editing this collection of chapters around the theme of education. Most were originally articles which had their first airing at the H-WRBI annual conference, but others were specially commissioned and the result is the work of an impressive array of international scholars that study women religious in the missions, as well as in Ireland, the United States, Canada, New Zealand and Australia. What is abundantly clear from all the chapters is that the educational reach of women religious was not contained rigidly within national borders but spilled into and out of various locations all over the world, as one would expect of such transnational religious institutes. This volume is also a response (hopefully one of many) to the historiographical text by Bart Hellinckx, Frank Simon and Marc Depaepe, *The Forgotten Contribution of the Teaching Sisters* (2009), which offered a thorough summary of the 'limited scholarly attention' paid to the role women religious played in schooling in the nineteenth and twentieth centuries.

This collection begins, as the conference did, with Phil Kilroy's introduction to the rich and complex lives of women, particularly women religious, in the Roman Catholic Church over the longue durée. Panoramic, passionate and emphatic, it does not always make for comfortable reading. It gives its readers much to think through, and vigorously discuss.

The other ten chapters are empirically rich and offer an array of historical approaches with which to interrogate material from the archives. Deirdre Raftery uses the theoretical lens of transnationalism to examine how the Sisters transmitted educational pedagogy as well as the excitement of the missions to Irish schoolgirls. Elizabeth M. Smyth employs the transnational lens to a different end, using it to link the continuity and change of the educational endeavours of two Canadian women's congregations. Barbra Mann Wall takes us into the mission field with her analysis of the education of Catholic Sister-physicians, surgeons and obstetricians, and illustrates how they merged their biomedical knowledge and therapeutics with their spiritual mission. Rosa Bruno-Jofré dissects one Canadian missionary congregation's understanding of education within an ecclesiocentric model of mission, considering the meanings, and cultural and political practices, that resulted. Margaret Susan Thompson suggests the diverse national backgrounds of the religious Sisters in the United States provided powerful challenges for those living within these multi-ethnic communities and are important to dissect in order to better understand the contributions of teaching Sisters to the education of the diverse student bodies they served. We travel to the Antipodes with Jenny Collins, who outlines the changing training regimen of a New Zealand Sister-teacher from 1871 to 1965, noting the key transitions in Sister teacher training. Jane Kelly examines Gonzaga Barry's contribution to Catholic education in Australia. Catherine Nowlan-Roebuck and Louise O'Reilly address the complicated position of Presentation Sisters teaching in Ireland. Nowlan-Roebuck highlights the tensions between their belief in the divine calling of their teaching vocation and the nature of the National System, which was becoming more secular. O'Reilly points to the obstacles arising from the autonomy of the individual houses and the resistance of the Sisters to amalgamation and formal teacher training. Michèle Milan, in her novel take on Catholic education, scrutinizes the dissemination of ascetical texts, introducing her reader to translation history. Her chapter brings us back, again, to the transnational links among religious congregations. These texts were translated and became a part of the 'network of religious and literary exchanges'.

Historians of education will find this edited collection a fine addition to the growing critical scholarship of education and the history of women religious. And yet, these chapters have an even broader remit and will feed the thinking of scholars who wish to examine the imbrication of gender and religion with social and cultural change.

Abbreviations

ACDA	Auckland Catholic Diocesan Archives
AL	autograph letter
ANZDS	Archives of the New Zealand Dominican Sisters
ASCRSI	Archives of the Sacred Congregation for Religious and Secular Institutes
BPP	British Parliamentary Papers
BVM	Sisters of Charity of the Blessed Virgin Mary
CPSHSB	Centre du Patrimoine, Société Historique de Saint-Boniface, St Boniface, Manitoba
CSJ	Congregation of the Sisters of St Joseph
CRC	Canadian Religious Conference
DDA	Dublin Diocesan Archives (Ireland)
FDA	*The Field Day Anthology of Irish Writing*
GHAD	George's Hill Archives Dublin
HL	Hocken Library (University of Otago)
HWRBI	History of Women Religious of Britain and Ireland
IBVM	Institute of the Blessed Virgin Mary
IHM	Servants of the Immaculate Heart of Mary
KDA	Kerry Diocesan Archives (Ireland)
KLDA	Kildare Leighlin Diocesan Archive
LCWR	Leadership Conference of Women Religious
MMM	Medical Missionaries of Mary
MMMA	Medical Missionaries of Mary Archives
MMS	Medical Mission Sisters
MMSA	Archives of the Medical Mission Sisters
MS	manuscript
NAI	National Archives of Ireland
n.d.	no date
n.p.	no page
OLM	Sisters of Charity of Our Lady of Mercy (South Carolina)
OP	Order of Preachers (Dominican)
PBVM	Presentation of the Blessed Virgin Mary

PCC	Presentation Convent Clondalkin
PCG	Presentation Convent Galway
PCL	Presentation Convent Limerick
PCT	Presentation Convent Thurles
PCWx	Presentation Convent Wexford
RNDM	Religieuses de Notre Dame des Missions
RNDMUK	Sisters of Our Lady of the Missions, Sturry, UK
RSCJ	Religious of the Sacred Heart of Jesus
SND	Sisters of Notre Dame de Namur
SSHA	Sisters of the Sacred Heart Archives (Auckland)
SSJ-TOSF	Sisters of St Joseph of the Third Order of St Francis
USMCA	University of St Michael's College Archives (Toronto)
WMC	Woman's Medical College (Pennsylvania)

Introduction

Deirdre Raftery and Elizabeth M. Smyth

For much of the nineteenth and early twentieth centuries, thousands of Catholic institutions of education were closely identified with women religious. Sisters founded schools, colleges and major teaching hospitals, and ran them with other women religious, and they often went unpaid for their labours. The significance of this work has not been fully explored. This is partly because these women operated within the male-dominated institution that is the Roman Catholic Church, which – as we shall see in this volume – managed to appropriate much of the kudos for the labour of women religious. It is also because Sisters operated at a remove from society, living within convents, wearing distinctive habits, and showing a kind of humility that does not demand public attention. Yet another reason why women religious have been side-lined in history until very recently, is that scholars simply did not turn their attention to the archival holdings of congregations. Indeed, sometimes scholars were not welcome in convents, which were, after all, the private homes of the Sisters. There has been a marked shift across the last fifteen years, with ever-increasing numbers of religious orders welcoming scholars into their archives. Relationships of trust have been developed between religious and historians, without ever compromising the academic independence of scholars. This volume represents work by lay scholars and also by scholars who are themselves women religious. They have looked at gaps in the historical narrative and found that Sisters – tens of thousands of Sisters – need to be woven into the fabric of this narrative.

Perhaps the most pressing question at the start of this volume is: why did the hierarchical Catholic Church, so highly dependent on the labour of women religious for the success of its enterprises in education, social service and health-care, render those women voiceless for centuries? This is the question that lies at the heart of the first chapter. To formulate a theoretical and practical response, Phil Kilroy situates the study of women religious within the fields of women's history, gender studies, feminist analysis and contemporary theology. Kilroy, a biographer of St Madeleine Sophie Barat, the founder of the Society of the Sacred Heart (RSCJ), grapples with the theoretical and methodological issues encountered in the study of women religious: hagiography, incomplete and edited sources, limited access to records housed in private archives, and active resistance to the articulation of the complex realities inherent in studying the human condition. Her chapter is a primer for present and future scholars of women religious. She guides the reader through two millennia of gender-based tensions within Christian thought, beginning with the portrayal of Eve as 'Christ slayer'. She elaborates on discourses around the virgin/whore dichotomy; the rise of women religious leaders in the Middle Ages; the suppression of convents and monastic life, and the eventual reform and re-growth of active, rather than contemplative, forms of religious life. Kilroy ends the chapter with a compelling analysis of the intersection of the reforms of the Second Vatican Council with the discourses and practices of feminism, before challenging readers to speculate on what may be the future of the vowed life.

Chapter 2 provides the first of several case studies of women religious in convents, classrooms and colleges across the globe. Here, Deirdre Raftery does a close analysis of sources at one convent, Drishane, situated on the Kerry–Cork border, in Ireland. Drawing on both school and novitiate records, she explores how the Infant Jesus Sisters, an order founded in seventeenth-century France, looked to Ireland to help them meet growing international demands to open more of their schools. She outlines how this order made strategic decisions to establish a foundation at Drishane, in the hope of providing much-needed teaching Sisters for their schools in Malaysia, Singapore and Japan. Situating her study in transnational historiography, Raftery also uses oral histories to demonstrate the subtle but sustained focus on mission activities in both the convent school and the novitiate, which influenced the pupils and the Sisters-in-formation. She concludes by challenging historians of women religious to employ transnational analytical tools as a means to theorize more effectively the missionary experience.

In Chapter 3, Elizabeth M. Smyth explores the theme of continuity and change in her analysis of two European congregations, one Irish and one French, which established women's colleges at the University of Toronto. Using a transnational framework, Smyth examines how the Irish Institute of the Blessed Virgin Mary (the Loretto Sisters: IBVM) and the French Congregation of the Sisters of St Joseph (CSJ), became independent of their European roots and developed identities that reflected the nascent English Canadian Roman Catholic Church. Smyth argues that both communities invested heavily in the education of their Sisters to ensure that they met the state-determined demands for teacher certification, thereby enabling their pupils to be competitive applicants to professional schools, and she concludes that their women's colleges furthered the goal of developing a Catholic professional class. Smyth's chapter suggests the need for further study to determine the extent to which professional needs trumped gender in the Catholic colleges at the University of Toronto.

In Chapter 4, Barbra Mann Wall presents a different cohort of women religious: Sister-physicians. She situates the late emergence of Sister-physicians in the medical profession, explaining how congregations began to support their members in obtaining specialized medical education, following the lifting of the papal ban on Sisters engaging in surgery and obstetrics. She also traces the evolution of congregations established specifically for the purposes of providing nursing and medical services. Mann Wall documents the experience of some of the pioneering Sister-physicians at the Women's Medical College (WMC) in Philadelphia, and the tensions that these women experienced as physicians, women religious and missionary workers. She concludes with an analysis of Sister-physicians' experience of their vows of poverty, chastity and obedience.

The Presentation Order (PBVM), a congregation founded in Ireland by Nano Nagle, is the subject of Chapter 5. Catherine Nowlan-Roebuck uses a series of core documents to uncover how this community, dedicated to the education of girls, ran a vast network of schools. While the Presentations would become a worldwide order, this chapter concerns itself with the earliest expression of Presentation schooling, clearly rooted in the ideas of Nano Nagle. The activity of the order, which managed to operate its schools within a state-funded (non-denominational) national school system, is explored in detail. Nowlan-Roebuck's study also presents to researchers a model for delving into the hidden world of classroom instruction, in order to better understand the agency of women religious who were teachers.

While many chapters in the collection show how external forces influenced the shifting identities of women religious, Margaret Susan Thompson looks outwards from her sources, so to speak, and explores how Sisters shaped American Catholic identities. Chapter 6 acknowledges the extent to which the American parochial schools were staffed by culturally, ethnically and linguistically diverse congregations of European Sisters. Thompson also provides an important analysis of congregational records and the published histories of congregations of women religious in the United States. She concludes that women religious effectively preserved the faith of the immigrant communities they served but that, in that service, they were also challenged by a contested concept: what did 'community' mean in the United States?

In Chapter 7, Jenny Collins tackles the question of how women religious were trained to become full members of teaching communities. Through the use of oral histories and archival document analysis, Collins studies how the Dominican (OP) order in New Zealand formed their novices into teaching Sisters. Her sources enable her to determine not only what was taught to the teachers-in-training, but also how the Sisters were themselves taught. In particular, she examines the values and attitudes that were imparted as part of the formation process. Collins concludes with a study of Loreto Hall, Auckland, a teacher-training college administered by the RSCJ. Collins finds that over its thirty-five-year history, the majority of its graduates were members of various religious orders. There is a need for comparative studies on higher education institutions for Sisters, many of which existed around the globe.

Chapter 8 provides a companion chapter to the earlier work of Nowlan-Roebuck, as it follows the Presentation Sisters (PBVM) into the twentieth-century, though here the focus is on the experience of the Sisters, rather than on the education they provided. In the chapter, Louise O'Reilly looks at tensions between the demands for teacher formation and the demands of the organizational structures of the community. Both created opportunities as well as challenges. She raises a question: did the struggle around autonomy and centralization help or hinder PBVM strategies for teacher training? Additionally, O'Reilly's chapter powerfully illustrates tensions between bishops and the women religious, and she documents how ecclesiastical rules and directives were sometimes openly – and indeed courageously – ignored.

Rosa Bruno-Jofré presents the reader with another example of tensions between women religious and their ecclesiastical superiors. The focus of Chapter 9 is on how members of pontifical religious orders from Lyons, France, adjusted to teaching in Canadian schools for Franco-Manitoban pupils, and to teaching aboriginal children on the Canadian Prairies. This chapter points out the importance of acknowledging the ethno-cultural and linguistic diversity in the North American mission fields, and clearly articulates the challenges they presented to European religious communities. The chapter is a reminder of the vast amount of analytical work that remains to be done, in order to develop a much deeper and more nuanced understanding of the education work of women religious around the globe.

Chapter 10 presents the reader with insights into the work of women religious as literary translators, rendering French works into English. Michèle Milan reminds the reader that the study of French was central to the 'female curriculum' of accomplishments, and a most necessary part of the education of any well-bred young woman. Milan focuses her studies on the translations of devotional-spiritual literature and the literature of religious life. She concludes that the study of women religious as translators is another indicator of the transnational context in which women religious lived, learned and taught.

The final chapter of the collection echoes themes from many earlier chapters. Here, Jane Kelly examines the influence of the Irish-born Mother Gonzaga Barry, a Loreto (IBVM) Sister who served as a Provincial Superior in Australia. Unlike the North American Loretto foundation studied by Elizabeth M. Smyth in Chapter 3, the Australian foundation was a province of the Irish mother-house. The challenges posed by desires for independence, not unlike those discussed earlier by Louise O'Reilly with reference to the PBVMs, surface once again in this study of the IBVMs. Kelly presents the reader with the biography of a strong-minded and immensely capable woman, similar to many other women represented in the pages of this book. Like both Smyth and Raftery in their chapters, Kelly draws upon the words of women religious themselves: Mother Gonzaga Barry's letters to her pupils sought to develop within them a sense of vocation. Further, through her extensive use of both public and private archival sources, Kelly illustrates the significant ways in which disparate sources can be drawn together to present subtle and rich understandings of complex historical events.

In conclusion, the eleven chapters in this collection lead readers on a journey that critically explores how women religious lived their professional lives, in parts of Africa, Australia, Canada, Europe, New Zealand, South East Asia and the United States. The authors reflect on the distinct stages in the lives of women religious. They study how Sisters were formed, what their vows meant in different contexts, and how the concept of vocation was communicated in schools and broader communities.

The authors use a variety of methodologies to collect their data and a number of theoretical frameworks to analyse it. While archival-based research is the most common strategy used, several of the authors delve into the realm of material culture to draw on additional sources. Significantly, several have used oral histories to supplement data retrieved from both private and public archives. Gender, feminism and transnationalism are among the theoretical optics used.

Some themes are common to several chapters. For example, tensions regularly emerged when highly competent women had to operate within structures that were overseen by a patriarchal Church, represented by bishops and priests who concerned themselves with affairs that the Sisters were already successfully managing. In several chapters, the changing ethno-cultural demographics of countries and cities provided new challenges to religious communities and their traditions. And Sisters, in many instances, are seen to have struggled with finding ways to respond appropriately to the changing needs of the times in which they lived and worked.

The authors of these chapters challenge the reader to look at the contributions that women religious made to education in schools, colleges, teaching hospitals, and in the wider constituencies they served. A vast amount of their work went unpaid, and its economic value has never been calculated. It may prove impossible for historians and economists to put a price on this labour. What scholars can do is mine the archives of religious orders; identify and critique art, music, translations and print culture created by women religious; and develop oral histories of communities while Sisters are still able to contribute. Such time-consuming and important groundwork will enable researchers to write women religious fully into the narrative of women's history, and history generally. This book represents the energies of scholars who recognize that there is much more work to be done.

Chapter 1

Coming to an edge in history
Writing the history of women religious and the critique of feminism[1]

Phil Kilroy

Introduction

The history of women religious can be studied within several contextual narratives. In this chapter the narrative is placed within the perspectives of women's and gender history, with particular reference to the history of women religious in the Roman Catholic Church in Europe and North America. This narrative forms part of the wider research of historians of women's and gender history which demonstrates how women in general were rendered invisible in the historical record, that an 'archaeology of exclusion' operated with regard to them.[2] With some notable exceptions, women were placed within the sub-narrative, the sub-text of history, in the minor role.[3] Historians of women and gender interrogate this narrative, this male model or archetype of history. Professional work of deconstruction and reconstruction of the historical record has disrupted previous, well-rehearsed narratives to the extent that radical shifts in interpretation have emerged. This historical research is supported by scholarly developments in the writing of historical biography. Biographers in particular study the interaction between the public and the private at all levels, personal, communal and institutional. These are perceived as the crossover places where major and minor narratives interact and fuller, truer pictures of individuals and their actions can be found. Until the last century these elements were largely ignored in biographical writing.[4]

Historians of women and gender show how down the centuries women have laboured within the confines of patriarchal, misogynistic societies. They were constricted in their personal lives, within the family, as single or married women, as mothers and widows, as women religious individually or as communities. Men assumed the right to control women with regard to money and property, to marriage and widowhood, single life and religious life. Undoubtedly some women fought with some success to assert their rights with regard to their property as landowners, as rulers and widows, as educators and healers. But these were exceptional, usually aristocratic, privileged women. The vast majority of women had no voice, no power, no position, and they lived in constant danger of violence and death, a condition described in early Christian Ireland by Adomnán in 697 CE in his Cáin (Law).[5]

Belief in the inferiority of women and their subordinate position to men pre-dated Christianity, but it was further deepened when the Christian Church evolved into a strongly hierarchical, clerical institution, especially after 300 CE. When patriarchal and misogynistic views were articulated within a religious context, within Christianity, by the institutional Church, by clerics, these increased anti-woman prejudices. The verdict of the Church was that all women were born inferior. They had weak minds, were led by emotions and sexual temptations, and they should be ruled and controlled by men. These judgements have had devastating effects on all women down the ages.[6]

The image of woman in Christianity

Negative, condemnatory views on women permeated the institutional Church from the earliest years of Christianity.[7] The Apostle Paul declared:

> Let a woman learn in silence with full submission. I permit no woman to teach or to have authority over a man; she is to keep silent. For Adam was formed first, then Eve. And Adam was not deceived, but the woman was deceived and became a transgressor.[8]

Tertullian (160–225 CE) saw all women as Eve, and responsible for the death of Christ:

> Do you not know that each of you is Eve? The sentence of God on your sex lives in this age; the guilt must of necessity live, too. *You* are the Devil's gateway. It was *you* who first violated the forbidden tree and broke God's Law. *You* persuaded him [Adam] whom the devil did not have the strength to attack. With what ease *you* shattered the image of God: man! Because of the death *you* deserved, the Son of God had to die.[9]

Similarly John Chrysostom:

> Yes, indeed: they are all weak and frivolous. For we are told, not that Eve alone suffered from deception, but that 'Woman' was deceived. The word 'Woman' is not to be applied to one, but to every woman. Thus all feminine nature has fallen into error.[10]

Men and women internalized these attitudes towards women and these were transmitted down the generations. An Irish eleventh-century poem reflected the views of a cleric, and expressed through the voice of a woman:

> I am the wife of Adam, Eve;
> For my transgression Jesus died;

> I stole Heaven from those I leave;
> 'Tis me they should have crucified.
>
> Dreadful was the choice I made,
> I who once a mighty queen;
> Dreadful, too, the price I paid
> Woe, my hand is still unclean!
>
> I plucked the apple from the spray
> Because of greed I could not rule;
> Even until their final day
> Women will still play the fool.
>
> Ice would not be anywhere
> Wild white winter would not be;
> There would be no hell, no fear
> And no sorrow but for me.[11]

Two centuries later Abbot Conrad of Marchtal (1226–75) expressed fears of women, of their danger to men:

> We and the whole community of canons, recognising that the wickedness of women is greater than all the other wickedness of the world, and that there is no anger like that of women, and that the poison of asps and dragons is more curable and less dangerous to men than the familiarity of women, have decreed for the safety of our souls, no less than for that of our bodies and goods, that we will on no account receive any more sisters to the increase of our perdition, but will avoid them like poisonous animals.[12]

Similar attitudes towards women were shown when English seminarians in the seventeenth-century, in a direct attack on women's bodies and sexuality, and especially on motherhood, were taught to revile the manner of their birth:

> For the manner of thy begetting is so foul that the name, nay the lightest thought of it, defiles the purest mind, so that our Blessed Saviour refused none of our miseries, but only that; and the matter so horrid, so foul, that all other dung is pleasant and grateful in respect of it; nay we dare not in discourse give it a name, for our own shame and others' offence.... I cannot imagine any prison so dark, so straight, so loathsome, as the womb of a woman, in which the child is enclosed and enwrapped ... for no less than nine whole months; so straightened and pressed, that neither hand nor foot can he stir or move; his food, the filthy menstrual blood of his mother, a thing so nasty and poisonous as that whatsoever it touches it infects, like the plague or leprosy.[13]

Such outright disdain of the processes of motherhood and birth reflected debates among theologians who wondered if woman was actually human, if she possessed a soul.[14] For example, Thomas Aquinas, the foremost theologian of the thirteenth-century, following the views of Aristotle, suggested that woman did not take part in the creation of the child but was merely the passive vehicle that brought the child to birth. Moreover, a female child was the result of a flawed process:

> For the active power in the seed of the male tends to produce something like itself, perfect in masculinity. But the procreation of the female is a result either of the debility of the active power, of some unsuitability of the material, or of some change effected by circumstances, like the south wind, for example, which is damp.[15]

Such negativity towards women was only further reinforced by the lofty position given to the Virgin Mary and the lowly one attributed to Mary Magdalene.

The Virgin Mary and Mary Magdalene

The perception of woman as Eve, the representative of evil in the world, found its polarity in the elevation of Mary, the mother of Jesus. The clerical Church placed Mary on a pedestal of unimaginable heights. She was the pure and immaculate Virgin and Mother. In the measure that woman, Eve, was reviled, the Virgin Mary was venerated and removed from the human condition. She alone was the 'immaculately conceived and conceiving', completely untouched by original sin. In effect, Mary was an archetype created by the clerical Church for its own worship, a goddess constructed by the world of patriarchy and misogyny.[16] She became the object of devotions, of hymns, of art and cathedrals, pilgrimages and liturgies down the ages. In polarity to the Virgin Mary, a composite figure of woman, Mary Magdalene the sinner, was created from three women in the Gospels: the woman who washed the feet of Jesus; Mary of Bethany; and Mary Magdalene, the first witness to the Resurrection.[17] This fiction, known as Mary Magdalene, became the clerical projection of women as evil, weak and sinful. And like the Virgin Mary, down the centuries Mary Magdalene also became, for different reasons, the object of devotions and hymns, of art and cathedrals, pilgrimages and liturgies.[18] Within the world of patriarchy and misogyny women were trapped between these two archetypes of the feminine: between Mary, the Virgin Mother, and Mary Magdalene, the sinner. Mary, the Virgin Mother, however attractive, was an unreachable model for women. Mary Magdalene, the sinner, signalled perpetual condemnation, at several levels. The body of woman was degenerate, she was a flawed being, and inferior to man and to be used as he thought fit.

Armed and justified by these theological constructions men assumed rights over women. Women's lives were firmly controlled in the family by fathers, sons, brothers, uncles and guardians, and in the institutional Church by popes, bishops and priests. An open door to shocking violence in word and deed had been created and indeed rationalized on religious grounds. In every age women have lived within the strictures of this patriarchal, misogynist world. Their experiences were largely undocumented and unacknowledged by chroniclers, unless they served to support the institutions of power in Church and in society, usually as examples of submission and humility. The archives of women religious contain vast material on the reactions of Church authorities to their initiatives and to their way of life. Until the advent of feminism and of women's and gender history, developed over the last 300 years, this situation remained unchallenged.

The impact of patriarchy and misogyny on women religious

Since the foundation of Christianity, women religious in every age have sought places and spaces where they could live their vision of the Gospel, of the following of Christ. Each community created its own narrative regarding how and why it was founded, its purpose and idealism, its rights to land and finance, and how the members wished to live within the Church and in society. Common to women religious was a life of personal and community prayer, singing of the Offices of the Church and attending the liturgy of the Mass. The culture surrounding these religious practices gave women religious access to basic education; to reading and writing; to music, especially singing; and to the decorative arts of painting, printing, sculpture, woodwork, dressmaking and embroidery. They held some endowments and dowries but tended to support themselves as much as possible economically as farmers and gardeners, as weavers and homemakers, as healers and cooks. Most communities had two ranks, that of Choir Sisters and Lay Sisters, reflecting the social norms of the time. Some communities were fully monastic and lived an enclosed life of prayer. Others were more oriented towards a visible service in society, especially in the sphere of education and health. All, however, underwent crises of reform and change, and either moved into new phases of growth or quietly disappeared, sometimes without trace.

Communities of women religious tended to have four features in common, often with different accents on one or other in any given time and place. First, they shared a common vocation and vision of life based on the following of Christ. With this as their focus they committed themselves to an agreed Rule of Life (sometimes called Constitutions), which was their commentary on and application of the Gospel to daily life. Second, communities of women religious usually acquired land and endowments (at least initially) which enabled them to live together with a certain autonomy and independence. Third, they watched over and developed their properties, took care of one another's material and spiritual needs, and were inventive in generating income from their own work which helped them become self-sufficient. In this way they created a monastic life with its rhythm of prayer and work and where each one in the community had her task and place. Finally, women religious sang the Offices and celebrated the feasts of the liturgical year. They expressed their religious culture in their buildings, their food, their art, music, dress, language and way of life.[19]

Impact of families and clergy on communities of women religious

However, communities of women religious lived within the wider social, political, religious and economic realities of their day. Families and clergy paid particular attention to them. Families became involved with communities and with individual members with regard to dowries and gifts of land. They also intervened in land disputes and succession rights. In the context of needing to secure large dowries for those daughters destined for dynastic marriages, families could force some daughters, sisters or aunts to join a community. This was an inexpensive way of providing for them, especially if they were unlikely to marry or if they were a financial burden on the family. On the other hand, if a woman in the family intended for a dynastic marriage declared her wish to join a community this could be staunchly resisted as she would take her all or some of her dowry with her. In these situations families often called on members of the clergy for their support when making their claims and demands on communities of women religious. These intricate political, social and economic aspects of family life were the manifestation of how the system of patriarchy, with its inherent misogynistic attitudes to women, operated in society and in the lives of women religious.

The institutional Church also exercised control over women religious who of necessity came into contact with local religious and diocesan clergy, as well as with bishops and popes. The records of women religious show how their vocation and their way of life, as well as their financial independence and access to learning, came under scrutiny from the Church. Indeed, their long history down the centuries shows that, while they certainly wished to be recognized by and affiliated to the institutional Church, women religious struggled to place limits on the interference of clerics in their lives, and on the restrictions which clerics wished to impose upon them. In many instances women religious either failed in their attempts or had to accept uneasy compromises. Clerics certainly assumed their right to intervene, not only in virtue of the patriarchal system which obtained in society with regard to all women, but also because such rights were confirmed in Church law and in theology as well as reinforced by discipline and punishment for any infringement. Within such perspectives clerics insisted on their authority to scrutinize communities of women religious, and there were consequences if they were not obeyed. Bishops could excommunicate individuals and communities and place a monastery under interdict, and so force submission. Records show a pattern of harassment and of public humiliation of leaders of women religious; some endured imprisonment, and even burning at the stake, for perceived disobedience.

Church law and its rulings hung over individual founders and communities of women religious and these affected every aspect of their lives, from the initial foundation of a community, which needed consent from clergy, as well as regular visitations and inspections. Vested interests in a parish or diocese could lead to the property rights of a community being challenged, as well as the dowries of individual women religious. In the sixteenth-century the Council of Trent further empowered bishops and priests to exercise control over women religious, and it especially recommended the imposition of strict rules of cloister to ensure that all women religious were strictly confined within the walls of enclosure. In effect, permanent enclosure/cloister was imposed by the Council of Trent on women religious of all traditions and ways of life. Apart from some minimal mitigations negotiated with difficulty after the French Revolution, the decrees of the Council of Trent remained in force in the Church until Vatican II.

Clerics had an armoury of Church law and theology, supported by the power of the Inquisition, which they could call upon to enforce their directives and assert their dominance over women religious in quite specific ways. For example, when women religious initiated a community they usually sought acceptance of their way of life from the institutional Church, as confirmation of their place in the Church and in wider society. In that process they encountered a minefield of obstacles. The history of the origins and developments of women's communities, as well as the biographies of their founders, reveals the nature of their crises and their difficulties in having their way of life accepted. It also shows the fate of those who stood up to clerics, how they were punished for actions taken beyond the place ascribed to women religious in the Church.

Clearly women religious were so pursued by Church authorities, even though they were not clerics; they did not belong to the governing institutions of the Church. They were lay people, at the periphery, not at the centre, of the Church.[20] Had they more influence than their position implied? And, for their part, how did women religious react to the exercise of clerical power? How did they carry this pressure? Did they bear it as a weight from within themselves, with a certain ambiguous, vague sense of foreboding? How aware could they have been of the pressures laid on them, and how could they express their reaction? What happened to them as they journeyed? Did they conform? Did they resist and how? What did they insist on protecting, and what could they let go of? Did they reach some understanding with clerics? Then again, maybe they were flattered by this attention and conformed to what was required, but did not grasp what they had conceded? Or did they wake up when an issue sparked a spontaneous reaction? And was that issue acknowledged, expressed or suppressed? The history of women religious reveals a broad spectrum of their responses to the actions of the institutional Church in their regard and which affected their lives intimately.

Virginity and the choice of religious life for women

Women's choice of vocation was severely curtailed and had to be exercised within the limits of Church thinking in their regard. The burden of guilt and shame inflicted on women had of necessity to be the basis and starting point of their spiritual journey. And yet over time the burden proved to be a foil, a challenge, for setting out on a long, unknown path into the future, beyond the immediate. For some women the path of voluntary virginity became an option, although it was founded on the denigration of a woman's sexuality, of her body, and in particular of her capacity to give birth and care for children. Jerome suggested virginity would free a woman's body 'which by natural law should have been subservient to a man'. It would even promote women to the status of being called a man.

> As long as woman is destined for birth and children she is different from man as body is from soul. But if she wishes to serve Christ more than the world, then she will cease to be a woman and will be called man.[21]

The eighth-century Irish Canons put it in another way when commenting 'on the honour due to veiled religious women': 'The Roman Synod says: Veiled women (*palliatae*) have great honour for they have conquered their sex, that is, their fragility, and have renounced the doings of the world.'[22] Indeed, Irish Canon no. 10 underlines the origin and significance of veiling for women religious:

> The word *pallium* 'veil' comes from *pulliditas* 'paleness', hence comes the word *palliata* 'veiled woman'; or, it comes from the goddess Pallas, that is Minerva, whose temple was *palladium* 'draped', and whose priestesses were virgins who were *palliatae*, that is 'veiled women'. With a change in meaning the word may be kept and one who under the New Law is veiled may be called *palliata*.[23]

Celtic Christianity, Anglo-Saxon England, the Frankish/ Carolingian Empire

In the early centuries of the Church, women, usually from the aristocratic or higher echelons of society, chose at first to live a life of virginity at home.

In time women sought more separation and they decided to leave their families and found places of solitude where they lived as hermits, alone or in small groups. As their numbers grew women began to settle on lands either inherited, donated or endowed by their families, and their way of life evolved into a rhythm of prayer, liturgical worship, and manual labour in the fields and in the community dwellings. This nascent form of religious life spread rapidly from East to West, and from the fifth-century monastic communities of women religious emerged in Celtic and Anglo-Saxon Christianity. As in the East, these communities were founded generally by women from royal families or families of distinction. Some had been married and had children, and then decided that they wished to found a monastic community. Other women declined marriage and chose to found monasteries.

Women became abbesses either of one monastery or of a group of monasteries, and some led double monasteries of nuns and monks. Monastic foundations were made in Ireland by Brigid of Kildare (c. 452–570),[24] Monnina of Killeavy (435–518),[25] Brónach of Kilbroney (d. 512), Ita of Killeedy (480–570)[26] and Samthann of Clonbroney (d. 793).[27] Similarly in Anglo-Saxon England, Frideswide (680–727) founded a monastery in Oxford. Cuthburga (d. 725) and later Tetta (d. 772) were abbesses of Wimborne in Dorset, a double monastery which prepared missionaries for different parts of Europe.[28] Ebba (615–83) was abbess of Coldingham; Etheldreda (c. 636–79) became abbess of Ely. Hilda (614–80), like Brigid of Kildare, was abbess of the double monastery of Streanaeshalch, where the 'Synod of Whitby' took place in 664. Monasteries also spread throughout the Frankish and Carolingian Empires, founded by women like Radegund (c. 520–87) of Poitiers,[29] Salaberga (c. 665) of Laon, Fara (c. 655) of Brie, Gertrud (626–59) of Nivelles, and Berta (c. 860) of Avenay.[30]

Most of the manuscripts recording these foundations were written by clerics, the chroniclers of the day. While they reveal undoubted admiration for the monastic founders, nevertheless it is clear that by exercising their leadership these women religious challenged the prevailing representations of women. Clerics record cautionary tales which portray women religious as sources of temptations for priests and monks. They also drew attention to the existence of double monasteries as another cause for tales of scandal.[31] The negative judgements contained in these tales find expression in the canonical laws passed by the Church synods concerning nuns. Clerics had their own model of women religious, portrayed for example in a Middle Irish homily on the life of St Brigid:

> Now there has never been anyone more bashful or more modest than that holy virgin. She never washed her hands or her feet or her head in the company of men. She never looked into a man's face. She never spoke without blushing. She was abstinent, innocent, liberal, patient, rejoicing in God's commandments, steadfast, humble, forgiving, and charitable.[32]

Brigid and the founders of so many monastic communities of women in Ireland, Anglo-Saxon England and the Frankish/Carolingian Empire were the antithesis of this clerical stereotype. They established their monastic way of life within a male world, and were most often supported and protected by their own aristocratic backgrounds, as well as by the patronage of royal houses and influential families. By so doing they laid the foundations of monasticism which provided spirituality, learning and culture for women religious which flourished for generations in Europe from the early Middle Ages.

Medieval communities of women religious

The monastic foundations in Ireland, Anglo-Saxon England and the Frankish/Carolingian Empire were succeeded by a new wave of monastic foundations for women inspired by the Benedictines and Cistercians. The lady abbesses Hildegard of Bingen, Elisabeth of Schönau and Héloïse of the Paraclete are representative of the scores of women religious who founded monasteries all over Europe which became centres of spirituality, learning, education and culture.[33] These women were gifted in the world of spirituality, theology and the arts, and they influenced the world around them. While monastic communities of women religious did not challenge clerical power, nevertheless conflicts arose over resistance to claims of clerical authority over communities of women religious.

For example, in 1178, in the closing months of her life, Hildegard, abbess of Bingen, drew the ire of the clergy of Mainz when she permitted the burial of an excommunicated nobleman in the monastery cemetery. Although the man had been reconciled to the Church before his death the clergy of Mainz still demanded the body be exhumed. This Hildegard refused and instead she solemnly blessed the grave with her abbatial staff. In retaliation, Hildegard and her community were placed under interdict, which deprived the community of Mass and the sacraments, and also banned the community from singing Divine Office, a singular punishment for Hildegard, who loved and composed liturgical music.

In a long letter to the clergy of Mainz Hildegard defended her actions, placing her light of conscience above clerical imperatives:

> In the vision that was fixed within my soul, by God the craftsman before I came forth in my birth, I was compelled to write on account of the fetter by which we have been bound by our superiors, because of a dead man, who at the direction of his priest, was buried without calumny in our midst. When a few days after his burial we were ordered by our superiors to fling him out of the cemetery, seized with no little terror at this order, I looked to the true light, as is my wont. And, my eyes wakeful, I saw in my soul that if we followed their command and exposed the corpse, such an expulsion would threaten our home with great danger,

like a vast blackness.... Yet, so as not to be wholly disobedient, we have till now ceased singing the songs of divine praises, in accordance with the interdict, and have abstained from partaking of the body of the Lord.[34]

Hildegard was an articulate preacher and teacher and she defended her position on the basis of her experience of God. Nobody had ever questioned her on these grounds, and at the end of her long life she could not understand the sinister opposition of clerics to a Christian burial.

Héloïse (1101–64), abbess of the Paraclete, had a quite different experience. In 1116 her uncle, Canon Fulbert of Chartres, appointed the theologian Pierre Abélard (1079–1142) as her tutor. They became lovers and had a child, Astrolabe. They were forcefully separated by Fulbert; Abélard resumed his teaching on the Trinity while Héloïse was sent away to become a nun. Some years later Abélard wrote his version of the affair which was swiftly refuted by Héloïse, which in turn drew a dark riposte from Abélard:

> The more subtle the tongue is in you, and the more flexible because of the softness of your body, the more mobile and prone to words it is, and exhibits itself as the seedbed of all evil. This defect in you is noted by the apostle when he forbids women to speak in church.[35]

It is hard to find a more misogynist citation from this period and one so misdirected. Fortunately, scholarship has retrieved the full stature of Héloïse, her monastic leadership and contribution to theology which in her lifetime won the admiration of many contemporaries. Peter the Venerable wrote to her: 'You have surpassed all women in wisdom and have gone further than almost every man.'[36]

From the thirteenth-century a host of women religious from different parts of Europe spoke openly and wrote extensively about their mystical insights into the life of Christ. Representative among them were Mechthilde of Magdeburg (1210–185), Angela of Foligno (*c*.1248–1309), Bridget of Sweden (1303–73), Catherine of Siena (1347–80) and Julian of Norwich (1342–*c*.1416). They invoked the testimony of personal experience and most lived within the accepted parameters of a monastic life, either in community or as hermits.[37] However, in the late thirteenth-century a group of women, called Beguines, came into existence in Liège, in present-day Belgium, whose way of life became questioned by the institutional Church. These women chose a new, distinctive form of religious life which blended the solitary and communal aspects of monastic religious life as before but lived out in a town setting. They wished to remain celibate but did not take vows of religion. Each one supported herself financially by either needlework, teaching children, or caring for the sick and the elderly. They tended to reside near a church, lived alone and met for prayer in common. They were free to choose another way of life at any time, although evidence shows that most remained as Beguines; those who left tended to join monastic communities. Some Beguines became writers and preachers. They commented in public on theology and spoke of their mystical experiences. They validated their vocation and way of life, and the content of their writing and theology, by invoking the authority of direct experience of God.

For a time the Beguines remained undisturbed, but in the measure that they became known Church authorities became suspicious. They considered this way of life beyond the accepted boundaries permitted to women in general and to women religious in particular. The Beguines were investigated and some of the members were accused of heresy and even witchcraft. One prominent leading member, Marguerite de Porete ($c.$1250–1310), a Beguine from Hainault, was accused of heresy, condemned to death and burned at the stake in the Place de Grève in Paris in 1310.[38] The following year, at the Council of Vienne, the Beguines were formally condemned by Pope Clement V:

> We have been told that certain women, commonly called Beguines, afflicted by a kind of madness, discuss the Holy Trinity and the divine essence, and express opinions on matters of faith and sacraments contrary to the catholic faith, deceiving many simple people. Since these women promise obedience to no one, and do not renounce their property or profess an approved Rule, they are certainly not 'religious', although they wear a habit and are associated with such religious orders as they find congenial. We have therefore decided and decreed with the approval of the Council that their way of life is to be permanently forbidden and altogether excluded from the Church of God.[39]

Clearly the Beguines posed a direct challenge to the Church. They encroached on the preserve of the clergy by daring to speak and write and publish on theological issues, and claimed the right to do so by invoking direct inspiration and experience from God. They exercised an unacceptable level of independence by the way they lived, and their practice of retaining their property rights drew criticism not just from the Church but from wider society.

Late medieval and early modern communities

Further developments in the lives of women religious occurred from the late fifteenth-century. Angela de Merici (1470–1540) founded the Ursuline community, and this initiative signalled both the introduction of the active teaching orders of women religious in the Church and their interest in missionary work.[40] A century later, in the wake of the Reformation and the Counter-Reformation, Mary Ward (1585–1645) founded the IBVM (The

English Ladies); Jeanne Frances de Chantal (1572–1641), with Francis de Sales (1567–1622) founded the community of the Visitation; Louise de Marillac (1591–1660), with Vincent de Paul (1581–1660) founded the Daughters of Charity; and Teresa of Avila (1518–52) reformed the Carmelite communities of women in Spain. As in previous centuries, these new enterprises in the lives of women religious led to prolonged disputes with the institutional Church, particularly concerning their way of life, as well as their presence and involvement in society.

In the early seventeenth-century, Mary Ward, an English woman, founded a radically new community called the Institute of the Blessed Virgin Mary (now the Congregation of Jesus). She modelled her Institute on the Jesuits and intended, contrary to the decrees of the Council of Trent, that it would not observe cloister, that its members would be seen and be active in the world. This intent set Mary Ward and her companions on a collision course with clerical authorities in Rome. In 1631 a series of censures were levelled against Mary Ward and the members of her Institute. Mary Ward was particularly criticized because she preached in England 'before the altar' and explained the Our Father; she gave her blessing; she travelled incognito. Moreover, she and the members of the Institute made long and expensive journeys, preached in missionary countries and wore the dress of the upper classes and the servant classes; they taught theology in their schools and allowed plays to be performed by the students. Finally, they did not observe religious cloister; 'they were proud, with a mania for liberty, and [were] garrulous'. These innovations, some of them intrusions on clerical territory, were roundly condemned. Mary Ward was imprisoned in a Poor Clare convent in Vienna by order of the Inquisition while awaiting her trial in Rome. She was denied papal approval for her community, which was suppressed, and while she was never tried by the Inquisition, she was forbidden to live in community or to leave Rome.[41]

Teresa of Avila, who reformed the Carmelite communities of women religious in Spain, was also investigated by the Inquisition but for different reasons. In the course of her life Teresa's writings, her spiritual visions and her reforming activities were continually under scrutiny. She defended herself vigorously with a distinctive rhetoric which both shielded her and enabled her to state her case.[42] The Inquisition was unable to recognize that a woman could be well versed in theology and have such profound direct experiences of God, to the extent that even after her death the Inquisition continued to condemn her work:

> That scholarly men should come to learn from a woman and recognise her as a leader in matters of prayer and spiritual doctrine is an argument for the novelty of this doctrine [Illuminism] in which this woman was wise and the men who subjected themselves to her were foolish. For in the ancient doctrine of the Church educated and learned men knew more than women.[43]

Thus, whether it was leadership, new enterprises, learning or education, writing or publishing, women religious faced and resisted as far as they could the relentless criticism of clerical patriarchy and misogyny.

This pattern continued into the seventeenth-century. In Mexico the scholar-nun Juana de la Cruz (1651–95), author of theological treatises, of plays, poetry and music, was renowned for her learning and knowledge. For a time she was protected by the Spanish viceroy of Mexico, but once he was recalled to Spain her work was examined by the Inquisition and condemned. At first Juana de la Cruz tried to resist pressures to repudiate her learning and literary work, but she was pursued so relentlessly that she disowned her own work. She became a broken woman and declared herself to be the 'worst of all sinners'.[44] In seventeenth-century France the community of Port-Royal (1608–1710), led by Mère Angelique Arnaud (1591–1661), was one of the main centres of Jansenism in France. The community was renowned for learning, theology, spiritual devotion, and music and publishing. These features, along with their austere way of life, drew the admiration of aristocratic women of the court and of men like Racine, Paschal and Le Maistre de Sacy. From the mid seventeenth-century Jansenist views held by the members of the community of Port-Royal brought them into conflict with the papacy in Rome. Louis XIV also viewed them with suspicion, seeing Port-Royal as a possible focus of opposition to his authority. With the support of Pope Clement XI the king first severely curtailed the influence of the community of Port-Royal and then finally destroyed it.[45]

However, bitter confrontations arising from Jansenism were widespread in eighteenth-century France and similar tensions continued between the Church and women religious. In the region of the Yonne (Burgundy), the most Jansenist part of France, Ursuline women religious came into conflict with the archbishop of Sens, Jean-Joseph Languet. He vigorously opposed Jansenism, and to counteract its influence he introduced a new catechism in his diocese. The Ursuline communities absolutely refused to accept this change, and in one house 'Sister Saint-Augustine and several others told him that the new catechism went against their conscience and that they would never accept it.'

The archbishop warned: 'You are damning yourself ... there is no salvation without obedience; it is so essential that even if I gave an unjust order, you would not be dispensed from obeying me.' To which she replied: 'Monseigneur, with your permission, what you have said goes against the gospel, which tells us that whoever follows a blind leader will also fall into the ditch.' Archbishop Languet wryly remarked how the nuns thought they were more learned than he, and apparently 'wished to teach him his catechism and reform his theology'. He fell back on the tools of the Inquisition.[46] Nonetheless, confrontations between the archbishop and communities of women religious in many other parts of his diocese, especially in Etampes and Joigny, continued.

From the Enlightenment and especially after the French Revolution an extraordinary surge of communities of women religious took place. These communities opened up choices and opportunities which many women grasped enthusiastically. They grew rapidly in numbers and became involved in education and nursing, and many communities had missionary outreaches beyond Europe.[47] In France alone 800 communities of women religious were founded between 1800 and 1880. By 1878, 135,000 women were women religious (7 in every 1,000 French women), and most were in teaching orders.[48] Typical among the founders of the new communities was Madeleine Sophie Barat (1779–1865). She was born in Joigny, Burgundy, and as a child had heard of the conflicts between the Ursuline communities and the archbishop of Sens. When she founded the Society of the Sacred Heart in 1800 she too ran into controversy. Her authority as Superior General was opposed regularly, sometimes by local clerics, or by school or community chaplains, or by diocesan bishops. She had prolonged clashes with two archbishops of Paris, Hyacinthe de Quelen (1778–1839) and Denis Affre (1793–1848). These concerned her leadership rights, an issue entangled with Gallican and Ultramontane disputes between the popes and the archbishops of Paris. Sophie Barat upheld and staunchly defended her rights and the rights of the Society of the Sacred Heart, and in a process characteristic of other contemporary women religious leaders, she developed a language and a style of leadership to achieve her goals.[49]

The evolution of women religious in the nineteenth–twenty-first centuries

Records of religious communities of women show deepening tensions throughout the nineteenth and twentieth centuries between the institutional Church and women religious, at local, diocesan and sometimes papal levels. These arose for several reasons. The historical context and position of the Catholic Church had shifted in the wake of the Reformation and Counter-Reformation, followed by the Scientific Revolution in the seventeenth-century and the Enlightenment in the eighteenth-century. The French Revolution in 1789 and the Empire of Napoleon were periods when the papacy was at its weakest and most humiliated by political forces. In the course of the nineteenth-century the Church had to come to terms with these forces and with the emergence of the modern nation-state in Europe. In that context, and to consider the stance the Church should take in this world, Pius IX convened the First Vatican Council. It met from 1869 to 1870, and in July 1870 the Council passed the decree *Pastor aeternus* asserting papal infallibility. Before it had time to debate the Church's attitude to liberalism, rationalism and materialism in modern society, the Council was dramatically interrupted by the outbreak of the Franco-Prussian War, followed by the loss of the Papal States, which were merged into the new state of Italy.

By December 1870 the papacy had lost its territorial power in Italy and had become a monarchy without a kingdom.

The First Vatican Council never reconvened but Pius IX and his successor, Leo XIII, set down measures to maintain discipline in the Church, planned a revision of the code of Canon Law and updated censorship procedures for placing books on the Index.[50] As a further strategy to gain authority and influence, the Church turned its attention to works of education and of nursing: that is to say, to schools and hospitals. This exposed women religious to even more claims of clerical authority, especially from priests and bishops, and they became absorbed into the overall political goals of the institutional Church. Just at the time when women in general were becoming aware of their rights in education, in politics, the family and society, and when feminism was gaining ground, women religious were travelling in another direction. Indeed, rules and regulations laid down for women religious in this period became more stringent than ever before and in minute, invasive detail, especially after the publication of the Code of Canon Law in 1917. This control on the lives and social works of women religious prevailed until 1962 when John XXIII convened Vatican II. This Council opened the debate on the place of the Catholic Church in the modern world and set out to evaluate all aspects of life in the Church, including religious life.[51]

In October 1965 Vatican II invited all religious, women and men, to re-visit their original, foundational records and evaluate the purpose and history of their community.[52] They were asked to update their original Rule of Life (Constitutions) and forward a new edition to Rome for approval. Vast bodies of historical material were gathered, catalogued and placed in archival holdings. The histories of the communities and the life of the founder/s were written, or re-written. The Rule of Life was revised, re-drafted by working parties, debated and accepted in General Chapters of women religious, and then forwarded to Rome for approval. Much of this material is currently in the process of being made available to researchers, and in this way the history of women religious, the biographies of individuals and of communities, their private and public records, are coming into the public domain. Prior to Vatican II records of women religious were not normally open to the public, and even within communities they were considered like relics, mementos of the past generations, rather like large family albums. They were passed down the generations and their purpose was to edify the members and confirm their way of life, and they were only released to the public for canonization purposes. Even then, only the Church authorities directly concerned with canonization, along with selected historians and witnesses, had access to them.

The act of gathering archives, writing the history of the community and re-drafting the Rule of Life (Constitutions) led to an awakening and to a critical self-assessment among women religious. For many it began to dawn on them what they as a body of women (or, at the very least, their leaders) had colluded with for quite some time. They saw the power and status they had enjoyed through material successes, which consciously or unconsciously they sought and indeed applauded along with the institutional Church. They had become identified with a centralized, militant Church and had lost the spiritual freedom which belongs to the nature and purpose of religious life, to live at the periphery rather than the centre. In a certain sense women religious had become pseudo-clerics, or clones of the clergy, trapped into an agenda not of their intention but of their own making. Many communities of women religious were genuinely taken aback at the pain and suffering which had been silently endured, sometimes for many years, by individuals and by groups. This only became public during consultations for General Chapters called after Vatican II which invited women religious to speak out, to begin to hear their own voices, and to move into new positions.

Research in the archives of women religious after Vatican II reveals material on the recovery of original sources and vision, and the enthusiasm with which this was received, as well as the practical steps women religious took to implement their new insights. Research also exposes the enormous efforts on the part of the institutional Church, in Rome and in dioceses worldwide, to prevent women religious taking new steps, especially reaching out to the poor and oppressed, to the marginalized in society. Sensing a loss of control, the institutional Church focussed on the dress of religious women. Indeed, the largest files, literally miles of paper, concern the issue of dress, of the habit, and especially of the veil. The male clergy required submission to a dress code, to a veil, to a type of veil, its length, its colour.

This obsession with dress/the habit was intense and prolonged. It side-lined the real issues which women religious wished to address. It led to lengthy negotiations, time-consuming meetings and pressure to conform. These processes lasted long after Vatican II ended in 1965, and some are still unfinished.[53] Instead of releasing all their energies into the future, women religious were obstructed in going forward, indeed strategically undermined by bureaucracy in Rome. Some leaders of women religious were dismissed, some were harassed and threatened, and some took the road of negotiation which in the end wore them down, often literally. Some leaders conformed, accepted, and some did not question at all. This led to a spectrum of deep divisions within communities, to serious splits in congregations, conflicted on issues of change, or on how far they wished to change, or preferred to leave things as they were and as Rome wished.[54] Many thousands of women decided to leave religious life at this time, quite disillusioned, and sensing they had another day, another life to live, somewhere else. Those who stayed tried to go forward with varying degrees of success, hard won but worn out by Vatican tactics, which could not hide its patriarchal, misogynist agenda for women religious.

Feminism and women religious today

Until the mid twentieth-century most women religious lived their lives parallel to the historical developments of feminism. They viewed feminism with distrust, perhaps intuiting the impossible polarity this would create in their lives and that it would ask decisions of them which they could not imagine taking. Certainly the institutional Church, recognizing the inherent challenge in feminism, ridiculed, even demonized the word and content of feminism, and most women religious agreed with this opinion. This was inevitable as those who live within a rigid, closed system of beliefs tend to become like those who control the system, to varying degrees. Some became identified with the system and could not see, maybe did not want to see, beyond that perspective. Others became resigned to their condition; many were flattered by belonging to it.[55]

In the middle of the twentieth-century Vatican II provided a path forward which would lead many women religious to the insights of feminism. From 1965 women religious set out on new paths and focussed on wider, more global directions. Women religious began studying theology, in addition to the arts and the sciences. They became in tune with the consciousness of their time, especially with justice and the rights of the poor, with human rights in all spheres of life: class, colour, creed, sex and gender; with the rights of women, the rights of the child, feminist movements internationally, globalization and care of the planet. These worlds, in their varying shades of clarity and opaqueness, were hard, even impossible to reconcile with the experience of women religious. How could these worlds meet? Could they meet? How avoid a split, in communities, in the leadership and with the long tradition of religious life? The questions are currently demanding resolution.

More than fifty years after Vatican II the institutional Church continues to systematically coerce women religious, demanding they submit to its definition of religious life. But the context has radically changed since debates in the Church today have become much wider than religious life. These concern women in general in the Catholic Church, particularly in the wake of the papal encyclical of Paul VI, *Humanae vitae*, published in July 1968.[56] Today intense debates surround the exclusion of women in general from full participation in the life of the Church, an exclusion constructed around law, scripture, theology and tradition, and founded on patriarchy and misogyny. In a bid impossible to enforce, the Vatican has forbidden even the discussion of the ordination of women. In 2012 a new translation of the liturgy removed previously approved inclusive language from the texts, a studied insult to women. On Holy Thursday, 28 March 2013, Pope Francis I washed the feet of twelve young prisoners, two of them women. Immediately objections were raised that the pope had washed the feet of two women. Clearly the archetypes of the Virgin Mary and Mary Magdalene continue to operate.

A signal of the hardening of attitudes towards women religious today was the action of the Vatican with regard to women religious in the United States in 2008. That year the American women religious were subjected to an Apostolic Visitation, imposed by the Vatican and carried out in its name by men and women religious who were to report their findings to Rome.

> From the start of the apostolic visitation women were not informed of how they came to be the objects of the investigation. Nor were they consulted on the process by which the investigation would be carried out. Nor were they to be, in any meaningful way, agents in the formation of the investigative report.[57]

The following year, 2009, a Doctrinal Assessment of the US Leadership Conference of Women Religious (LCWR) was instigated. Women religious in the USA were accused of being more concerned with the poor and justice and human rights than with promoting the teaching of the Church on the ordination of women, contraception, abortion and homosexuality. They were also accused of corporate dissent and of radical feminism:

> The Cardinal noted a prevalence of certain radical feminist themes incompatible with the Catholic faith in some of the programs and presentations sponsored by the LCWR, including theological interpretations that risk distorting faith in Jesus and in his loving Father who sent his Son for the salvation of the world. Moreover, some commentaries on 'patriarchy' distort the way in which Jesus has structured sacramental life in the Church; others even undermine the revealed doctrines of the Holy Trinity, the divinity of Christ, and the inspiration of Holy Scripture.[58]

Several years of investigations of American women religious followed, and in December 2014 the Apostolic Visitation Report was issued in Rome. The language of the Report is remarkably different in tone from the announcement of the investigation in 2008. This was due to the election of Pope Francis I in 2013, leadership changes in the Roman Curia and the criticism of Catholics internationally at the manner in which American women religious have been treated by the Vatican. In their perception, and that of the wider public, the entire process was an exercise of male power and institutional violence. Within the perspective of the history of women, the treatment meted out to American women religious fits into the pattern of abuse women have endured in the Church for centuries. At no time in their history have polarities been so clearly drawn between women religious and the clerical institution of the Church. The abyss widens, resolution seems unattainable and the paradigm of victim/oppressor seems solidly cast. The Vatican considers radical feminism as a challenge to the teachings of the institutional Church. The real issue is that women religious are thinking for themselves, are coming to an understanding of how they have been treated and why they allowed this to happen.[59]

But as well as a growing consciousness among women religious of how they have been treated historically in the Church is the recognition of an even more difficult truth: that women religious have had their part in the historical abuses cases which have surfaced internationally in recent decades. Thus, in the very process of distancing themselves from the abusive structures of the institutional Church women religious have begun to acknowledge how they have been part of those same structures. Knowingly or not, they have colluded with the power structures of the Church, especially in the last 100 years. Trapped as prisoners themselves in the structures, they in turn imprisoned those they set out to serve. This painful realization in no way denies the compelling record of historical abuse exercised by the institutional Church on women religious down the centuries.[60]

Certainly feminism profoundly challenges the Church today. But so do all the abused children, who were bullied into silence, rendered mute. They have found their voice as adults and told the world their terrible truths. Their revelations exposed the power systems which operated in the Church and in religious life.[61] All members of the clergy are tarnished by the sexual abuse of children by some clerics. So are all women religious tarnished by the abuse perpetrated by some women religious on children and women in orphanages, industrial schools, Magdalene Laundries, and Mother and Baby Homes. An honest shame, shared by all clerics and religious, could create new spaces for reflection, dialogue and action.

The history of women religious down the centuries shows countless instances of how their intuitions and views were either ignored or roundly rejected by clerics. This could change. The life of Mary MacKillop (1842–1909), founder and Superior General of the Sisters of Joseph of the Sacred Heart in Australia, stands as model for future action. In 1870, along with her community, she reported a case of clerical child sexual abuse to the bishop of Brisbane, Laurence Sheil (1815–72), an Irish Franciscan. He and his clergy rejected the accusation, and the bishop countered the accusation by excommunicating Mary MacKillop, charging her with disobedience and insubordination. In the presence of her Sisters, he forced her to kneel down in front of him for a long time while he pronounced the sentence of excommunication. He then set out to crush her community, causing her and her companions interminable problems. They persisted and won through. This quality of courage and truth is needed today at all levels if change is to take place in the Church. Such a task will be daunting, if it is undertaken.

Conclusion

This chapter has tracked some representative and typical incidents of patriarchal, misogynistic violence towards women religious throughout the centuries. Women religious have been questioned, called to account, harassed, bullied, imprisoned; forbidden the sacraments; silenced and humiliated; rendered invisible and powerless. This treatment happened in parishes by local clergy, in dioceses by bishops, or in Rome by popes. However, the evolution of religious life for women from 1850 to 1962 in particular could be described as a form of colonization by the institutional Church, an invasion of the space of religious life.[62] The historical experience of women religious fits well into the pattern of colonizer/colonized. The colonizer, in this instance the institutional Church, moved in, offered security on condition of submission and cooperation. If women religious complied they were rewarded, given status, and they were expected to execute all the policies of the colonizer. If they objected they were silenced or cast out, certainly side-lined.

Women religious today in Europe and North America have come to an edge, to another edge, in their history. Some may continue to stand attentively within the space of present realities within the Church. Some may break their canonical links with the Church, following those communities which have taken this decision already. Others may leave their communities, as so many have done since Vatican II. In any event, profound changes are inevitable since the majority of women religious in North America, Europe, Australia, New Zealand and Japan are fast ageing. Furthermore, given the present state of the Church, and especially its attitude towards women, the attraction of religious life for women in these countries has greatly diminished. In the future those researching and writing the present history of women religious will place their narrative at this historical edge, mindful of the rich tradition and lived experience of women religious over the centuries.

Notes

1 A shorter version of this chapter was given as the keynote address at the History of Women Religious in Britain and Ireland Annual Conference, 21–22 June 2012, University College Dublin.
2 Michelle Zancarini-Fournel, *Histoire des femmes en France, XIXe–XXe siècles* (Rennes: Presses Universitaires de Rennes, 2005), 23–35. Also Diarmaid MacCulloch, *Silence: A Christian History* (London: Allen Lane, 2013), 191–202.
3 Laurel Thatcher Ulrich, *Well Behaved Women Seldom Make History* (New York: First Vintage, 2007); Michelle Perrot, *Mon histoire des femmes* (Paris: Seuil, 2006); Michelle Perrot, *Les femmes ou les silences de l'Histoire* (Paris: Flammarion, 1998); Olwen Hufton, *The Prospect before Her: A History of Women in Western Europe*, Vol. I, *1500–1800* (London: HarperCollins, 1995); Carolyn Heilbrun, *Writing a Woman's Life* (London: Women's Press, 1989); Carolyn Heilbrun, *Women's Lives: The View from the Threshold* (Toronto: Toronto Press, 1999); Gerda Lerner, *The Creation of Feminist Consciousness: From the Middle Ages to Eighteen-Seventy* (Oxford: Oxford University Press, 1993); Elizabeth Dufourcq, *Histoire des Chrétiennes: L'autre moitié de l'Evangile* (Paris: Bayard, 2008).
4 John Batchelor, *The Art of Literary Biography* (Oxford: Oxford University Press, 1995); Mark Bostridge (ed.), *Lives for Sale: Biographer's Tales* (London: Continuum,

2004); Peter France and William St Clair (eds), *Mapping Lives: The Uses of Biography* (Oxford: Oxford University Press, 2002); Hermione Lee, *Body Parts: Essays on Life-Writing* (London: Chatto and Windus, 2005); Hermione Lee, *Biography: A Very Short Introduction* (Oxford: Oxford University Press, 2009); Michael Holroyd, *Works on Paper: The Craft of Biography and Autobiography* (London: Little, Brown, 2002).

5 'Cáin Adomnán (The Law of Adomnán)', in Angela Bourke, Seamus Deane and Andrew Carpenter (eds), *The Field Day Anthology of Irish Writing*, 5 vols (hereafter cited as *FDA*), Vol. IV, *Irish Women's Writing and Traditions* (Cork: Cork University Press, 2002), 18–22. See also Máirín Ní Dhonnchadha, 'The *Lex innocentium*: Adomnán's Law for Women, Clerics and Youths, 697 AD', in Mary O'Dowd and Sabine Wichert (eds), *Chattel, Servant or Citizen: Women's Status in Church, State and Society* (Belfast: Queen's University Belfast, 1995), 58–69. For the position of women in early Irish society see essays in *FDA*, Vol. IV: Donnchadh Ó Corráin, 'Early Medieval Law, *c.* 700–1200' (6–12); and Máirín Ní Dhonnchada, 'Mary, Eve and the Church, *c.* 600–1800' (45–57).

6 Sandra M. Schneiders, 'The Effects of Women's Experience on Their Spirituality', *Spirituality Today*, 35:2 (1983), 100–16.

7 Anne Baring and Jules Cashford, *The Myth of the Goddess: Evolution of an Image* (London: Penguin, 1993), 486–546.

8 Paul to Timothy, 1 Timothy 2:11–14.

9 Tertullian, *On the Apparel of Women* [*De cultu feminarum*], Book I, Chapter 1, trans. Sydney Thelwall, in Alexander Roberts and James Donaldson (eds), *The Ante-Nicene Fathers* 10 vols, Vol. IV (New York: Christian Literature Company, 1890), p. 14.

10 Bonnie S. Anderson and Judith P. Zinsser, *A History of Their Own: Women in Europe from Prehistory to the Present*, 2 vols (London: Penguin, 1990), Vol. I, 79.

11 'Mé Éba (I Am the Wife of Adam, Eve) (11th Century)', in *FDA*, Vol. IV, 125.

12 Cited in Brian Griffin, *Different Visions of Love: Partnership and Dominator Values in Christian History* (Denver: Outskirts Press, 2008), 370. For comment on the text, see Caroline Walker Bynum, *Holy Feast and Holy Fast: The Religious Significance of Food to Medieval Women* (Oakland: California University Press, 1992), 15–16.

13 Daniel Edward, *Meditations Collected and Ordered for the Use of the English College of Lisbon: By the Superiors of the Same College*, 2nd edn (Douai: Baltazar Bellere,1663). See MacCulloch, *Silence*, 196.

14 Tertullian, *Liber de anima*, XXXVI.

15 Baring and Cashford, *The Myth of the Goddess*, 521. Also Marina Warner, *Alone of All Her Sex: The Myth and the Cult of the Virgin Mary* (New York: Vintage, 1983), 39–44.

16 Baring and Cashford, *The Myth of the Goddess*, 547–608.

17 Feminist theologians have deconstructed this representation of Mary Magdalene and restored her to her rightful position in the Gospel as key witness to the Crucifixion and Resurrection of Christ.

18 For a detailed discussion of these issues, see Baring and Cashford, *The Myth of the Goddess*, 486–546.

19 Patricia M. Rumsey, *Women of the Church: The Religious Experience of Monastic Women* (Dublin: Columba Press, 2011).

20 Until Vatican II women religious were commonly considered as members of the clergy. Canon Law Society of Great Britain and Ireland, *The Code of Canon Law* (London: Collins, 1983), Book II, Part I, no. 207, 1–2 states clearly that women religious are members of the laity in the Church.

21 Anderson and Zinsser, *A History of Their Own*, Vol. I, 83.
22 'Hibernensis, Irish Canons, *c.* 716–25', in *FDA*, Vol. IV, no. 13, 101. According to the Roman Synod women were veiled very young, even at twelve years of age; ibid., no. 11, 101.
23 Ibid., no. 10, 101.
24 'Giraldus Cambrensis (Gerald of Wales), *Topographia Hiberniae, c.* 1187', in *FDA*, Vol. IV, 74–6.
25 'The Latin Life of Saint Darerca alias Mo-ninne (14th Century MS)', in *FDA*, Vol. IV, 82–6.
26 'The Latin Life of Saint Íte (13th Century MS)', in *FDA*, Vol. IV, 76–80. Also, 'Ísucán (Saint Íte and the Child Jesus, Old Irish)', in *FDA*, Vol. IV, 80–1.
27 'The Latin Life of Samthann (14th Century MS)', in *FDA*, Vol. IV, 86–8.
28 Leoba (*c.*700–80) and Walburga (710–99) left Wimborne to found monasteries in Germany. Mary T. Malone, *Women and Christianity*, 3 vols (Dublin: Columba Press, 2000–3), Vol. I, *The First Thousand Years*, 203–15.
29 Rumsey, *Women of the Church*, 126–461; Malone, *Women and Christianity*, Vol. I, 189–92.
30 'Sedulius Scottus, *fl.* 860', in *FDA*, Vol. IV, 107. Also Anderson and Zinsser, *A History of Their Own*, 183–7.
31 Hagiographical lives of the saints in Ireland and Anglo-Saxon England. Rumsey, *Women of the Church*, 137–43. Also *FDA*, Vol. IV, 118–19.
32 'A Homily on the Life of Saint Brigit (Middle Irish)', in *FDA*, Vol. IV, 73.
33 MacCulloch, *Silence*, 120.
34 Letter of Hildegard of Bingen to the Mainz prelates, in Hildegard of Bingen, *Hildegard of Bingen: An Anthology*, ed. Fiona Bowie and Oliver Davies (London: SPCK, 1992), 149–51. Barbara Newman, *Sister of Wisdom: St Hildegard's Theology of the Feminine* (Aldershot: Scolar Press, 1987), 14. It is clear that this dispute was part of a long power struggle between the clergy of Mainz and Hildegard. See Newman, *Sister of Wisdom*, 9–14.
35 Cited in Malone, *Women and Christianity*, Vol. II, 74; see also 72–6. Barbara Newman, *From Virile Woman to Woman Christ: Studies in Medieval Religion and Literature* (Philadelphia: University of Pennsylvania Press, 1995), 46–75.
36 Malone, *Women and Christianity*, Vol. II, 73.
37 For example, Julian of Norwich has been the subject of major studies in recent decades. See Julian of Norwich, *The Writings of Julian of Norwich*, ed. Nicholas Watson and Jacqueline Jenkins (University Park: Pennsylvania State University Press, 2006); Denys Turner, *Julian of Norwich, Theologian* (New Haven: Yale University Press, 2011); Veronica Mary Rolf, *Julian's Gospel: Illuminating the Life and Revelations of Julian of Norwich* (New York: Orbis, 2014). See also Newman, *From Virile Woman to Woman Christ*, 19–136; Rumsey, *Women of the Church*, 186–210.
38 Newman, *From Virile Woman to Woman Christ*, 137–67; MacCulloch, *Silence*, 121–3, 141.
39 Pope Clement V, *Cum de quibusdam mulieribus* (1311), cited in Malone, *Women and Christianity*, Vol. II, 131–2.
40 Belinda Jack, *The Woman Reader* (New Haven: Yale University Press, 2012), 164–6; Natalie Zemon Davis, *Women on the Margins: Three Seventeenth-Century Lives* (Cambridge, MA: Harvard University Press, 1995), 63–139.
41 Henriette Peters, *Mary Ward: A World in Contemplation* (Leominster: Gracewings, 1994), 468–9, 585.
42 Alison Weber, *Teresa of Avila and the Rhetoric of Femininity* (Princeton: Princeton University Press, 1990).

43 Ibid., 160. For Illuminism in the lifetime of Teresa of Avila, see 22–8.
44 Juana Inés de la Cruz, *Sor Juana Inés de la Cruz: Selected Writings*, ed. Pamela Kirk Rappaport (New York: Paulist Press, 2005); Michelle A. Gonzales, *Sor Juana: Beauty and Justice in the Americas* (New York: Orbis Books, 2003); Octavio Paz, *Sor Juana; or, The Traps of Faith* (Cambridge, MA: Harvard University Press, 1988).
45 Clement XI condemned Jansenism in the papal decree *Unigenitus* in 1713. Laurence Plazenet, *Port-Royal: Une anthologie* (Paris: Flammarion, 2012). See also Daniella Kostroun, *Feminism, Absolutism, and Jansenism: Louis XIV and the Port-Royal Nuns* (Cambridge: Cambridge University Press, 2011). For the spiritual attraction Jansenism held for aristocratic women, see Benedetta Craveri, *The Age of Conversation*, trans. Teresa Waugh (New York: New York Review of Books, 2005), 97–135.
46 Elizabeth Rapley, 'Jansénisme au féminin', in *A Social History of the Cloister: Daily Life in the Teaching Monasteries of the Old Regime* (Montreal: McGill-Queen's University Press, 2001), 69–77.
47 See Sarah A. Curtis, *Civilizing Habits: Women Missionaries and the Revival of French Empire* (Oxford: Oxford University Press, 2010).
48 Rebecca Rogers, *From the Salon to the Schoolroom: Educating Bourgeois Girls in Nineteenth-Century France* (University Park: Pennsylvania State University Press, 2005), 58. Claude Langlois, *Le catholicisme au féminin: Les congrégations françaises à supérieure générale au XIXe siècle* (Paris: Editions du Cerf, 1984).
49 Phil Kilroy, *Madeleine Sophie Barat: A Life* (Cork: Cork University Press, 2000); Phil Kilroy, *The Society of the Sacred Heart in Nineteenth-Century France* (Cork: Cork University Press, 2012). See also Curtis, *Civilizing Habits*; Margaret MacCurtain, *Ariadne's Thread: Writing Women into Irish History* (Dublin: Arlen House, 2008); Mary Peckham Magray, *The Transforming Power of Nuns: Women, Religions and Cultural Change in Ireland, 1750–1900* (Oxford: Oxford University Press, 1998); Caitríona Clear, 'The Limits of Female Autonomy: Nuns in Nineteenth-Century Ireland', in Maria Luddy and Cliona Murphy (eds), *Women Surviving: Studies in Irish Women's History in the 19th and 20th Centuries* (Dublin: Poolbeg, 1990), 15–50.
50 The Congregation for the Index existed from 1571 to 1917. After 1917 the Index was directed by the Holy Office, formerly the Inquisition and now the Congregation for the Doctrine of the Faith (CDF). The Index was regularly updated until 1948 and finally abolished in 1966.
51 It is not possible in this short article to detail the experience of women religious from the late nineteenth-century until Vatican II. However, it is clear from their positive responses to Vatican II that women religious had been living under heavy burdens in the preceding decades, with varying degrees of consciousness. See Kilroy, *The Society of the Sacred Heart*, 235–7.
52 Decree on the Adaptation and Renewal of Religious Life (*Perfectae caritatis*), 28 October 1965.
53 Enclosure remains an issue for monastic communities of women religious. Rumsey, *Women of the Church*, 239–73.
54 The archives of women religious contain detailed records of these issues. Access to such archives is sensitive since many of the members are still living.
55 See Peckham, *The Transforming Power of Nuns*, 129–30 for a discussion of the quality in the leadership of women religious from the late nineteenth-century.
56 Dufourcq, *Histoire des Chrétiennes*, 1142–98.
57 Thomas C. Fox, 'Abuse of Episcopal Authority in Apostolic Visitation Created Deep Wounds', *National Catholic Reporter* (17 December 2014). The Doctrinal Assessment announced in 2009 has not yet been completed.

58 Doctrinal Assessment of the Leadership Conference of Women Religious, II, no. 3. There was widespread public response to the Vatican's statement in the USA and internationally, supportive of the LCWR and women religious in general. On the other hand, there are women religious who support the position taken by the Vatican. See website of the LCWR (https://lcwr.org); and of the *National Catholic Reporter* (http://www.ncronline.org). Also Sandra M. Schneiders, *Prophets in Their Own Country: Women Religious Bearing Witness to the Gospel in a Troubled Church* (New York: Orbis, 2011); Gary Wills, 'Bullying the Nuns', *New York Review of Books*(24 April 2012).
59 In the measure that they engaged with the women's movement, with Feminism in all its phases and with concrete life experiences, many women religious reached awareness of how they mimicked, or submitted to, their male counterparts, bishops, priests, and religious Brothers. See Anne E. Patrick, *Conscience and Calling: Ethical Reflections on Catholic Women's Church Vocations* (Bloomsbury: T. & T. Clark, 2014).
60 Camillus Metcalfe, *For God's Sake: The Hidden Lives of Irish Nuns* (Dublin: Liffey Press, 2014).
61 MacCulloch, *Silence*, 202–7.
62 Sarah Mills, *Gender and Colonial Space* (Manchester: Manchester University Press, 2005).

Chapter 2

From Kerry to Katong
Transnational influences in convent and novitiate life for the Sisters of the Infant Jesus, c. 1908–1950

Deirdre Raftery

Introduction

Research on teachers and on classroom routines has, particularly in the last decade, attempted to give voice to teachers and to the experience of schooling. In the British context, for example, the work of McCulloch (1998); Grosvenor, Lawn and Rousmaniere (1999); and Cunningham and Gardner (2004) has widened our perspectives on 'the realities of teachers' and students' work'.[1] As research in the history of education has also clearly shown, there has been a strong relationship between the experience of schooling and the influence of religions – that is, the various denominational groups that provided schooling.[2] There is a substantial literature on the history of Anglican and Catholic missionaries and education;[3] the contributions of particular churchmen and clergy to schooling has been examined;[4] the influence of charitable societies, the Sunday School movement, and evangelicalism on education has attracted scholarship,[5] as have some of the Catholic teaching orders of nuns, priests and Brothers.[6] There is also considerable research on the impact of religious discord and dissent on education.[7]

Some of this work has appeared since 1992, when the distinguished historian of education Harold Silver drew attention to the need to bring 'the Catholic, the Christian, the religious experience into the canon of educational history.'[8] Yet despite the considerable burst of attention to religions in the history of education, there are areas that still demand attention, including using different theoretical lenses to re-examine how education was provided and experienced in the past. This chapter attempts such an exercise, using the optic of transnationalism to examine how education at convent schools and novitiates prepared girls and young women for missionary life, as nuns.[9] The chapter takes one Irish convent, the Infant Jesus Convent, Drishane on the Cork–Kerry border, as a case study, and looks at how life in the boarding school prepared pupils for life in the novitiate and convent. It will be seen that pupils were educated not only by the nuns who were *in situ*, but also by transnational networks that included visiting missionary nuns and overseas visitors. These people brought the international mission field into school, via presentations and talks, magic lantern slide shows, and films. They also fostered transnational networking for pupils via pen-pal clubs and school magazines, and deposited 'foreign' educational souvenirs and ephemera in schools as they continued on their travels. Missionary nuns were influential educators who grew vocations[10] to Catholic religious life, yet they have received little attention in scholarship, and no attention as transnational actors.

Theoretical perspective and sources

The informing theoretical lens used in the analysis is that of transnationalism. As I have argued elsewhere,

> in the history of women's education, the conceptual tool of transnationalism has been utilized by many scholars ... [but] in writing on women religious, it has not been utilized explicitly, although some scholars have made substantial contributions to our understanding of how women religious moved between countries and influenced educational ideas in different countries.[11]

This chapter demonstrates how convents and novitiates were transnational spaces, influenced directly by the transmission of ideas and culture that travelled across countries and continents.

The chapter draws on several sources, subjecting them to analysis in order to better understand the convent as a transnational space.[12] The main sources used are archival materials, which were located at archives in Singapore, Paris and Dublin, and reflect the religious life and educational mission of the Infant Jesus Sisters.[13] Convent annals, novitiate annals and mission annals are particularly relevant to the chapter. However, annals are not without limitations; they may reflect the biases of the annalist writing at the time in her description of events, and they are often very general. They describe 'important' events, but convent annalists were not allowed to make personal comments or value judgements, so annals can be somewhat lifeless. Information from the annals is corroborated and enlivened by the addition, in this chapter, of oral accounts.

The value of using oral interviews and life histories has been discussed by a number of scholars, including Ivor Goodson and Pat Sikes.[14] They also recognize the limits of oral accounts, which are always subjective, and which tend to rely on 'storytelling', rather than analysis. As Goodson and Sikes observe, 'Most people, in telling their lives, will try to impose some order, however spurious, because they are concerned to make sense of things that happened.'[15] Respondents also tend to use the narrative available to them, which reflects their own culture. As will be seen in this chapter, because the respondents were women religious, the particular 'culture' of the novitiate and convent schools, and the specialist vocabulary of religious life – particularly pre-Vatican II life – had a direct impact on how they tried to make sense of their lives. Sisters engaged in acts of translation, unpacking exactly what it meant to 'Live by the Rule', or to conduct a 'Chapter of Faults', for example.

Researchers using oral evidence tend to agree that a respondent's facility with language – that is, general fluency and articulacy – also has an impact on the quality of the interviews. I would argue that women religious, as respondents, are often particularly articulate; this is not only because of their own education but because the very nature of religious life is reflective; Sisters are used to regular formal and informal periods of self-examination, such as religious retreats, confession and prayer. Many of them exhibited a high level of awareness of their own shortcomings, and few had idealized notions about nuns as educators.

Aware of both the challenges and strengths of supplementing archival data with oral histories, I suggest it is possible to research convent and novitiate education in ways that will allow insight into an era in education which is now at its end. In this chapter, both types of source illuminate an understanding of transnational influences on life at a school, novitiate and the convent near County Kerry known as Drishane, which belonged to the Sisters of the Infant Jesus. The chapter reflects a desire to move away from the kind of research on religious that gives a panoramic sweep, and instead to 'drill down' into the records of one institution, with a view to illuminating an understanding of daily lives, routines, customs and practices, in one school and novitiate. This method responds to Tom O'Donoghue's comment that there is a need for research on the 'lived experience' of religious who worked in education, particularly in the Irish context. In his book *Come Follow Me and Forsake Temptation*, O'Donoghue develops a set of hypotheses, on how Catholic religious recruited within their schools and thereby 'retained' pupils who entered religious life and worked as teachers.[16] O'Donoghue, inviting further research, states that his hypotheses 'are in need of much testing ... for various sub-periods, for various religious orders, and for various settings'.[17] In some respects, this article involves this kind of testing: the sub-period is the first half of the twentieth-century, the religious order is the largely unexamined Infant Jesus order, and the setting is Drishane.

The Sisters of the Infant Jesus: from France to Ireland via Singapore

The institute of the Infant Jesus Sisters had originated in France, in 1666. Their founder was Nicolas Barré, a Minim priest from Amiens who was dedicated to the education of the poor. A scholar of theology and philosophy, in 1653 he was appointed head of the Minim library at the Place Royale, Paris, which was at that time one of Europe's most prestigious libraries. He took up priestly duties in Rouen in 1659, and his contact with pauper children – particularly girls – who lived on the streets lead him to his decision to found small schools with the support of two aristocratic women, Françoise Duval and Marguerite Lestocq. Their aim was to raise girls from abject poverty, so that they could earn their living. The women were joined by three others, Catherine Lestocq, Marie Deschamp and Anne Corneille, and they were known as the Charitable Mistresses.[18] By 1669, they had established seven schools in Rouen. Fr Barré proposed that they should live as a lay community; most female religious orders at that time were cloistered but he did not think that they could carry out their work if they did not live within the community in which they worked. He also wanted the Charitable Mistresses to be free of endowments and obligations to patrons, so that they could travel freely to pursue their mission to educate the female poor. Agreeing to live as a lay community, the women formed the Soeurs Maîtresses des Ecoles Charitables du Saint Enfant Jésus.

By 1686, they had had established a novitiate and over twenty schools in Paris, and they had also established schools at Rheims. At that time, the lay community became an official congregation with a religious Rule of Life, and thereafter were known as the Infant Jesus Sisters. The congregation continued to expand in France and the Sisters were in ninety-six French villages by the outbreak of the French Revolution. Though the congregation emerged diminished from the Revolution, the Sisters continued to work in education and chose to expand outside France in 1852 when they began a mission school in Malaysia (then Malaya). This marked a new stage in the work of the congregation, under the generalship of a strong-willed and charitable woman, Mother de Faudoas. The congregation gained support from Rome, and became an order in 1866, after which time the Sisters took religious vows. There began a period of expansion, as they opened convents in Japan, Singapore, Thailand, Africa, Australia, the Americas and many parts of Europe.

By the late nineteenth-century, the order was opening schools at a rapid rate in Malaysia. In part the Sisters responded to a need for Christian education in British colonial settlements, and they also pursued their own mission to spread Christianity and provide education to the poor. Christianity in Malaysia can be traced to the arrival of the Portuguese in 1511. Francis Xavier and his missionaries came later, converting thousands of native people to Christianity.[19] The colony came under Dutch rule in the seventeenth-century, and from the end of the eighteenth century was under British rule. At that time a large number of English-speaking missionaries went to work there, including the De La Salle Brothers, the Jesuits and the Good Shepherd Sisters. In the vanguard of this wave of Catholic missionary activity was the Infant Jesus order, which sent a group of Sisters to found a school in Penang in 1852, and this was followed in 1854 with the founding of a convent and school at Victoria Street, Singapore. The Sisters followed the expansion of roads and towns in Malaysia in the 1890s, building their new convents and schools in Katong, Taiping, Malacca, Kuala

Lumpur and Seremban. There they taught not only the fee-paying boarders (daughters of prosperous Eurasian families) but also pupils whose families could afford less. Fees from these boarding schools supported the work of the orphanages. At the schools, English was the medium of instruction, and by 1900 the order found that they could not provide a sufficient supply of English-speaking Sisters for their schools. They had hoped that their English convents in Wolverhampton and Weybridge would provide English-speaking Sisters and, indeed, there were some vocations, but not the numbers they needed. It was this situation that brought the order to think of Ireland, a Catholic country in which the majority by then spoke English.

The founding of Drishane: an exercise in transnational networking

When the Infant Jesus Sisters began to turn their attention to Ireland for vocations, they were directed and influenced strongly by Père Charles Nain, a talented and sophisticated strategist. He was a priest from the Séminaire des Missions Etrangères de Paris, which was located in rue du Bac, just around the corner from the Mother-House of the Infant Jesus Sisters. Père Nain had spent many years in Singapore and, while serving in the Church of SS Peter and Paul there, he was the architect for the Infant Jesus convent chapel, completed in 1904, among other significant religious houses. He therefore knew the order very well, and was sensitive to their need in Singapore for more English-speaking Sisters. In 1908, he drafted a document in which he set out for the order a rationale for establishing a novitiate in Ireland.[20] Nain made the prudent decision to involve an Irish man, Cornelius Duggan, as an agent and negotiator for the Sisters. Duggan was the brother-in-law of an Irish member of the order, Sr St Beatrice Foley, who had entered the order in Paris in 1875. Sr St Beatrice had spent most of her life at the convent in Singapore with which Père Nain was involved, and he knew of her Irish connections. Cornelius Duggan surveyed several Irish properties, and communicated his findings in English to Nain, who in turn wrote to the Mother General in Paris, to update her on developments.

Late in 1908, Duggan finally suggested Drishane Castle and its surrounding land as a possible location for the proposed convent and school, and Père Nain travelled to Ireland on 1 October 1908 to see the property. He arrived in Cork from Paris in the morning, left straightaway for Drishane in the afternoon, and wrote to Mother General in Paris the following morning, expressing his pleasure at everything he had seen.[21] It would, he wrote to Mother General, be hard to find a place more contemplative, more poetic and also more suited to the silence and calm of religious life.[22] Drishane was purchased, and the Duggan family helped to prepare it for the arrival of the first group of Infant Jesus Sisters, who took up residence on 29 March 1909.[23]

Drishane convent school and novitiate: recruitment to religious life

For religious orders involved in education and missionary activity, successful expansion relied on being able to constantly recruit new members. Recruitment has been examined by several scholars, who agree that the education delivered in convent schoolrooms included the kind of routinized behaviour that prepared girls for novitiate life. This was certainly the case at Drishane, and other convent schools in Ireland at that time. Scholars such as Tom O'Donoghue, Máire Kealy and Emmet Larkin all emphasize the effects of what Larkin calls the 'devotional revolution' that had taken place in Ireland from the second half of the nineteenth-century.[24] The reforms that followed the Synod of Thurles (1850) were

> put into practice by means of parish missions, and the introduction of devotional exercises which included the rosary, forty hours' adoration of the Blessed Sacrament, benediction of the Blessed Sacrament, devotion to the Sacred Heart, novenas and triduums, pilgrimages to shrines, processions and retreats.[25]

In boarding schools, it was important to establish the Children of Mary sodality, as many girls who joined this also went on to enter the novitiate. These devotional exercises within the boarding school meant that 'pupils had some experience of the rhythms of the religious way of life from an early age'.[26] Initiation into religious life began in school, rather than in the novitiate, and the very ordered communal life experienced by boarders prepared for religious life.

Evidence indicates that the boarders at Drishane were directly affected by the routines of religious life. Research into the annals and records of Drishane shows that the level of recruitment to the order from within the school was high. Out of a total of 298 Irish-born members, 75 per cent had themselves been at school in Drishane. Sr Hannah Slevin reflected a view shared by many other nuns:

> school life was permeated by a living awareness of Christ's example and teachings. Every school day began with religious education ... St Joseph's feast day and the Corpus Christi procession were important events in the school calendar. Many of the students were members of the Children of Mary Sodality. At mid-day, all the students went to the convent chapel to say the rosary.
>
> (Sr Hannah Slevin, interview, 2010)

In a similar vein, Sr Karen Grogan described her convent schooling saying:

> Right from the beginning there was a special family atmosphere ... there was an openness ... [and] the chapel was central to everything. We were

encouraged to go to daily mass, to make visits during the day. It was all part of the rhythm of life. There was quite a big number [of schoolgirls] who entered the novitiate, and always with the intention of going on the missions.

(Sr Karen Grogan, interview, 2010)

The novitiate (or noviceship) at Drishane, like that at many convents, was situated close to the boarding school, and pupils were always aware of the activities of the novitiate. Sometimes schoolgirls moved into the novitiate even before their second-level schooling had finished. Sr Paula Smyth recalled:

> year after year, even some of those at school with me, they entered before they had completed their education. I remember Barbara Fogarty, she was in the Leaving Certificate class ... she [didn't] return after Christmas. And the next thing she was back as a postulant ... and that was something, you know. We had been with her, played with her, and she [was gone] already before completing her secondary education.

Another respondent, Sr Nancy O'Flynn, who would spend much of her religious life in South East Asia, moved from the sixth-form dormitory of her Irish convent school into the novitiate in 1935. As she attempted to articulate the atmosphere at school that fostered vocations and missionary zeal, she drew repeatedly on war imagery: 'You're caught up in it – like the army – the spirit of it [had] a very great influence on the students there ... It was like a pre-novitiate ... Mass and visits to the Blessed sacrament, retreats etc. They nurtured a missionary vocation.'

When a young woman entered the novitiate, she became a postulant. Typically the period of postulancy would last six months, and the postulant wore simple clothes such as a short black veil and a black dress, but not a religious habit. After those six months, if she decided to continue religious life, she became a novice. The ceremony which marked this was called Reception (some orders refer to 'Clothing'). At the start of the ceremony, the novices wore a white dress and veil, like a bridal dress, and later in the ceremony they were robed in the habit. This ceremony of 'clothing' the novice was significant, and for many it marked the start of the next stage of the journey towards full and final vows. However, Reception was a very private ceremony in most orders, with few outsiders attending, and before the middle of the century it was rarely photographed. It is a part of convent life about which there are few in-depth accounts, and it was often experienced as a period of intense spiritual and intellectual development for many Sisters. The daily routines were described by Sr Hannah Slevin:

> [It was] ... highly structured with specific times for rising, prayer, meals, work, recreation and retiring. Meals were taken in silence, with Sisters taking turns to read aloud to the rest of the community ... from the *Lives*

> *of the Saints*, or bulletins of the Congregation. During recreation periods, Sisters might go out walking together ... The Great Silence lasted from the end of Night Prayer to after breakfast the next morning.
> (Sr Hannah Slevin, interview, 2010)

Several Sisters commented on their unquestioning acceptance of everything that was taught to them in the novitiate. Sr Karen Grogan said

> the early years were routine. We went along with it ... I never questioned it ... we had Bible reading, the Constitutions of the Congregation; we were introduced to the Office Book and we had other things like needlework and other diversions ... [that was the] Spiritual Year.
> (Sr Karen Grogan, interview, 2010)

While Sr Karen was unquestioning as a novice, other women religious found the routines challenging. Sr Patricia Fogarty, who entered the novitiate in the 1950s, recalled that she had felt impatient and irritated by some parts of novitate life. She could not sing and did not like music but, at she said wearily, the novices were 'always singing ... learning all the masses, hymns, Gregorian chant, stuff in parts, there was huge singing.'

Transnational communication and missionary impulse

The experience of novitiate life was fairly uniform across religious congregations. This had the advantage that professed Sisters in all congregations had some shared experiences, that transcended geographical location. For example, in a French religious order such as the Infant Jesus Sisters, many novices spent some of their novitiate at their mother-house in Paris. There they met, albeit briefly, with other young women religious from different countries, who were also embarking on religious life. But perhaps the earliest 'transnational' experience that fostered a vocational impulse in young women was experienced in school. Sr Nancy O'Flynn recalled watching the young Sisters depart from Drishane to go to Japan, Malaysia and Singapore, noting the kind of fervour that this stirred up:

> And you know, [when] the missionaries [were] going out – there was a big ceremony ahead of it. And a hymn ... that we had learned to sing for them, 'twas blood curdling: 'Go forth adieu, for life, oh dear sisters / Proclaim afar the sweetest name of God / We'll meet again in Heaven, Land of Blessings / Adieu, sisters, adieu' ... seeing them, so brave, so courageous, you know, you catch the spirit, don't you? They went out untrained with their secondary education, just that, and they ended up running schools ... it was pretty general at the time, that the

nuns weren't trained at all. They trained ... [by] experience.... Like the recruits being sent to war before finishing their training.

(Sr Nancy O'Flynn, interview, 2010)

In addition to prayer and religious observances, there were other school practices that generated enthusiasm for religious life. One Sister recalled how, in her convent school, there were regular 'Crusade' meetings, where the pupils would gather to pray and to hear about life on the missions. She recalled that singing the Crusaders' song made her think, 'What am I going to do with my life? What would make it worthwhile? The rallying words of the Crusaders' song went: "Who has a blade for the splendid cause? To live and fight for the grandest thing"' (Sr Nancy O'Flynn, interview, 2010).

Meetings of 'Crusaders', and other sodalities, were vivified by talks from visiting missionary nuns. For example the annals note in 1931 that 'Mother St Therese, Visitatrice of Japan, is going to spend a week in Drishane on her way back to the Far East, also Mother St Rosalie, Mistress of Novices in Tokyo.'[27] These talks gave missionaries the opportunity to describe the challenges and rewards of overseas teaching, and the purpose of evangelizing non-Christians. Talks were often illustrated with lantern slides, and photographs, that valorized the work of the missionaries. The 'exotic' elements of missionary life were instantly realized in such images, which not only conveyed information about mission life but also – doubtless – tantalized young viewers. On occasion, if a Sister became ill overseas and could not continue her work, she would be sent back to Drishane to recuperate. One such woman was Sr St Teresa O'Donoghue, who had been the first Irish Sister to go from Drishane to Japan in 1910. She had to return in 1922 owing to ill health, and thereafter she promoted mission life to the pupils at Drishane, where she lived – despite predictions to the contrary – to a great age, dying in 1981.

Conclusion

Though scholarship on the history of women religious is enjoying attention, and is a growth area in research in Europe and North America, there are countless ways in which historians can still interrogate records, and there is much work to be done on creating data sets, oral histories, and digital visual collections. The history of Catholic missionary initiatives, and the role of women religious in mission schools, colleges and hospitals offer immense scope for research. Deploying theoretical perspectives can add to the interpretive work, and in this chapter the optic of transnationalism has been useful in helping to focus on ways in which orders involved in missionary activity were deeply involved in transnational networks, and in the kind of cultural transfer that characterizes much transnational education activity. For example, although it is outside the scope of this chapter, it is important to note that just as returning missionary Sisters 'imported' ideas to the girls at this school, the girls who eventually joined the order and left for the mission field brought something of Ireland with them, to Infant Jesus convents at Katong, Klang, Seremban, Singapore, Yokohama, Tokyo and other parts of South East Asia.[28] Like many other Irish missionaries, they taught Irish songs, and staged dramatic productions of Irish legends, in their mission schools. It seems appropriate to refer in the closing lines of this chapter to one Infant Jesus Sister who, on going to Yokohama in 1949, exported a little of Drishane in her suitcase, providing a curious metaphor for the missionary impulse. Writing back to her Mistress of Novices, Sr St Marie Noelle recounted:

> you and Drishane and each and every one in it ... were the exhaustless topic of conversation. Indeed so impregnated was the air with Drishane ... that it was hard not to dream at odd moments that one was back there ... it was a lovely surprise to find that some of Sr St Stanislaus's [flower] seeds had travelled with us, so now we shall see a spot of Drishane blooming on the Bluff ...[29]

Notes

1 Gary McCulloch, *Failing the Ordinary Child? The Theory and Practice of Working Class Secondary Education* (Buckingham: Open University Press, 1998); Ian Grosvenor, Martin Lawn and Kate Rousmaniere (eds), *Silences and Images: The Social History of the Classroom* (New York: Peter Lang, 1999); Peter Cunningham and Philip Gardner, *Becoming Teachers: Texts and Testimonies, 1907–1950* (London: Woburn Press, 2004).

2 See for example Marjorie Cruickshank, *Church and State in English Education: 1870 to the Present Day* (London: Macmillan, 1963); Zvi E. Kurzweil, *Modern Trends in Jewish Education* (New York: T. Yoseloff, 1964); Uriah Zevi Engleman, *Jewish Education in Europe, 1914–1962: Annotated Bibliography* (Jerusalem: Institute of Contemporary Jewry of the Hebrew University, 1965); T. A. Fitzpatrick, *Catholic Secondary Education in South-West Scotland before 1872: Its Contribution to the Change in Status of the Catholic Community* (Aberdeen: Aberdeen University Press, 1986); Caroline Bowden, '"For the Glory of God": A Study of the Education of English Catholic Women in Convents in Flanders and France in the First Half of the Seventeenth Century', *Paedagogica historica*, Supplementary Series 5 (Ghent: CSHP, 1999), 77–95; Camilla Leach, 'Religion and Rationality: Quaker Women and Science Education, 1790–1850', *History of Education*, 35:1 (2006), 69–90; Ahmed Noor Khan, 'The Educational System in Muslim India: A Historical Perspective', *Paedagogica historica*, 23:1 (2006), 67–83; John T. Smith, 'Ecumenism, Economic Necessity and the Disappearance of Methodist Elementary Schools in England in the Twentieth Century', *History of Education*, 39:5 (2010), 631–57; Rashida Keshavjee, 'The Elusive Access to Education for Muslim Women in Kenya from the Late Nineteenth Century to the "Winds of Change" in Africa (1890s–1960s)', *Paedagogica historica*, 46:1–2 (2010), 99–115.

3 See for example Patricia T. Rooke, 'The Pedagogy of Conversion: Missionary Education to Slaves in the British West Indies, 1800–1833', *Paedagogica historica*, 18:3 (1978), 356–74; Patricia T. Rooke, 'Missionaries as Pedagogues: A Reconsideration of the Significance of Education for Slaves and Apprentices in the British West Indies, 1800–1838', *History of Education*, 9:1 (1980), 65–79; Alan Cumming, 'Strife and Dissension: Missionary Education in New Zealand, 1840–1853', *Paedagogica historica*, 25:2 (1985), 486–502; Andrew Porter, *Religion versus Empire? British Protestant Missionaries and Overseas Expansion, 1700–1914* (Manchester and New York: Manchester University Press, 2004); Rosa Bruno-Jofré, *The Missionary Oblate Sisters: Vision and Mission* (Montreal and Kingston: McGill-Queen's University Press, 2005); Hugh Morrison, '"Little Vessels" or "Little Soldiers": New Zealand Protestant Children, Foreign Missions, Religious Pedagogy and Empire, c. 1880s–1930s', *Paedagogica historica*, 47:3 (2011), 303–21.
4 See for example P. B. Pritchard. 'Churchmen, Catholics and Elementary Education: A Comparison of Attitudes and Policies in Liverpool during the School Board Era', *History of Education*, 12:2 (1983), 103–19; Gerald T. Rimmington, *The Rise and Fall of Elected School Boards in England* (Peterborough: Iota Press, 1986); John T. Smith, 'The Real Milch Cow? The Work of Anglican, Catholic and Wesleyan Clergymen in Elementary Schools in the Second Half of the Nineteenth Century', *History of Education*, 31:2 (2002), 117–37.
5 See for example E. A. G. Clark, 'The Early Ragged Schools and the Foundation of the Ragged School Union', *Journal of Education Administration and History*, 1 (1969), 9–21; Robert Hume, 'Interest with Impotence: The Influence of the SPCK as a Directive Force for the Development of Education in Eighteenth-Century Kent', *History of Education*, 11:3 (1982), 165–72; Timothy Allender, 'Anglican Evangelism in North India and the Punjabi Missionary Classroom: The Failure to Educate "the Masses", 1860–77', *History of Education*, 32:3 (2003), 273–88.
6 See for example Rebecca Rogers, 'Retrograde or Modern? Unveiling the Teaching Nun in Nineteenth-Century France', *Social History*, 32:2 (1998), 146–64; Bruce Blyth, *Counting the Cost: Christian Brothers and Child Care in Australian Orphanages* (Perth: P. & B. Press, 1999); Elizabeth M. Smyth and Linda F. Wicks (eds), *Wisdom Raises Her Voice: The Sisters of St Joseph of Toronto Celebrate 150 Years. An Oral History* (Toronto: Transcontinental Press, 2001); Maurice Whitehead, '"To Provide for the Edifice of Learning": Researching 450 Years of Jesuit Educational and Curricular History, with Particular Reference to the British Jesuits', *History of Education*, 36:1 (2007), 109–43; Carmen Mangion, '"Good Teacher" or "Good Religious"? The Professional Identity of Catholic Women Religious in Nineteenth-Century England and Wales', *Women's History Review*, 14:2 (2005), 223–42; Deirdre Raftery and Catherine Nowlan-Roebuck, 'Convent Schools and National Education in Nineteenth-Century Ireland: Negotiating a Place within a Non-Denominational System', *History of Education*, 36:3 (2007), 353–65; Máire Kealy, *Dominican Education in Ireland, 1820–1930* (Dublin: Irish Academic Press, 2007); Margaret Susan Thompson, 'Adaptation and Professionalisation: Challenges for Teaching Sisters in a Pluralistic Nineteenth-Century America', *Paedagogica historica*, 49:4 (2013), 454–70.
7 See for example Matthew Mercer, 'Dissenting Academies and the Education of the Laity, 1750–1850', *History of Education*, 31:1 (2001), 35–58; David A. Reid, 'Education as a Philanthropic Enterprise: The Dissenting Academies of Eighteenth-Century England', *History of Education*, 39:3 (2010), 299–317.
8 Harold Silver, 'Knowing and Not Knowing in the History of Education', *History of Education*, 21:1 (1992), 97–108.

9 In the nineteenth-century Catholic Church, women in religious orders took solemn vows and received the title 'nun', and women in congregations took simple vows and were called 'Sister'. Throughout the article, the terms nun, woman religious, and Sister are used interchangeably, as is common in scholarship. See Mary Peckham Magray, *The Transforming Power of the Nuns: Women, Religion, and Cultural Change in Ireland, 1750–1900* (New York and Oxford: Oxford University Press, 1998), 138.
10 The term 'growing vocations' was used with reference to the novitiate at Drishane Convent in 1909, when the convent was established with the purpose of providing English-speaking nuns for a French order (Infant Jesus Sisters) that needed them for their missions in Singapore and Malaysia. See Catherine KilBride and Deirdre Raftery, *The Voyage Out: Infant Jesus Sisters Ireland 1909–2009* (Dublin: Origin, 2009).
11 Deirdre Raftery, 'Teaching Sisters and Transnational Networks: Recruitment and Education Expansion in the Long Nineteenth Century', *History of Education*, 44:6 (2015), forthcoming.
12 The oral history project proposal underwent the usual university ethical review process, and a series of interviews took place between 2008 and 2010, with the permission of the interviewees, the Provincial and the relevant Superiors. Pseudonyms were given to respondents, as agreed before interviews took place. This author has permission to cite the interviews in research.
13 Infant Jesus General Archives, Paris; Infant Jesus Provincial Archives, Dublin; National Library of Singapore. For a discussion of the preparation of Irish women religious for missionary activity see Deirdre Raftery, '"*Je suis d'aucune Nation*": The Recruitment and Identity of Irish Women Religious in the International Mission Field, c. 1840–1940', *Paedagogica historica*, 49:4 (2013), 513–30.
14 Ivor Goodson and Pat Sikes, *Life History Research in Educational Settings: Learning from Lives* (Buckingham and Philadelphia: Oxford University Press, 2001).
15 Ibid., 46.
16 Tom O'Donoghue, *Come Follow Me and Forsake Temptation* (Bern: Peter Lang, 2004).
17 Ibid., 32.
18 See Elaine Meyers, *Convent of the Holy Infant Jesus: 150 Years in Singapore* (Penang: Convent of the Holy Infant Jesus, 2004); see also *The Charitable Mistresses of the Holy Infant Jesus, Known as the Dames de St Maur* (Dornach: Braun, 1924).
19 Daniel Murphy, *Irish Emigrant and Mission Education* (Dublin: Four Courts Press, 2000), 505.
20 Père Nain documents, 1908–9, Infant Jesus Provincial Archives, Dublin.
21 MS letter from Père Nain to Mother St Henri, 2 October 1908, Infant Jesus Provinical Archives, Dublin.
22 Ibid.
23 Drishane Papers, 6M 2-1 Drishane 1909–67, 9–10. Infant Jesus General Archives, Paris.
24 Kealy, *Dominican Education in Ireland*, 7.
25 Ibid.
26 O'Donoghue, *Come Follow Me*, 113.
27 MS Drishane Convent Annals, October 1931, Infant Jesus Archives, Dublin.
28 While cultural transfer and cultural exchange are outside the scope of this chapter, they are provoking and complex areas in mission history. They are treated in my forthcoming monograph on the history of Irish women religious in the international mission field, 1840–1940.
29 Sr St Marie Noelle to Revd Mother Anthony, 1 February 1949, Mission Annals, 1949, Infant Jesus Provincial Archives, Dublin.

Chapter 3

Continuity and change within the Toronto Convent Academies of the Sisters of St Joseph and the Loretto Sisters, 1847–1950[1]

Elizabeth M. Smyth

In the autumn of 2007, the Vatican's Congregation for Catholic Education issued the document *Educating Together In Catholic Schools: A Shared Mission between Consecrated Persons and the Lay Faithful*, in which the critical role of a teacher was highlighted. Asserting that 'Poor quality teaching, due to insufficient professional preparation or inadequate pedagogical methods, unavoidably undermines the effectiveness of the overall formation of the student and of the cultural witness that the educator must offer', the Congregation recommended:

> Educating the young generations in communion and for communion in the Catholic school is a serious commitment that must not be taken lightly. It must be duly prepared and sustained through an initial and permanent project of formation that is able to grasp the educational challenges of the present time and to provide the most effective tools for dealing with them within the sphere of a shared mission. This implies that educators must be willing to learn and develop knowledge and be open to the renewal and updating of methodologies, but open also to spiritual and religious formation and sharing. In the context of the present day, this is essential for responding to the expectations that come from a constantly and rapidly changing world in which it is increasingly difficult to educate.[2]

These twenty-first-century words would have had profound resonance with the members of the IBVM (the Loretto[3] Sisters), who journeyed from Ireland, and the Congregation of the Sisters of St Joseph (CSJ), who journeyed from France, to teach children in what was then the English-speaking colony of Upper Canada some 160 years ago. From their initial missions, the roles played by these communities – and indeed, their physical presence – grew and changed to meet the needs of the times, with core elements of their charisms remaining constant.

This chapter analyses continuity and change within the Toronto convent academies and women's colleges of the Loretto Sisters and the Sisters of St Joseph. During the period under study, both grew from small single-convent academies delivering a specialized curriculum to a network of state-inspected schools. Further, the two religious congregations established women's colleges, first within their convent academies and later housed in purpose-built facilities. Taught by Sister-professors, graduates were awarded degrees from the secular, non-denominational University of Toronto.

The research upon which this chapter is built is drawn from an ongoing study of women religious and education in English Canada.[4] Defining education broadly to include the primary, secondary, tertiary and professional levels, the chapter presents the experience of the pupils and women religious who learned and taught in the convents, classrooms and colleges of the Toronto Sisters of St Joseph and Loretto Sisters. Through an analysis of sources drawn from an array of public and private archives, this chapter argues that the convent academies and institutions of higher education established by these communities were characterized by continuity and change. Within the hundred-year period between 1850 and 1950, the Loretto Sisters and Sisters of St Joseph operated as agents of the Church and of the state: protecting the Catholic faith – while educating pupils from many denominations – and enhancing the status of women in secular professional society, while maintaining the norms of the consecrated life.

The chapter develops in three sections. The first sets the historical and historiographical context for the study of these two communities of women religious in Canada, by situating them in the larger fields and tracing the historical identities. The second presents a composite image of the educational experience of teachers and pupils in the communities' convent academies and women's colleges. The third outlines key elements of continuity and change and suggests directions for future research.

The historical and historiographical context

There is a certain irony in the contemporary study of the history of women religious. At the same time as their numbers and public presence are shrinking in North America and Europe, scholarly interest in them is expanding. Over the past decade, a number of books, edited collections and special issues of journals have analysed and documented the history of the growth and development of congregations of women religious and their enterprises.[5] In addition, scholars from the sciences and social sciences have been drawn to study congregations of women religious using discipline-specific tools to generate fascinating results. The 'Nun Study', David Snowdon's collaboration with the School Sisters of Notre Dame, is a longitudinal study of ageing and Alzheimer's disease in an example of one such study.[6] As well, the current work of many religious communities in the area of female human trafficking has drawn scholars of criminology and social work to collaborate with Sisters in studying their work.[7]

Significantly, the emerging field of transnational history has provided a dynamic and exciting new theoretical home for scholars of the history of women religious. Many communities, like the two studied in this chapter, can be seen through a transnational lens. Akira Iriye has defined transnational history as 'the study of movements and forces that have cut across national boundaries'.[8] And certainly, the history of the Loretto Sisters and Sisters of St Joseph is the study of women who moved across countries and continents in the course of their histories. Sven Beckert noted that transnationalism is a means to study 'the interconnectedness of human history as a whole, and while it acknowledges the extraordinary importance of states, empires, and the like, it pays attention to networks, processes, beliefs, and institutions that transcend these politically defined spaces'.[9] As vowed women within the Roman Catholic Church, these women religious operated within personal, religious, political and professional networks, bound to their Sisters-in-religion by such visible signs as habits and by the invisible bonds that are evident through the congregational Constitutions. Simon Macdonald commented in his 2013 essay 'Transnational History: a Review of Past and Present Scholarship' that 'transnational history forms one of a series of terms which have developed in order to help study engagement beyond the terms of state or nation-centred history, and especially so as to revise, renew or go beyond comparative approaches'.[10] Thus, this chapter challenges the observation made by German Historian Jürgen Osterhammel that while 'religion can be seen as a key worldwide communication network during the nineteenth century … it would be "banal" to describe such a network, which predated and outlived many nineteenth-century nations, as transnational'.[11] For, as historian Patricia Clavin concludes, transnationalism is 'first and foremost about people: the social spaces they inhabit, the networks they form and the ideas they exchange'.[12] In the case of these two congregations of women religious, these habited women were parts of congregations that had international presences, and while they may have separated from a governance perspective, their vows, congregational cultures and Constitutions nested them within transnational organizations. For, it was from Europe that both of these communities, like the pioneering teaching Sisters and teaching nurses before them, came to serve God through meeting the spiritual and physical needs of the North American Church.

Teaching Sisters, convent/college pupils

To understand the educational work of the Loretto Sisters and Sisters of St Joseph in the nineteenth and twentieth centuries, it is necessary to situate them within a Canadian historical context. The history of education in Canada is intertwined with the history of Roman Catholic religious orders. In 1615, four members of the Recollects, a male branch of the Order of St

Francis, came as missionaries to Quebec. They were joined in 1625 by members of the male Society of Jesus (the Jesuits). By 1639, the settler population of New France had sufficiently stabilized, as had the clear mandate to evangelize the indigenous population, that the two religious women's congregations, the Order of St Ursula (Ursulines of Tours) – a teaching order – and the Religious Hospitallers of St Augustine (Hospitallers of Dieppe) – a nursing order – were recruited to establish schools and hospitals. The professions of teaching and nursing were in their infancy as the practitioners worked in institutions operated outside state control – and funding. In the Roman Catholic and later Anglican traditions (and indeed associations of lay women in other Christian traditions) like-minded women gathered together, funded by personal philanthropy; charitable agencies; or occasionally with the support of local churches, diocese or congregations; to provide schools, hospitals and other agencies of social service to serve populations.

As educators, one task charged to the Ursulines was the education and conversion of aboriginal girls and young women. The voluminous correspondence of Mother Marie de l'Incarnation Guyart (1599–1672), widow, mother and first Superior the Ursulines of Quebec, documents that the women religious had much more success with the children and adults of the settler societies than they did with the children of the indigenous population.[13] She wrote to her son in 1668:

> His Majesty desires, so it is said, that the Reverend Fathers should raise a number of little Savage boys, and we a number of little girls to be French. If His Majesty desires this, we are willing to do so because of the obedience we owe to him and above all because we are all prepared to do whatsoever will be for the greatest glory of God. However, it is a very difficult thing, not to say impossible, to make the little Savages French or civilized. We have more experience of this than anyone else and we have observed that of a hundred that have passed through our hands we have scarcely civilized one. We find docility and intelligence in these girls but when we are least expecting it they clamber over our walls and go off to run with their kinsmen in the woods, finding more to please them there than in all the amenities of our French houses. Such is the nature of the Savages; they cannot be restrained and, if they are, they become melancholy and their melancholy makes them sick. Moreover, the Savages are extraordinarily fond of their children and when they know they are sad, they leave no stone unturned to get them back and we have to give them up.[14]

The themes identified here in the letters of Canada's first teaching Sisters – responding to the mandate of salvation of souls, struggling with cultural clashes with the indigenous population and between and among immigrant groups, and responding to shifting demands of the patriarchal Church and state – characterize the experience of congregations of teachers throughout Canadian history.

In the aftermath of the British conquest of 1759 and the imposition of the Quebec Act (1774), the colony of Lower Canada (Quebec) was dominated by institutions and agencies of the Roman Catholic Church. Further, it witnessed a blossoming of foundations by European religious congregations, and saw the rise of new congregations established by bishops and women in Quebec. Some of the latter spread not only across Canada but also internationally. Religious life attracted a small but significant number of Canadian women, reaching its apex in 1965 when 65,254 women were members in 183 religious congregations.[15]

The foci of this chapter are two congregations of women religious, one Irish in origin, one French in origin, that would have a significant role in the development of education, higher education, social service and health-care, nationally and internationally.

As the Roman Catholic Church spread its organizational structures across the continent beyond Quebec, Rome had to deal with the fact that the ethno-cultural makeup of the population was shifting. Beginning with the American Revolution, English-speaking settlers came to occupy indigenous lands in what would become the provinces of Ontario, Nova Scotia and New Brunswick. Waves of migration caused by political, economic and environmental factors led Anglo-Celtics to be the dominant populations in Upper Canada. This led to new dioceses being created – and the need to recruit European religious communities to serve the needs of the population – not only the Catholic adherents but also the populations at large.

Loreto becomes Loretto

The first bishop of the newly created diocese of Toronto was Michael Power.[16] Born in the colony of Nova Scotia of Irish parents, Power was educated for the priesthood in Montreal and Quebec. He was consecrated as the first bishop of the newly created diocese of Toronto in 1842. Shepherd to some 50,000 Catholics dispersed over a huge geographic area, he quickly began plans for building the infrastructure for his new diocese: recruiting priests and Sisters to tend to the spiritual and social needs of his scattered souls and building a cathedral. He would barely live to see the fruits of any of these activities. In 1847, he travelled to Ireland, where he successfully negotiated with the IBVM (the Loreto Sisters) to staff a school for girls and young women.

The creation of IBVM was the actualization of the dream of seventeenth-century Englishwoman Mary Ward (1585–1645). As her collected writings indicate, Ward was a highly intelligent woman who, befitting her class and her times, was educated by private tutors. Responding to a powerful call to serve God as an educator, Ward gathered around her a group of exiled English Catholic women to establish a community whose purpose it was to educate girls and young women. Taking the Jesuits as her model, Ward established a community of uncloistered, vowed educators: women who were centrally governed and spiritually Ignatian.[17] By the nineteenth-century, the Bar Convent in York, England was the mother-house of the Institute. It was from that foundation that Frances Ball, an Irish woman who was sent there for her own education, returned to Ireland to establish a foundation in Rathfarnham, Dublin, in a house she named Loreto. As Mother Teresa Ball, she oversaw the growth of the Irish community and exported her Sisters and their teaching mission to Calcutta (1840), Mauritius (1845), Gibraltar (1845) and Toronto (1847). The Canadian Foundation became independent of the Irish mother-house in 1881, reuniting in 2003 as the Canadian Province of the Loreto Branch of the Institute of the Blessed Virgin Mary.

Mother Teresa Ball was persuaded by Bishop Michael Power to establish a foundation in Upper Canada, even though he was candid in his assessment of the financial and cultural challenges the community might experience. He wrote:

> I cannot inform you of the number of scholars (boarders) you might have ... I am aware that for a short time there may exist among the Protestants slight prejudice, but when the parents will find that they can obtain a cheaper and better education for their daughters in the Convent than in any other establishment, they will certainly avail themselves of its advantages ... You remember that the people (Catholics, mostly Irish or of Irish descent) are not rich.[18]

Power's remarks were both prophetic and accurate. Led by Mother Teresa Dease, five Sisters journeyed from Ireland to establish a day and boarding school in Toronto and later to teach in the city's Catholic schools. Yet, one of the first activities in which the Loretto Sisters engaged was to nurse the dying prelate. Within two weeks of their arrival, their bishop was dead. This was the first of a series of challenges that rocked the community's fragile foundation. The tiny boarding school in their convent closed after four years as the Sisters were taxed not only by the demands of their enterprises but by the harsh environmental conditions. Bishop Armand de Charbonnel, Power's successor, wrote:

> These good ladies have suffered more than I can say. Deprived of a bishop, of a house, and of many things during three years, I am amazed at their having got through the numberless difficulties they contend with ... There is a good spirit in the house, they are esteemed and cherished by their pupils and all who are acquainted with them; they have done and will do much good among the Catholics and protestants ... Still the members of the house are few; the Reverend Mother is very delicate; Sister Gertrude keeps to her bed [she had had a foot amputated

because of frostbite], one has died; in fact they are overwhelmed ... they have suffered heroically; they are sinking under the hardships of their situation.[19]

Yet, in spite of this inauspicious beginning, the Institute began to flourish, with numbers of Sisters complemented by the arrival of Sisters from Ireland and by Canadian women who presented themselves as postulants. The community established schools throughout southern Ontario, Michigan and Illinois. While each school delivered a Loretto education, the Sisters adapted it to meet the changing needs of the times. Most significantly, in the late nineteenth-century, urged by the local priest, the Sisters of the Loretto School in the farming town of Lindsay, Ontario presented their pupils for the provincial examinations. Henceforth, the majority of Ontario convent schools were state-inspected, offering a state-regulated secondary school diploma that was accepted for entrance to both Canadian and American universities, teachers' colleges and schools of nursing, while nonetheless developing and maintaining a unique local character as a congregationally affiliated convent school.

The Sisters of St Joseph

The second congregation of women religious to establish a foundation in Toronto was that of the Sisters of St Joseph. In 1851, they were recruited to Toronto by Bishop Power's successor, Armand de Charbonnel. Like himself, the Sisters of St Joseph had their origins in France. While the Loretto Sisters' sole orientation was education, the Sisters of St Joseph were engaged in social service and health-care – as well as in education, especially the education of exceptional children. The Sisters of St Joseph were established in 1650 when a Jesuit priest, Jean Pierre Médaille, gathered six women in Le Puys, to establish a non-cloistered community of pious women dedicated to serving God through the service of neighbour. Initially organized as small groups of women housed in small houses, the community expanded until it was disestablished during the French Revolution. In its aftermath, under the leadership of Mother St John Fontbonne of Lyons, France, the community was re-born.

In 1836, six members of the community travelled to Carondelet, Missouri, to engage in works of education – including the establishment of a school for the deaf – as well as working in social service and health-care. The congregation spread eastward, establishing a foundation in Philadelphia, Pennsylvania in 1847. Four years later, four Sisters, led by Mother Delphine Fontbonne, the niece of Mother St John, responded to the call of Bishop de Charbonnel, and journeyed from Philadelphia to Toronto to administer an orphanage. In 1852 the Sisters expanded their work to education, and in 1854, established a convent academy for girls and young women. Further growing their work into social service, the Sisters established the House of Providence in

1857, to meet the needs of the socially marginalized and elderly. With the opening of St Michael's Hospital in 1892, the Sisters formalized their work in health-care. The community expanded across Ontario, establishing independent foundations in Hamilton, Peterborough, Pembroke, London and Sault Ste Marie. In the course of the late nineteenth and twentieth-century, these communities expanded their reach not only across Canada but also into Central and South America.

Expanding educational enterprises

From very modest beginnings in the mid nineteenth-century, by the mid twentieth-century the educational enterprises of the Loretto Sisters and the Sisters of St Joseph had expanded at an impressive rate, evolving to meet the changing societal needs, while maintaining features drawn from their historical roots. Both communities operated a variety of schools: Catholic elementary schools that, in the province of Ontario, were state-funded; secondary schools that were partially funded and private in the higher grades; private schools that accepted no state funding; music schools that were housed within the convents; schools of nursing and residential schools for First Nations students. This chapter focusses on the schools within that were convent academies, for they were the sites of demonstrable continuity and change. The most significant changes are interrelated: the aligning of the curriculum from that of the 'accomplishments curriculum' with emphasis on fine arts and languages to one which enabled the pupils to sit the state examinations and qualified them for admissions to professional programmes; creating linkages with external agencies to qualify their graduates to meet the changing concepts of women's work; establishing a tertiary department within the schools that would become a college affiliated to a university.

It is noteworthy that in Ontario the Catholic school system was publicly funded. Teaching Sisters would have to meet the same state certification standards as their secular colleagues, and thus they attended state normal schools. With the exception of a small teachers' college briefly operated in an anglophone community in the province of Quebec by the Sisters of St Joseph of Pembroke in the mid twentieth-century, neither community operated a freestanding institution of teacher education. As part of the novitiate, and congregational infrastructure, there were supports for the development of a Sister teacher, but in order to teach in state-funded schools, Sister-teachers required state certification. If they were planning to teach in state-funded schools, both potential postulants and novices attended the state-run normal schools. In the case of the novices, they did so in full habit. As noted above, both congregations did operate private, fee-paying schools, parts of which, such as the music and arts programmes, were not state-inspected. It was within these programmes, and the private music and arts lessons given within either local convents or in private music and art studios within the publicly funded schools, that uncertified Sisters could and did in fact teach.

Both Toronto academies advertised their curricula through contemporary media. From the annually produced *Prospectus* to public examinations reported in the press, both communities stressed that their programmes prepared young women socially, spiritually and academically to live rich and productive lives. Yet, in the course of the period, the focus shifted to reflect the changing social context in which they were living. Young women could opt for programmes certified through business colleges, or the Royal Conservatory of Music, and, by the first decade of the twentieth-century, could enrol in a university programme housed within the convent academies.

The emergence of women's colleges

In spite of the wishes of Sisters of St Joseph and Loretto Sisters to establish women's colleges that would be independently affiliated with the University of Toronto, this would not be the case. They were forced to defer to their brother institution, St Michael's College. In 1852, Bishop de Charbonnel recruited members of the Congregation of St Basil's to establish a school for boys. In the course of the nineteenth-century, the boys' academy grew to offer higher education, and in 1906, St Michael's College federated with the University of Toronto. While the two women's colleges tried to negotiate affiliation agreements, there was insufficient political will on the part of both the university and the Canadian ecclesiastical hierarchy to support them. Thus, the women's colleges were affiliated through their brother college and:

> All girls proceeding to a degree in the faculty of arts should be enrolled in St Michael's; lectures in college subjects were to be given at both St Joseph's and Loretto ... lecturers in religious knowledge, ethics, logic and psychology were to be supplied by St Michael's; university subjects were to be taken at the university proper as was the case with men; degrees should be conferred by the university through St Michael's.[20]

Initially women's college programmes were taught within the convent academies until in the course of the early twentieth-century they were delivered in their own physical space and, by mid-twentieth-century, were offered in purpose-built buildings that contained academic, residential, social and spiritual space.

The Rainbow and The Lilies

Each of the three schools had their own periodicals that pre-dated the existence of the colleges. An analysis of the publications of Loretto (*The Rainbow*),

St Joseph's (*The Lilies*) and St Michael's (*The College Yearbook*) shows how they document the extent to which each of these three Catholic colleges maintained and encouraged a separate identity. Yet, all three publications clearly state that the dual purpose of the colleges was the protecting of the faith and preparation for the professions. As the Basilian Fathers explained to parents:

> All university men admit the great danger to young men thrown on themselves for the first time ... Catholic boys cannot be entrusted to secular university, and yet by leaving them at home we yield our heritage and must in time reconcile ourselves to a position of inferiority ... By not securing the benefits of higher education, Catholics place themselves in a position of inferiority and weakness; on the other hand, by attending non Catholic institutions they subject themselves to influences that will almost necessarily undermine their Catholicity.[21]

St Michael's College, they explained, provided a spiritual and academic home offering 'close fatherly supervision, intimate association of priests and student, religious exercises, frequent communion, everything to foster strong faith. Students leave the college grounds only when necessary'.[22] The Calendars of Loretto College and St Joseph's College echoed the same notes:

> Young women can receive as high a training as given in any University in the world, and hardly leave convent walls. Not only is the success of the sisters in other work a sufficient guarantee of what they will accomplish here but the examinations are a test that makes efficiency essential.[23]

Catholic culture

At recruitment, during the years of study and at graduation, elements of Catholic culture shaped the students' lives. The elements of the faith and its practice were evident on a daily basis and devotional activities were nested within the academic year. Terms began and ended with Mass. Spiritual retreats were scheduled into the academic calendar. In addition to feast days and holy days, congregational celebrations such as those of the patrons of the orders and saints who held special significance for the community (in the case of the Sisters of St Joseph, St Joseph, and in the case of Loretto, St Michael the Archangel), and milestone events in the lives and histories of the orders were celebrated with special liturgies and other rituals (including the singing of hymns, the eating of special foods and the staging of concerts and entertainments). Membership in sodalities – devotional and charitable societies – and other Catholic clubs such as the Catholic Women's League and the Newman

Club – were encouraged by the students and the faculty alike, as evidenced by comments drawn from student publications: 'A Catholic Student must not confine himself [*sic*] to the duties of the lecture room and those of society. There are other higher duties that the Church demands of him';[24] and 'Faith without good works is dead.'[25] At graduation, students were reminded that their alma maters had

> but one mind, one heart, one intention – to impart to our Catholic young men and women all that is best in higher education and to cherish the high ideals of Catholic manhood, of Catholic womanhood and of the Catholic family.[26]

Co-curricular activities

Both colleges had a full complement of co-curricular activities including sports. The value of participation in these activities beyond their intrinsic values was documented by students writing in the college periodicals. The value of participation in student government was highlighted by two students, one of whom assessed its worth through a gendered lens, noting:

> In these days when woman is competing with man for big positions, she must have some acquaintance with the problems of the government of affairs. She must have a sense of individual responsibility and initiative and a capacity to deal with those annoying incidents that occur in the business world.[27]

Meanwhile the second writer focussed on skill development: 'In student government there is an opportunity for giving direct play and exercise to the faculty of judgment and thus it is a true basis of education for active and inventive powers necessary and useful in any walk of life.'[28]

Sister-professors

One feature of student life that differentiated these Catholic women's colleges from other denominational and secular women's colleges was the presence of Sister-professors. Sister-professors were highly visible models of an alternative life choice for women – a life outside marriage, motherhood or spinsterhood. The choice of this lifestyle was purposefully presented as an option to the women students. Mother Estelle Nolan, founding Dean of Loretto College, wrote persuasively in *The Rainbow* of the need for vocations to the Institute, inviting current pupils and members of the alumnae to follow in the footsteps of centuries of vowed women:

> A college cannot be maintained without an ample endowment and the best possible endowment is that of professors who have devoted their lives to this work demanding only the means of subsistence and without any claims of family ... had you lived in the middle ages, a number, even a majority of you having your present talents, tastes and inclinations, would have found happiness, sanctity and a full development of the intellectual life in some of the various monasteries in which perhaps self-actualization was more possible than at any other period of the world's history. If then, why not now ... the new-won freedom affords women many attractive avenues of experience ... we now stand on the threshold of a time which demands the fullest possible intellectual development if we are to make effective this new application of it to the needs of university students. This, then, the religious life could offer you.[29]

Following in the pattern established in their convent academies, a number of pupils from both Loretto and St Joseph's did join their Sister-professors as members of the community.[30]

The graduates

Yet, most graduates of the colleges lived out their lives as single or married women. Their achievements were recorded and celebrated in the college periodicals. One student explained their significance thus:

> It should be the end or purpose of a school journal to encourage and stimulate effort on the part of the student; first for his [*sic*] own sake, secondly for the sake of those to whom he owes his education, and thirdly, to justify, in some slight measure, the hopes of those who have planted and nourished the seeds of learning and wisdom.[31]

A glimpse into the 1925 issue of *The Rainbow*, which celebrated ten years of graduates of Loretto College and focussed on 'modern working women', provides evidence of the extent to which the College achieved its goal of promoting the professions while protecting the faith. Two graduates who practised law shared their observations, strongly grounded in First-Wave maternal feminism. Florence Daly wrote:

> It seems only natural a woman takes a more sympathetic view of trouble and does not leave untouched the smallest detail ... As for the problems affecting women and children in particular, it is undoubtedly true that a woman acquainted with the laws relating thereto is able to treat the matter in a more logical manner.[32]

Kathleen Lee observed:

> Women students are on equal footing with the men, whether it be in professional life or as a student of the law ... [where] a woman is preparing herself for a business career ... If her avocation, on the other hand is to be a Club woman or one which brings her in public contact with great numbers of people who have diverse views, a clear conception of the law in all subjects, concerning everyday life, and especially those laws relating to the welfare of women and children, will be of inestimable value.[33]

While most graduates of the two colleges did in fact live their lives as wives and mothers, one author outlined how these roles were changing and had been changed by women's access to higher education. In the aptly entitled article '*A College Education Does Not Unfit a Girl for Married Life*', the curiously anonymous writer asserts:

> The average woman of yesterday entering matrimony depended for her livelihood upon the generosity of some male, the woman of today – especially is it true of the college woman – acknowledges her master in no such sense ... The modern college woman believes in economic independence and that equality will make it possible to come nearer realizing an ideal marriage [*sic*] ... The two entering a marriage contract must determine to share their dangers and responsibilities or it is unfair to both.[34]

The fact that these words are included in the collection is not surprising; the fact that the author does not choose to sign her name is telling.

Women and the professions

A few more observations are worthy of note. The majority of the women graduates did enter the traditional women's professions; education, social service and heath-care. The women teachers scattered far across Ontario, taking positions in the public non-denominational high school system. As noted earlier, Catholic high schools were publicly funded – but at a lower rate and only to the end of grade 10. Thus, Catholic high schools through to secondary school leaving were the domain of the religious orders – out of necessity – for they worked for very low wages that were frequently ploughed back into the operational budgets of the schools. For a woman to earn a living wage as a secondary school teacher, a public secondary school appointment was her only route. Some of these women who chose such paths did experience discrimination because of their religious affiliation.

Continuity and change

There are many similarities and differences in the historical development of the Loretto Sisters and the Sisters of St Joseph in English Canada. While both were European in origin, both quickly attracted postulants through their Canadian and American schools. After the 1880 separations of both congregations from their founding houses (in the case of the Loretto Sisters, Rathfarnham in Ireland; in the case of the Sisters of St Joseph, Lyons, France by way of Carondelet, Missouri), there are few examples of Sisters journeying from the foundational mother-houses to join either community. Both quickly became Canadian. The postulants presenting themselves to Sisters of St Joseph were predominantly Irish and quickly lost overtly French customs, traditions and language in their community celebrations. While they received few native-born Irish postulants, the Loretto Sisters retained and promoted their Irish heritage. Reflecting the ethno-cultural orientations of the English Canadian Church, postulants from the waves of immigrants drawn to Canada in the course of the twentieth-century joined and ascended to leadership in both communities. With a few notable exceptions, few First Nations women or racialized women joined either community.

For both communities, the 1950s marked the high points in community expansion. Both undertook major building projects that would culminate in modern college residence buildings. Both expanded their Mother-House facilities, anticipating an ongoing expansion in the number of women presenting themselves as novices. But the winds of change were beginning to blow. Neither initially seemed to heed the warnings presented to the Canadian Religious Conference by sociologists of religion that the growth was unsustainable.[35] Neither seemed to see that the cosmetic changes in religious habits, and the calls for attention to congregational governance signalled by the creation of the meetings of the International Union of Superiors General by Pope Pius XII, would be followed by the major changes in religious life that accompanied the Second Vatican Council. Neither foresaw that the activities the congregations undertook in their work with African Americans and First Nations communities would both further their commitment to social justice and cause them challenge – and indeed be challenged by – societal norms.

Soon after the 1950s dawned, the three Catholic Colleges at the University of Toronto began to more fully cooperate with each other. Classes quickly became coeducational and the tight community bonds that cemented the identity of Loretto and St Joseph's College began to loosen. By the early years of the twenty-first-century, St Joseph's College has disappeared, memorialized by the establishment of the Sisters of St Joseph's Chair in Systematic Theology at the University of St Michael's College. While Loretto College continues to exist, it serves as a women's residence and houses offices that support the Loretto community's local and international initiatives.

The theme of continuity and change, using the metaphor of a river, was the framework used by Loretto Superior Sister Helen Cameron at the ceremony in 2005 to mark the community's departure from Loretto Niagara.[36] This iconic school situated on a hill above Niagara Falls was the favourite convent – and final resting place – of pioneering Sister, Mother Teresa Dease. Sister Helen recalled:

> Teresa [Dease] was always a woman of faith; so are we. We all know what a privilege and gift it has been to have a convent overlooking Niagara, to work there, to pray there, to enjoy its beauty. Are we now invited to experience a kind of gift, a more painful one – that of moving forward to another form of mission, a work that is still not clear? Are we meant to be like the waters of the Niagara River, always on the move?[37]

The history of these two communities is one of flow and change: a history of two European congregations that shaped and were shaped by their North American experience. While loyal to the charism of their founders, both changed and adapted to meet the needs of the times.

This chapter has begun to explore the experience of the women students and their Sister-professors in the two Catholic women's colleges at the University of Toronto. While it provides some evidence that their goals of protecting the faith and preparing women for the professions were to some extent met, only continued research and analysis can further unpack how transnational connections both helped and hindered the achievement of these goals.

Notes

1 The author acknowledges the support of the Social Sciences and Humanities Research Council of Canada; the Archivists and Leadership Teams of the Institute of the Blessed Virgin Mary, Canadian Province and of St Joseph of Toronto; and the Archives of the Archdiocese of Toronto and of the University of St Michael's College in the University of Toronto.
2 Congregation for Catholic Education, *Educating Together in Catholic Schools. A Shared Mission between Consecrated Persons and the Lay Faithful* (Vatican City: Congregation for Catholic Education, 2007), 20 (available at http://www.vatican.va/roman_curia/congregations/ccatheduc/documents/rc_con_ccatheduc_doc_20070908_educare-insieme_en.html).
3 The Canadian province of the IBVM spells their name with two 't's: Loretto.
4 English Canada is defined as the nine provinces and three territories outside Quebec that make up Canada.
5 In addition to the work of the authors represented in this collection and the bibliographies accompanying the chapters, see for example the 2013 special issue of *Paedagogica historica*, 49:4: *Catholic Teaching Congregations and Synthetic*

Configurations: Building Identity through Pedagogy and Spirituality across National Boundaries and Cultures. For work on women religious in Australia, see for example Heather O'Connor, *The Challenge of Change: Mercy and Loreto Sisters in Ballarat, 1950–1980* (Ballan, VIC: Connor Court, 2013). For Europe, see for example Bart Hellinckx, Frank Simon and Marc Depaepe, *The Forgotten Contribution of the Teaching Sisters: A Historiographical Essay on the Educational Work of Catholic Women Religious in the 19th and 20th Centuries* (Leuven: Leuven University Press, 2009). For a bibliography produced by the HWRBI, see http://historyofwomenreligious.org/women-religious-bibliography/modern-2/.

6 David Snowdon, *Aging with Grace: What the Nun Study Teaches Us about Leading Longer, Healthier, and More Meaningful Lives* (New York: Bantam, 2001).

7 See for example the work of criminologist Christine Gervais, 'Alternative Altars: Beyond Patriarchy and Priesthood and towards Inclusive Spirituality, Governance and Activism among Catholic Women Religious in Ontario', in Brenda Cranney and Sheila Molloy (eds), *Canadian Woman Studies: An Introductory Reader*, 3rd edn (Toronto: Innana Publications, 2015), 54–64.

8 Akira Iriye, 'Transnational History', review article, *Contemporary European History*, 13 (2004), 211–22.

9 C. A. Bayly, Sven Beckert, Matthew Connelly, Isabel Hofmeyr, Wendy Kozol and Patricia Seed, '*AHR* Conversation: On Transnational History', *American Historical Review*, 111:5 (2006), 1440–64. This is an interview and the specific quotation from Beckert is on p1459.

10 Simon Macdonald, 'Transnational History: A Review of Past and Present Scholarship' (2013), https://www.ucl.ac.uk/cth/objectives/simon_macdonald_tns_review, 6.

11 As quoted in Simon MacDonald, "Transitional History", 16.

12 Patricia Clavin, 'Defining Transnationalism', *Contemporary European History*, 14:4 (2005), 433–4.

13 J. Marshall, *Word from New France: The Selected Letters of Marie de l'Incarnation* (Toronto: Oxford University Press, 1967), 31.

14 Marie de l'Incarnation to her son, Claude, 1 September 1668, in ibid., 341.

15 Marc A. Lessard and Jean Paul Montminy, *The Census of Religious Sisters of Canada* (Ottawa: Canadian Religious Conference (CRC), 1966). CRC, *Statistics of the Institutes of Consecrated Life and Societies of Apostolic Life in Canada* (Ottawa: CRC, 2004), 29.

16 Mark George McGowan, *Michael Power: The Struggle to Build the Catholic Church on the Canadian Frontier* (Montreal and Kingston: McGill-Queen's University Press, 2005).

17 Ward's revolutionary vision would cause her much personal and professional grief. The Church was unwilling to support her vision of women's education and she was excommunicated by papal bull. Upon her death in 1645, her memory was erased and it was not until 1909 that she was recognized as the founder of the community.

18 Bishop Michael Power to Mother Teresa Ball, 25 June 1847, as reprinted in *Life and Letters of Rev. Mother Teresa Dease*, ed. 'a member of the community' (Toronto: McClelland, Goodchild and Stewart, 1916), 37–9.

19 Archbishop Armand de Charbonnel to Bishop Daniel Murray, as cited in Kathleen McGovern, *Something More than Ordinary* (Richmond Hill, ON: The I Team, 1989), 103–4.

20 Laurence K. Shook, *Catholic Post-Secondary Education in English-Speaking Canada: A History* (Toronto: University of Toronto Press, 1971), 158.

21 University of St Michael's College Archives (USMCA), St Michael's College Calendar (1912–13), 12.
22 Ibid., 15–16.
23 USMCA, *The Echo* (1913), 48.
24 USMCA, 'Mission Work', *St Michael's College Yearbook* (1922), 52.
25 USMCA, 'Our Sodality', *St Michael's College Yearbook* (1922), 63.
26 USMCA, Revd L. O'Reilly, Baccalaureate Sermon, 15 May 1918, 'Convocation', *St Michael's College Yearbook* (1919), 24.
27 USMCA, 'Student Government', *St Michael's College Yearbook* (1919), 45.
28 USMCA, 'Students' Council at St Joseph's', *St Michael's College Yearbook* (1921), 49.
29 Mother Estelle Nolan, 'The College of the Future', *The Rainbow: College Alumnae Number 1915–1925*, 4–7.
30 For a more detailed analysis, see for example the anniversary displays for both colleges, available at http://stmikes.utoronto.ca/onehundred/timeline.
31 USMCA, 'Some Early Steps in School Journalism', *St Michael's College Yearbook* (1917), 39.
32 Florence Daly, 'The Woman Lawyer', *The Rainbow: College Alumnae Number 1915-1925*, 28.
33 K. Lee, 'Law from a Woman's Viewpoint', *The Rainbow: College Alumnae Number 1915–1925*, 29.
34 Anon., 'A College Education Does Not Unfit a Girl for Married Life' (presented under the authorship of Mrs Hinzmann, Mrs McGradey, Florence Daley, Kathleen Lee, Elsie Irvine and Eleanor Mackintosh), *The Rainbow: College Alumnae Number 1915–1925*, 24–5.
35 For a fuller discussion see Lessard and Montminy, *Census of Religious Sisters of Canada*.
36 For a fuller discussion, see Elizabeth M. Smyth, 'Loretto Academy Niagara (1861–1969)', *Encounters*, 2, (2006), 25–42.
37 Sister Helen Cameron. 28 September 2005, available at http://ibvm.org/content/view/98/139 (accessed 1 September 2010).

Chapter 4

Sister-physicians, education, and mission in the mid-twentieth-century

Barbra Mann Wall

Introduction

When Sister Helen Lalinsky, a Medical Mission Sister, graduated from medical school in 1935 in the United States, she was the first Catholic woman as a member of a religious community to become a qualified physician and surgeon.[1] Sister Helen attended the Woman's Medical College (WMC) of Pennsylvania and in doing so, crossed both religious and gendered boundaries in a field dominated by men. Through case studies, this chapter traces the education of Catholic Sister-physicians, surgeons and obstetricians who trained for the medical mission field in the mid-twentieth-century. It explores the educational experiences of Sisters, or nuns, and the respective curricula and destinations after education. It also examines how Sister-physicians negotiated their professional roles while working under the benefits and constraints of the male-dominated medical profession and the hierarchical Catholic Church.

The chapter highlights the experiences of the Medical Mission Sisters (MMS), established by Anna Dengel in 1925 in Washington, DC. Dengel was born in Austria, and with the encouragement of Dr Agnes McLaren, a Catholic convert and Scottish missionary to India, Dengel trained as a medical doctor at University College, Cork. After her 1919 graduation, she worked as a physician in Rawalpindi, India, where she became convinced that women trained in medical science were needed to care for other women. Dengel envisioned a group of women who were not only educated in scientific medicine and nursing but were also dedicated to God. She acknowledged the endeavours that missionary priests and Sisters had carried out over the centuries, but she emphasized that her religious community would provide 'organised, systematic medical care by people ... who have been trained in the medical field as doctors, nurses, or technicians'.[2] Her religious congregation (sometimes called order or community) became the first of its kind to include women in the medical field who were both professional and religious, and the first Catholic congregation of women to work as physicians, surgeons and obstetricians.[3] From the beginning, the MMS congregation was international in its composition: the four original members were from three different countries. In the late 1930s, the MMS moved their Mother-House, the authoritative structure for women's religious orders, to Philadelphia, Pennsylvania. The MMS initially worked in India, but after the Second World War they expanded to other parts of the world.

Two other women's religious congregations will be considered when discussing certain themes. The Foreign Mission Sisters of St Dominic, or Maryknoll Sisters, were established in 1912 under the leadership of Sister Mary Joseph Rogers. This was the first American-based Catholic women's religious congregation to be established specifically for overseas missions. Then, in 1937, Marie Martin founded the Medical Missionaries of Mary (MMM) in Nigeria. Although they concentrated their work in Africa and on other continents, the congregation initially consisted of Irish women, and they specifically focussed on health-care for women and children. This broke with the earlier Irish mission tradition of establishing schools.[4]

Review of historiography

This chapter builds on scholarship of women from faith-based backgrounds in medicine. Angelyn Dries has analysed Catholic Sister missionaries in the American context, but she only touched on the Sisters as physicians and she did not discuss medical education. Dana L. Robert has written extensively about Christian women's place in global medical missions, but she centred much of her work on Protestant women.[5] In my own work, I have argued for the centrality of women in medicine, nursing and health-care in the United States. The Catholic hospital system that began in the late-nineteenth-century was primarily the work of Catholic Sisters.[6] Secular women also established hospitals so that women could have opportunities to join the medical profession. Women often justified their position by working in paediatrics, public health and obstetrics, considered the domain of women; and while Sister-doctors did so as well, they also were surgeons and thereby penetrated a more masculine space.[7]

As Catholic Sisters prepared for the mission field, they benefited from growing educational opportunities for women. Ellen S. More, Elizabeth Fee, Manon Parry, Regina Morantz-Sanchez and Steven Peitzman have noted how women in the United States struggled to obtain a place for themselves in the world of medicine. They have described how the burgeoning women's medical movement that began in the late-nineteenth-century came to a halt by the early-twentieth-century as women faced increasing costs for medical education, pressures to postpone marriage and childbearing, and exclusion from internships and residencies. By 1950, only 6.1 per cent of practising physicians were women.[8]

Medical histories in the colonial context also have grown over the past several decades.[9] Megan Vaughan's *Curing Their Ills* has had a lasting influence.

She has analysed British Protestant medical missionary discourse during the colonial era and how physicians and Church leaders represented their subjects in Africa. She asserted that missions used their medical work as 'part of a program of social and moral engineering through which "Africa" would be saved'.[10] Women's voices in this discourse usually came from physicians' wives and a few nurses. None of the sources mentioned here focussed on Catholic Sisters and their education for the medical profession. This chapter bridges that gap and illustrates broader historical trends that consider the significance of gender and religion in medicine.

Scholars of Africa such as E. A. Ayandele, Elizabeth Isichei and Augustine S. O. Okwu have been critical of white missionaries who, they claim, did not act on behalf of blacks but instead pushed their own interests. While Ayandele wrote his book during the African independence movement, Isichei and Okwu are more recent publications.[11] By contrast, Lamin Sanneh documents evidence that a 'new and educated class of African leaders' began taking greater responsibility for modernizing Africa 'as a postslavery society that is as committed to reform as it is to renewal of custom and tradition. The instrument for this double task belonged with the idea of mission as an intercultural process.'[12] Indeed, in Catholic hospitals and clinics today, indigenous workers constitute the majority of personnel. Yet European and American Sisters were the ones who established Catholic hospitals or administered them for the local diocese. They went to the mission field with the specific goal of training African nurses and midwives to replace the European and American Sisters. Not only did this sustain what the Sisters began, but it also was a means to ensure acceptance of their religious and medical ideas about health-care.

A distinct Catholic trajectory

At the turn of the twentieth-century in the United States, the power of science increasingly took command in American hospitals, and institutions organized with recovery and cure as realistic goals to be brought about by professionally educated personnel who worked in an increasingly technological environment.[13] Within this environment, Catholic Sisters worked as nurses and hospital administrators, and they adapted to the scientific advances that occurred over the twentieth-century. Significantly, Catholic congregations of women as physicians, surgeons and obstetricians were latecomers into the medical field because they faced certain Church restrictions. Although surgery in hospitals had grown in the early-twentieth-century with the expansion of asepsis that made procedures safer, until 1936 Catholic canon law prohibited Sisters from performing surgery or delivering babies. They could nurse, however, and, rarely, a few Sisters obtained medical education before they entered the convent. Sisters took vows of poverty, chastity and obedience, and most scholars attribute the prohibition in surgery and obstetrics to fears that Sisters' vow of chastity would be violated if they even looked at private parts of men or women's bodies. Indeed, as early as the seventeenth-century in France, Vincent de Paul expressed his fears that scandal would occur if the Daughters of Charity cared for women in labour, and he warned them not to tend women in childbirth.[14] These ideas persisted over the centuries. In 1901 the Congregation of Bishops and Regulars issued the *Normae*, which explicitly forbade Sisters to work with maternity cases. Then in 1917 under Pope Benedict XV, Sisters' lives became more restricted when the Code of Canon Law mandated that all religious orders, both men and women, had to have separate living quarters. If they were part of an institute such as a hospital or college, they had to live in a separate building where no member of the opposite sex was allowed.[15]

These issues became even more significant as Sisters prepared for the mission field in the mid-twentieth-century. In 1935, a woman physician pleaded for Catholic women to play a greater role in medicine. The woman doctor was particularly needed in the fields of gynaecology and obstetrics. She wrote:

> We are all too dimly cognizant of the menace of birth control, sterilization, and so-called therapeutic abortions. Do we realize that over the whole of this country, numbers of young women, who are every year being graduated in medicine, form a great and ever increasing corps for the propagation of these iniquities? ... For women are going more and more to women for medical help. And among the women doctors graduated each year, not ten per cent are Catholics.[16]

The topic of birth control had escalated in public discourse since the 1920s, and in the 1930s both chemicals and condoms were being perfected for use. The Catholic Church was one of the few organizations that took a public stand against the practice. The writer also advocated for more Catholic medical schools. The few Catholic women who entered medicine had to go to 'pagan schools' where birth control was broadly presented and discussed. To her, Catholic medicine meant not only feeding the hungry and caring for the sick but also that

> the unwanted child [could] be saved to Catholicity, the unbaptized child to be brought to Baptism, the 'problem', wayward child to be guided aright, the unmarried mother to be fortified, the married mother to be saved from modern birth control.[17]

The writer's worries were realized in 1937 when the American Medical Association adopted birth control as a standard part of medical school curricula.[18]

While the writer saw the need for Catholic women in medicine as a means to fight the evils of abortion and birth control, Dengel and others had broader plans. Both at home and in distant mission fields, bishops needed hospitals for women that would be run by the Sisters. In India, for example, women of the Muslim faith could not be tended by men, and Dengel particularly was concerned for Muslim women who practiced purdah.[19] Indeed, many of the problems that society faced affected women, and Dengel and McClaren, along with American, Irish and Australian bishops, lobbied the Vatican in Rome to overcome the ban on Sisters practising surgery and obstetrics. As Margaret MacCurtain asserts, 'tensions came from within the [C]atholic structure of authority'.[20] Eventually both lay and religious personnel were able to get the pope to lift the ban in the 1936 publication *Constans ac sedula*, which allowed Sisters to do surgical and obstetric work and encouraged them to enter medical schools. Although they faced uphill battles to belong to the male world of medicine, by the late 1930s they had succeeded. The role of physician or surgeon gave Sisters medical authority, and this separated them from the religious authority of priests. Thus, as medical women with a distinct body of knowledge, they gained an unusual respect from the patriarchal Church.

Medical education

After 1936, Catholic Sisters were able to obtain medical education with the help of their religious congregations. Although Sisters as individuals took vows of poverty, their religious communities did not, and the congregation paid for the Sister's medical education. Yet it was not easy, and often Sisters had to borrow medical textbooks. At the same time, medical schools offered a limited number of scholarships, and nuns applied for and received them. While American Sisters had to go to Europe for midwifery training, others could get medical degrees in both the United States and Ireland.[21] In Ireland, university degree programmes had gained popularity for Sisters in the 1920s, and Dengel earned her medical degree there. Educational endeavours were enhanced when the MMM opened Our Lady of Lourdes Hospital in Drogheda, Ireland, in 1940, which became a training school for general nursing and a postgraduate hospital recognized by the Royal College of Obstetricians and Gynaecologists. In 1957 Our Lady of Lourdes officially became an International Medical Missionary Training Center.[22]

Sisters in the United States did not run their own centres for the education of physicians, however, and their educational trajectories varied. After graduation, they also worked in very different settings from most women physicians. Of the Sisters who obtained medical degrees in the United States, the MMS made up the majority. Sister Helen Lalinsky was one of the pioneer Sisters in the MMS congregation in the United States. Before she entered the convent, however, she trained as a laboratory technician. When she joined the MMS in 1928, she knew their focus was to improve health-care in developing countries, and she planned to continue her work in the laboratory. Yet

Mother Anna (Dengel) had other plans and asked Sister Helen if she had ever considered medicine. Significantly during those years, Superiors of women's religious congregations made the decisions as to the different roles nuns would undertake. Based on aptitude and credentials, Sisters went into nursing, medicine, teaching or other professions. Their vow of obedience assured that they would go wherever their Superiors deemed necessary. Therefore, Sister Helen entered medical school after a pre-medical education at Trinity College in Washington, DC, a Catholic college for women that had been in existence since 1897. Yet finding a medical school that accepted a woman was difficult, and Sister Helen benefited by the WMC in Philadelphia where she obtained her medical degree in 1935.[23]

The WMC opened in 1850 as the first college organized for women's medical education in the world.[24] It provided an important place for women's entry into medicine, and many of its students went into missionary work. Indeed, in the late nineteenth and early twentieth centuries, several religious denominations provided opportunities for women to work in the mission field. Protestants were initially reluctant to hire women for missions, but they eventually became active as wives or as single women with professional skills such as teaching, nursing or evangelism. Some also went into medicine.[25] At WMC, faculty consisted of both men and women, and by 1893, all students had to take a four-year course of study. In 1930 the college constructed a new hospital in East Falls, a suburb of Philadelphia, where students could obtain both classroom and hospital experience in one facility.[26] By then medical schools throughout the United States included better laboratory and clinical experiences as they became associated with hospitals. The changes during these years shaped medical education over the entire twentieth-century.[27]

When Sister Helen began classes in 1932, the MMS congregation paid $400 for general tuition. All students had to buy their own microscopes (at $45), pay additional laboratory fees and cover costs for textbooks. The total cost of the four-year programme was approximately $2,200.[28] Although the MMS congregation supported Sister Helen, it was only seven members strong at the time and poor. She had to borrow textbooks, and she won the Dr Julia P. Horton Memorial Scholarship, which was a boost for her struggling congregation. Secular women students rented rooms in nearby lodgings that the Dean's Office had approved. Yet because of canon law restrictions, when Sisters went away to colleges and medical schools, they had to find other Sisters with whom to live. Thus Sister Helen found a room with the Sisters of St Joseph, who had a Catholic house a few blocks from the WMC.[29]

Sister Helen followed the general plan of instruction, which was heavy in the sciences. The first year included lectures and laboratory experiences in physiological chemistry, anatomy, histology and embryology. Students also took a course in individual health maintenance. Second-year students had classes in physiology, pathology, bacteriology, public hygiene and sanitation, physical diagnosis, surgery, obstetrics, pharmacology, and post-mortem techniques. The third year had more lectures and laboratory experiences in applied anatomy and physiology, pathology, applied therapeutics, toxicology, surgery, medicine, obstetrics, gynaecology, paediatrics, industrial hygiene, nutrition, obstetric and neurological diagnosis, operative surgery, orthopaedics, and additional clinical instruction in the WMC's hospital and dispensaries. The final year featured lectures in medicine, surgery, obstetrics, paediatrics, oto-laryngology, orthopaedic surgery, ophthalmology, medical law, roentgenology, epidemiology and public hygiene. Bedside instruction took place not only in the WMC hospital but also in five other clinical facilities in the city.[30] Sister Helen claimed she never regretted her decision to enter medical school, but she equivocated when she spoke about her frustrations over medicine's technological emphasis. She stated, 'I wish I could somehow have been a nurse. Nurses are closer to the people than most doctors.'[31]

After her graduation in 1935, Sister Helen had to complete a one-year novitiate. This period included the formation of candidates to the religious life to help them attain unity in their lives and work, along with an intense spiritual indoctrination. The novitiate was a time for all Sisters to absorb community ideals, develop mental toughness and a sense of obedience, and take on a group identity and common purpose. Commitment mechanisms involved de-individualizing practices to decrease one's sense of separateness, even as they created boundaries between Sisters and the outside world.[32] In the convent, a hierarchical authority structure was modelled on that of the Catholic Church, with a Sister Superior as head of the community. Although Sister-physicians had to undergo religious formation in the convent along with all their other Sisters, the MMS physicians held an advantage. In the 1920s and early 1930s, the MMS introduced a class distinction among their membership – that only Sister-doctors could be Superiors. By 1938, however, these distinctions disappeared. The Sisters changed their *Constitution* to note, 'All the members form one class. ... In the community all were to be addressed as Sister.'[33]

Following her novitiate, Sister Helen once again re-entered the secular world of medicine through an internship and residency. Internship and residency programmes in areas of specialization had become commonplace in American medical education since the early-twentieth-century,[34] and although women faced discrimination in their choices, Catholic Sisters benefited from their status in the Catholic Church. They typically obtained positions in Catholic hospitals. For example, Sister Helen accepted an internship at Misericordia Hospital, a Catholic facility in Philadelphia, and then she served a gynaecological and surgical residency at Georgetown University Hospital, a Catholic institution in Washington, DC.[35] In March 1938, she sailed for Rawalpindi, India, where she expected to assist two lay doctors. Unfortunately, they left before she came, and she had to quickly assume the role of doctor-in-charge. Sister Helen spent the next forty years of her life in

India and Pakistan, and she did surgery; attended outpatient clinics; assisted in deliveries; and taught doctors, nurses and laboratory assistants. Refresher courses in obstetrics and gynaecology could be taken in Bombay, India, or in other large cities.[36] After Sister Helen graduated from the WMC, a new cadre of scientists joined the faculty to fulfil a demand to increase full-time chairs in the science department. By 1937, there were twelve women and two men who were full-time science faculty.[37]

Expansion of medical missions

The experiences Sisters gained in medical schools prepared them to practise in an expanding international medical mission field after the Second World War. European colonial rule was disintegrating, and nationalist governments began organizing their own health-care institutions and schools. The MMS' work had been hampered by the war, but now they saw themselves playing a supportive role in these endeavours, and they expanded their medical missions to Africa.[38] This was a time of tremendous growth in the missionary movement; by the 1950s more foreign missionaries, both Protestant and Catholic, were in Africa than ever before.[39]

Florence Young (who took the religious name of Sister Mary Benedict) trained for the mission field in this context. She entered the WMC to study medicine in the early 1940s. Her four-year instruction included classes from 9 a.m. to 6 p.m. every day of the week and some Saturdays. Admission requirements included graduation from an accredited college with a baccalaureate degree; completion of the Scholastic Aptitude Test; and, as a recommendation, the Graduate Record Examination. Table 4.1 is a summary of hours for courses in the first two years of Sister Benedict's programme. It shows how heavily the sciences dominated the curriculum.

Clinical courses in medicine, obstetrics, gynaecology, paediatrics and surgery took up much of the curriculum in the third and fourth years, while dermatology, psychiatry, proctology, neurology and oto-laryngology commanded fewer hours. Sister Benedict graduated in 1946.[40] She had a clear understanding of the sciences, pathology, surgery, germ theory, the role of sanitation in disease prevention, and the positive outcomes of care for pregnant women and their children. She and other Sisters translated this knowledge to their patients in the mission fields. Sister Benedict went on to serve as physician and surgeon in India and Pakistan; and in 1957 she became Superior of the American province of the MMS. In this role, she travelled all over Asia, South America and Africa to inspect MMS hospitals.[41] She also became a fellow of the International College of Surgeons.[42]

A Maryknoll Sister entered the WMC in the late 1940s. Her congregation had to pay an annual tuition of $625 for her. She had to complete four sessions of thirty-two or more weeks of instruction for the medical degree. As in earlier years, instruction centred on the sciences and included lectures, laboratory work, clinical conferences, and clinical experiences in hospitals and outpatient facilities. Examinations had to be passed before matriculation to the next year. The 1947-8 *Bulletin* noted, 'To be eligible for promotion a student must be without condition, and her grades in the major subjects of the year must average more than the minimum passing grade [75-9 per cent].' The clinical courses continued to use the College Hospital and other facilities in Philadelphia. Rotations in the four main services – medicine, obstetrics, gynaecology and paediatrics – began in the third year and expanded in the fourth.[43]

Sister-doctors were needed in even greater numbers in the 1950s when papal encyclicals began focussing on an expanded mission. Although the MMS were heavily concentrated in India and Pakistan and the Maryknolls had been in other parts of Asia, each responded to Pope Pius XII's 1957 encyclical, *Fidei donum* ('On the Present Condition of the Catholic Missions, Especially in Africa'), which called for mission expansion to Africa. As African independence movements were growing, he was concerned that 'blind nationalism' would lead the countries 'into chaos or slavery'. He wrote, 'The present situation in Africa, both social and political, requires that a carefully trained Catholic elite be formed at once from the multitudes already converted.'[44] The Sisters were ready for this endeavour.

In 1957, Sister Jane Gates became the first MMS doctor assigned to Africa. Eventually the MMS elected her Superior of the congregation. Sister Jane followed yet another educational trajectory. She joined the MMS in 1945 and, after a formation period, became a full member of the congregation in 1948. She then attended Georgetown University Medical School and graduated in 1955. For her residency, Sister Jane rotated through various services, including a year's surgical residency at Sacred Heart Hospital in Allentown, Pennsylvania. Her medical education also was part of a larger movement in the Catholic Church that escalated in the 1950s when the Sister Formation Movement began focussing on the need for more education, or formation, for the Sisters' specific works. As with the earlier Sisters who went to medical schools, most of the nuns' education took place in non-Catholic settings, and they were exposed to secular values in new ways. In the 1950s, for example, they confronted increasingly diverse beliefs and people.[45] The educational investment spurred by the Sister Formation Movement prepared a whole new generation of Sisters, and in 1956, the movement culminated in the establishment of the Conference of Major Superiors of Women. These women were highly educated and, like the Sister-physicians who preceded them, they enhanced nuns' status within the Catholic Church.[46] Thus, by the mid-twentieth-century, a large group of women emerged who were educated not only in medicine but also in nursing, theology and teaching. They supported themselves and their Sisters and increasingly earned respect as experts in their fields.[47] As Jay P. Dolan asserts, these Sisters were 'at odds with the authoritarian

Table 4.1 Summary of hours in courses, 1945–6

Year 1		Year 2	
Anatomy	689	Bacteriology	192
Body mechanics	6	Clinical diagnosis (laboratory)	75
History of medicine	14	Medicine	89
Health maintenance	11	Nutrition	9
Library studies	7	Obstetrics	10
Statistics	20	Pathology	308
Mental hygiene	10	Paediatrics	8
Chemistry	238	Pharmacology	184
Physiology	126	Physiology	154
		Psychobiology	8
		X-ray technology	8
		Sanitation	30
		Surgery	16
		Tropical medicine	30
TOTAL	1,121	TOTAL	1,121

Source: 96th Annual Announcement of the Woman's Medical College of Pennsylvania, Session of 1945–6, Legacy Center, Drexel University College of Medicine and Archives and Special Collections, Philadelphia, PA.

and hierarchical Roman model that [had] emerged in the early-twentieth-century'.[48] By 1967, the MMS had 738 professed Sisters in thirteen different countries. Medical doctors numbered 53, of which 8 were graduates of the WMC. A further 11 were medical students.[49]

Mission medical practices

When the Sisters went to the mission fields, they took their full arsenal with them: their Christian faith, and their own biomedically trained physicians, surgeons, obstetricians, nurses and midwives. Using mission practices in sub-Saharan Africa as an example, it can be seen that although Sisters were well trained in colleges and universities, when working in the bush or holding clinics during wartime or other periods of violence, as often occurred in the missions, they faced new challenges. There were rarely enough Sister-doctors for mission hospitals, and sometimes they had to perform unfamiliar surgical procedures. As an example, Sister Pauline Dean was a member of the MMM who worked at St Mary's Hospital in Urua Akpan, Nigeria, during the country's civil war. As people with unusual injuries poured into her hospital, sometimes she had to read instructions from a textbook as she operated. Sister Pauline had joined the congregation after receiving her medical education from Liverpool, and she did postgraduate work in paediatrics in the United States.[50]

Catholic Sisters' medical practices incorporated both science and religion. Even though they performed surgery in sterile operating rooms, Sisters also included religious feasts, processions and rituals in their hospitals, and they celebrated holy days. They also commanded respect in their white habits with their distinct gender and religious identities. Mission hospitals were sites where one could witness a variety of healing practices. One hospital administered by the Maryknoll Sisters in Tanzania was such a space. In 1949 a Sister delivered a premature baby who did not thrive, and after performing life-saving measures, she eventually gave up and baptized the infant. Yet she had also allowed an indigenous practitioner into the delivery room. This person beat 'some sort of a cooking pot which she held over the baby's head, and chant[ed] a pagan song to ward off the evil spirits'. Soon the baby started breathing.[51] Blending of cultural practices was not common in Africa in the 1940s, and the Sisters strongly believed in the superiority of their scientific medical practices. Yet they also believed in miracles. In this case, the Sister attributed the baby's survival to the baptism rather than to the work of the indigenous healer.

It must be added here that when considering Catholic Sisters' work, a conception of health-care exclusively in terms of scientific practice and prevention of illness is inadequate. The significance of their practice was much broader. They believed in both religious and non-religious explanations of illness. As I have argued elsewhere,

> These included a concept of disease as a deviation from normal health, caused and potentially correctable by natural means, but also other perspectives that involved an emphasis on supernatural causes and healing by religious measures.... Often, however, natural causes were subsumed under ultimate supernatural causes that only divine intervention could ameliorate.[52]

Catholic hospitals were distinct in other ways. One of the defining characteristics was the way in which religious and professional boundaries altered authority structures. Significantly, the MMS, MMM and Maryknoll Sisters ran their own mission hospitals and clinics, and secular physicians had limited control. As an example, the MMS recruited doctors from the United States, the Philippines, the Netherlands, England and Ireland, and they typically were men who were accustomed to managing hospitals in their home countries. Conflicts sometimes erupted over hospital control in the mission. At Holy Family Hospital in Berekum, Ghana, for example, a Sister-nurse wrote to Mother Anna in 1952 and noted that the doctors

> are a problem ... They said if they would never be in charge they would not want to stay. I pointed out that they were in charge of the medical side of the work and they say they are not.

The physicians had disagreed with the Sisters over where patients should be allowed to die. Ghanaians' tradition was to die at home, and they often took their dying relatives out of the hospital, against the doctors' wishes. The Sister added,

> When patients are about to die the people insist on taking them home. There are several reasons why and the doctor will not let them go. But the doctors are only in the ward a few minutes but the relatives pester the life out of the poor Sister all day, and too, the patients and their relatives have human rights. We do everything to keep them; we are just as anxious for their recovery as the doctors are, but as I told the doctors this is not a jail. We cannot keep them by force.[53]

The Sister prevailed. Indeed, as tensions developed between medical men and Catholic Sisters in mission hospitals, each group expected to have power. Factors involving gender and religion often determined how conflicts would work out. Sisters – either nurses, midwives or physicians – were the administrators, which was a role men traditionally held. As well, if a Sister-physician was at the hospital, she would be in charge of the medical department. In these positions, Sisters had unusual authority, which was very different from secular hospitals.[54]

Although Catholic Sisters were motivated by religious beliefs, they used their religious networks to disseminate scientific knowledge in the missions. Their hospitals had a large role to play in training indigenous nurses, laboratory technicians and auxiliary workers. The MMS, for example, taught nursing students about germ theory, anatomy and physiology, specific diseases, medication administration, preventive care, and the need for vaccinations.[55] Although by the 1980s African healers had become more influential in the nuns' medical practice, Sisters' schools of nursing continued to be based on the biomedical model and British educational standards. Significantly, Catholic Sisters did not establish medical schools in the mission field. These institutions were far too expensive to operate. Nuns did provide indigenous medical students learning experiences when they worked in the Sisters' hospitals, went on treks with the Sisters into the bush, and accompanied them to women's and children's clinics.[56]

As an example of a small but interesting diaspora, some Nigerian women trained in Ireland under the direction of the MMM. Afterwards, they returned to Nigeria where they became teachers, midwives, nurses, social workers and medical doctors.[57] By the 1980s, Catholic mission personnel had globalized as American and European Sisters increasingly left their convents to serve in new ways. The Sisters who remained refocussed their mission away from acute care to primary health care. Sister Pauline Dean, who had worked in Nigeria during its civil war, began writing *Primary Health Care Links*, a periodical that she used to educate her Sisters in their different destinations. These writings became a significant influence in helping them rethink their mission as they grew more open to local customs. She suggested new ways to teach and learn from local populations. In 1987, for example, she advocated a whole new training scheme for Sisters going into medicine. Rather than beginning with anatomy and physiology, they should start the curriculum with classes on how to live and communicate in groups. They needed to learn skills in listening and how to dialogue with others. They also needed to focus more on the causes of poverty and oppression in the different regions, how power was distributed, and information about unjust land laws. She recommended the Sisters read Paulo Friere's *Pedagogy of the Oppressed*. This did translate to new endeavours, as the MMM today attend to issues of income insecurity, social and economic discrimination, and security issues for women.[58] This was a far cry from their own curricula in medical schools that had focussed exclusively on the sciences and clinical work.

Conclusion: both medical and religious

Catholic Sisters, educated to be scientific practitioners in the mid-twentieth-century, were convinced that they could bring established biomedical knowledge and therapeutics to the missions in order to provide health-care access as one answer to an uneven distribution of health-care. Beginning in the late 1930s women of the Catholic Church began playing greater roles in the Church's healing mission. Under the leadership of Anna Dengel and others, Sisters established a new position for themselves that combined religious commitment and medical science. The Catholic Church provided a structure for women in religious congregations as vowed, celibate women to obtain a medical education and eventually to cross national borders as they developed care networks all over the world. Dengel and others had worked to change a centuries-old policy that prohibited Catholic Sisters from practising medicine, and after 1936, they became surgeons, midwives and obstetricians. They worked alongside nurses in new initiatives and, for the most part, embraced the power structure of the Catholic Church and what it could provide them. Their personal negotiations of their religious and gendered identities in secular medical schools and later in their mission hospitals reveal the possibilities of professional roles for Catholic Sister-doctors; and they set the stage for their work as both doctors and missionaries in an international health-care endeavour.

Significantly, Catholic Sisters viewed illness in both biological and spiritual frameworks. Education in medicine came in medical schools, and spiritual formation came from convent training, with each having equal influence. To maintain their medical skills, nuns attended continuing education classes; and for their vocations, they went to Mass, prayed daily and attended yearly retreats. Through their vow of chastity, Sisters distanced themselves from other women, which sometimes was difficult in the secular world of a medical school. Yet their distinct religious and medical identities claimed respect for them not only as Roman Catholic Sisters but also as physicians, surgeons and obstetricians. At the same time, by professing religious vocations, Sisters could leave behind many of the traditional gender constraints experienced by secular women physicians. This helped them as they obtained internships and residencies in Catholic institutions and also when they expanded into other countries in the name of the Catholic Church. And through their vow of obedience, they could be trusted to carry out not only scientific care but also spiritual healing wherever they went, even as they performed surgery on both men's and women's physical bodies. Yet as religious women, when they stepped beyond traditional gender roles, their religious identities had to project an asexual persona; this afforded them exemption from much of the gender discrimination of that era. Church authorities demanded it, and secular society benefited by having skilled medical women at the helm.

Notes

1 'Sister Helen Lalinsky', alumna file, Records of WMC/Medical College Pennsylvania Registrar, 1921–75, accession number 266, Legacy Center, Drexel University College of Medicine and Archives and Special Collections, Philadelphia, PA (hereafter cited as Legacy Center). Her religious name was Sister Alma.
2 Anna Dengel, *Mission for Samaritans* (Milwaukee: Bruce, 1945), 1.
3 Angelyn Dries, *The Missionary Movement in American Catholic History* (Maryknoll, NY: Orbis Books, 1998).
4 Medical Missionaries of Mary, *Medical Missionaries of Mary* (Dublin: Three Candles, 1962).
5 Dana L. Robert, *Christian Mission: How Christianity Became a World Religion* (Chichester: Wiley-Blackwell, 2009); Dana L. Robert (ed.), *Converting Colonialism: Visions and Realities in Mission History, 1706–1914* (Grand Rapids, MI: Wm B. Eerdmans, 2008).
6 Barbra Mann Wall, *Unlikely Entrepreneurs: Catholic Sisters and the Hospital Marketplace, 1865–1925* (Columbus: Ohio State University Press, 2005).
7 Ellen S. More, Elizabeth Fee and Manon Parry (eds), *Women Physicians and the Cultures of Medicine* (Baltimore: Johns Hopkins University Press, 2009).
8 For statistic, see ibid., p. 5. See also Steven J. Peitzman, *A New and Untried Course: Woman's Medical College and Medical College of Pennsylvania, 1850–1998* (New Brunswick, NJ: Rutgers University Press, 2000), Regina Morantz-Sanchez, *Sympathy and Science: Women Physicians in American Medicine* (New York: Oxford University Press, 1985).
9 See, for example, Anne Digby, *Diversity and Division in Medicine: Health Care in South Africa from the 1800s* (Oxford: Peter Lang, 2006); David Hardiman (ed.), *Healing Bodies, Saving Souls: Medical Missions in Asia and Africa* (Amsterdam: Rodopi, 2006); and Claire L. Wendland, *A Heart for the Work: Journeys through an African Medical School* (Chicago: University of Chicago Press, 2010). J. D. Y. Peel, *Religious Encounter and the Making of the Yoruba* (Bloomington: Indiana University Press, 2000).
10 Megan Vaughan, *Curing Their Ills: Colonial Power and African Illness* (Stanford, CA: Stanford University Press, 1991), 74.
11 E. A. Ayandele, *The Missionary Impact on Modern Nigeria* (New York: Humanities Press, 1966); Elizabeth Isichei, *A History of Christianity in Africa: from Antiquity*

to the Present (Grand Rapids, MI: William B. Eerdmans, 1995); Augustine S. O. Okwu, *Igbo Culture and the Christian Missions, 1857–1957* (New York: University Press of America, 2010).

12 Lamin Sanneh, 'Bible, Translation, and Culture: From the KJV to the Christian Resurgence in Africa', in Andrea Sterk and Nina Caputo (eds), *Faithful Narratives: Historians, Religion, and the Challenge of Objectivity* (Ithaca, NY: Cornell University Press, 2014), 187.

13 Charles E. Rosenberg, *The Care of Strangers: The Rise of America's Hospital System* (Baltimore: Johns Hopkins University Press, 1987).

14 Colin Jones, *The Charitable Imperative: Hospitals and Nursing in Ancien Regime and Revolutionary France* (London and New York: Routledge, 1989), 190; and Laurence Brockliss and Colin Jones, *The Medical World of Early Modern France* (Oxford: Clarendon Press, 1997). See also Barbra Mann Wall, 'Science and Ritual: The Hospital as Medical and Sacred Space, 1865–1920,' *Nursing History Review*, 11 (2003), 51–68.

15 Dom. Jean Prou and the Benedictine Nuns of the Solesmes Congregation, *Walled about with God: The History and Spirituality of Enclosure for Cloistered Nuns* (Leominster: Gracewing, 2005).

16 Elise Whitlock-Rose, 'The Ball and the Cross,' *Catholic World*, 141 (May 1935), 223.

17 Ibid., 225.

18 Kristin Luker, *Abortion and the Politics of Motherhood* (Berkeley, CA: University of California Press, 1984); Patricia Walsh Coates, *Margaret Sanger and the Origin of the Birth Control Movement: 1910–1930. The Concept of Women's Sexual Autonomy* (Lewiston, NY: Mellen, 2008); and https://laurawelsh93.wordpress.com/2014/04/14/1960s-the-sexual-revolution/ (accessed 15 February 2015).

19 Purdah was a practice by some Muslims in which women had to live separately or behind curtains so they would not be seen by strangers or men.

20 Margaret MacCurtain, *Ariadne's Thread: Writing Women into Irish History* (Galway: Arlen House, 2008), 288.

21 Medical education for women in the United States began in 1848 when Elizabeth Blackwell entered Geneva Medical College. See Peitzman, *A New and Untried Course*; MacCurtain, *Ariadne's Thread*; Margaret O'Hogartaigh, *Quiet Revolutionaries: Irish Women in Education, Medicine and Sport, 1861–1964* (Dublin: History Press Ireland, 2011); Dries, *The Missionary Movement*, 247.

22 Mary Duff, Gerard Fealy and Isabelle Smyth (eds), *Nursing Education in Drogheda, 1946–2004* (Drogheda: Nursing Education Commemorative Committee, 2004); Sister Margaret Mary Nolan, *Medical Missionaries of Mary: Covering the First Twenty-Five Years of the Medical Missionaries of Mary, 1937–1962* (Dublin: Medical Missionaries of Mary, 1962); Medical Missionaries of Mary Archives (hereafter cited as MMMA); O'Hogartaigh, *Quiet Revolutionaries*.

23 'Sister Helen Lalinsky'.

24 In 1969 the school became coeducational. Today this institution continues as the Drexel College of Medicine.

25 Angelyn Dries, 'American Catholic "Woman's Work for Woman" in the Twentieth Century', in Dana L. Robert (ed.), *Gospel Bearers, Gender Barriers: Missionary Women in the Twentieth Century* (Maryknoll, NY: Orbis Books, 2002), 127–42; Jonathan J. Bonk (ed.), *The Routledge Encyclopedia of Missions and Missionaries* (New York: Routledge, 2007); Annette Vance Dorey, *'Miss Dr Lucy' and Maine's Pioneering Female Physicians, 1850s–1920* (Lewiston, ME: Van Horn Vintage Press, 2013).

26 *91st Annual Announcement of the Woman's Medical College of Pennsylvania*, Session of 1940–1, Legacy Center. See also Peitzman, *A New and Untried Course*.

27 Peitzman, *A New and Untried Course*.
28 *86th Annual Announcement of the Woman's Medical College of Pennsylvania*, Session of 1935–6, Legacy Center.
29 Sue Chastain, 'A 50-Year Reunion of 3 "Lady Doctors"', *Philadelphia Inquirer* (29 May 1985); and 'Sister Helen Lalinsky'.
30 *86th Annual Announcement*.
31 'Sister Helen Lalinsky'.
32 Wall, *Unlikely Entrepreneurs*; Rosabeth Moss Kanter, *Commitment and Community: Communes and Utopias in Sociological Perspective* (Cambridge, MA: Harvard University Press, 1972); Carole K. Coburn and Martha Smith, CSJ, 'Creating Community and Identity: Exploring Religious and Gender Ideology in the Lives of American Women Religious, 1836–1920,' *US Catholic Historian*, 14 (Winter 1996), 94–7.
33 MMS *Constitution*, 1938, Archives of the Medical Mission Sisters, Philadelphia, PA (hereafter cited as MMSA).
34 Rosenberg, *The Care of Strangers*.
35 *86th Annual Announcement*; 'Sister Helen Lalinsky'.
36 'Sister Helen Lalinsky'.
37 Peitzman, *A New and Untried Course*.
38 This is a theme of my new book, *Into Africa: A Transnational History of Catholic Medical Missions and Social Change* (New Brunswick, NJ: Rutgers University Press, 2015).
39 Adrian Hastings, *African Catholicism: Essays in Discovery* (London: SCM Press, 1989), 122.
40 *96th Annual Announcement of the Woman's Medical College of Pennsylvania*, Session of 1945–6, Legacy Center.
41 Anon., 'Nun Wages Global War on Disease', *Citizen Advertiser*, Auburn, New York (2 May 1963), n.p.
42 Anon., 'Featuring Sister Doctors', *The Medical Missionary* (January–February 1958), 20.
43 *98th Annual Announcement, Bulletin of the Woman's Medical College of Pennsylvania*, 1947–48. Quotation is on p. 37.
44 *Fidei donum*, 1957, available at http://www.vatican.va/holy_father/pius_xii/encyclicals/documents/hf_p-xii_enc_21041957_fidei-donum_en.html (accessed 18 February 2015).
45 Ritamarie Bradley, 'A Survey of a Decade Past', *Sister Formation Bulletin*, 10:4 (1964), 32–6; Marjorie Noterman Beane, *From Framework to Freedom* (Lanham, MD: University Press of America, 1993); Kenneth Briggs, *Double Crossed: Uncovering the Catholic Church's Betrayal of American Nuns* (New York: Doubleday, 2006).
46 Marie Augusta Neal, *From Nuns to Sisters: An Expanding Vocation* (Mystic, CT: Twenty Third Publications, 1990); Briggs, *Double Crossed*.
47 Leon Joseph Cardinal Suenens, *The Nun in the World* (London: Burns and Oates, 1962); Briggs, *Double Crossed*.
48 Jay P. Dolan, *In Search of an American Catholicism: A History of Religion and Culture in Tension* (New York: Oxford University Press, 2002), 234. I discuss this theme further in Wall, *Into Africa*.
49 Sister M. Regis Polcino, 'The Medical Mission Sisters', *Transactions and Studies of the College of Physicians of Philadelphia*, 35:1 (July 1967), n.p.
50 Sister Pauline Dean, Biafra War Diary, MMMA.
51 Diary Digest, 18 October 1949, Diaries, Africa, Mauritius and Tanganyika, Box 1, Maryknoll Sisters Archives, Ossining, New York.

52 Wall, *Unlikely Entrepreneurs*, 130.
53 Letter to Mother Dengel, 7 December 1952, Ghana box, MMSA.
54 Wall, *Unlikely Entrepreneurs*.
55 Holy Family Hospital Berekum, 'Works for the First Three Quarters of 1965', MMSA.
56 Summary of discussions with Mother Benedict, 1 February 1964, MMS.
57 Isichei, *A History of Christianity in Africa*.
58 Paulo Friere, *Pedagogy of the Oppressed* (New York: Continuum, 1970).

Chapter 5

Sisters as teachers in nineteenth-century Ireland

The Presentation Order

Catherine Nowlan-Roebuck

Introduction

The nineteenth-century was a period of significant change in the spheres of Roman Catholicism and national education in Ireland. The gradual dismantling of the penal code that had begun during the last quarter of the eighteenth-century gathered pace, culminating in Catholic Emancipation in 1829. At the same time the Catholic Church embarked on a campaign of improvements that saw the refurbishment of existing churches or the construction of new ones. James Kelly identifies the 'swelling ranks' of priests and nuns as an important index of the growing strength of the Church at this time.[1] In education, the establishment of the National System (1831) brought elementary education to children throughout the country and the Intermediate Education Act (1878) laid the foundation for progression to second level in the latter decades of the century and beyond. A distinctive feature of life in the Catholic Church across Europe was the emergence and growth of female religious congregations. This growth was represented in a move away from enclosure to more open and active congregations. The Church viewed these female institutes as a new missionary force to focus on the areas of welfare, health-care and education.[2] The Presentation Order (1775) was the first of the modern Irish congregations to be established and has been dedicated to the education of girls since its foundation. The growth and development of the institute during the nineteenth-century was based solely on its mission to provide religious, literary and industrial instruction to the daughters of the poor. That the expansion of the Presentation network of convents and schools took place in tandem with the developments in national education provides a valuable opportunity to examine how the order carved out a role for itself at the heart of Irish education.

All of the schools established by the order were opened and operated by the Sisters, ensuring for them a dual identity as women religious and teachers. Tom O'Donoghue points to the developments in international research into the history of teachers as a general field of research since the 1980s in the United States and Canada, and more recently within the British context.

He identifies the history of Catholic teachers as a specific area within this and describes a growing body of literature internationally. Notwithstanding these developments, he states that the history of teachers' lives is still much under-researched, particularly 'regarding the intersection of religion and education'.[3] Deirdre Raftery notes that whilst international research, especially in the last ten years, has attempted to make the schools and classrooms of the past more accessible by drawing on a variety of sources, within the Irish context little has been done on teachers' lives. In particular, she states that research into the work of religious orders engaged in teaching has tended away from exploring the experiences of religious as educators, focussing instead on the histories of orders or schools they founded.[4] This is in contrast to the direction taken by international scholars who have begun to examine the contribution of nuns to education.[5] Existing research within the Irish context includes the work of Tony Fahey and Caitríona Clear, both of whom focus on the establishment, growth and development of the orders and congregations that opened in Ireland from the end of the eighteenth-century and into the nineteenth-century.[6] Mary Peckham Magray's work examines the way in which religious women became central to the religious and cultural change that occurred in Ireland during the nineteenth-century, and how nuns used the powerful position they gained through the course of their work.[7] Maria Luddy and Rosemary Raughter place the establishment and growth of the new congregations and orders within the context of the philanthropic movement that had come to prominence during the eighteenth-century, and continued into the nineteenth-century.[8] In her study 'The Journey Out', Suellen Hoy traces the pattern of migration whereby young Irish women went out to the New World as nuns, aspirants, postulants, novices and professed Sisters. Starting in 1812, Hoy identifies two waves, the first lasting from 1812 until 1881, and the second beginning in the 1860s and continuing into the twentieth-century.[9] In the area of education Máire Kealy documents the lives and contributions of Dominican Sisters to Irish education at a time of significant change (1820–1930).[10] This study seeks to build on her contribution by examining the work of the Presentation Sisters as women religious who were teachers. Using documents and material from a number of convent archives and information from the Records of the Commissioners of National Education, what follows is an account of some aspects of the way in which the Presentation Sisters established and ran their schools in Ireland during the nineteenth-century.[11]

Background

Although its start was delayed until the end of the eighteenth-century, Ireland experienced the significant growth in the number of women religious and convents that became a distinguishing feature of life in the Roman Catholic Church across Europe during the nineteenth-century. In 1800 there were

6 religious orders with 11 houses of women religious between them. This accounted for 120 nuns, a total that rose to over 8,000 in 1901, with the second half of the century experiencing a dramatic growth from 1,552 in the 1851 Census to 8,031 in the Census of 1901. Clear points out that between 1841 and 1901 the number of nuns increased eight-fold, in spite of a decline of almost one half in the Catholic population during the same period. By 1900, the number of orders and congregations had increased to 35 with the number of convents standing at 368.[12] This expansion had the dual effect of fulfilling the obligations of the Church to respond to the vast amount of poverty and distress that existed in the country at the time, whilst at the same time providing relatively wealthy single women with the opportunity to engage in socially active work. The modern native Irish congregations were founded by independently wealthy women, who had engaged in charitable work before establishing religious communities. Nano Nagle (Presentation Order), Mary Aikenhead (Sisters of Charity), Frances Ball (Loreto), Catherine McAuley (Sisters of Mercy) and Margaret Aylward (Sisters of the Holy Faith) had all been involved in philanthropic work.[13] These institutes were established between the 1770s and 1850 and were complemented by Irish houses of congregations with continental origins, and adapted versions of female orders with a more traditional heritage. The organizational basis was thus laid for the growth that took place after 1850.[14]

In addition to the new Irish foundations, many European congregations such as the Sisters of the Sacred Heart, the Daughters of Charity of St Vincent de Paul, the Good Shepherd Sisters and the St Louis Sisters set up convents in Ireland during the nineteenth-century. Equally the older orders like the Dominicans, who became significant educators of the daughters of the wealthier Catholics, and the Poor Clares, who became involved in the institutional care of orphans, were revived. The numbers of women in Irish convents in 1800 represented roughly 6 per cent of the total number of Catholic priests and nuns. This rose to 38 per cent in 1850 and 70 per cent by 1901. By including the approximately 1,100 teaching Brothers that were in the country by 1901, women religious still numbered 64 per cent of the total.[15] This growth in women religious occurred at the same time as the Catholic Church was re-emerging and re-organizing, and the development of women's religious orders constituted an integral element in its transformation. By their work as teachers, nurses, visitors of the sick and poor, and social workers generally, nuns were in immediate contact with Catholics of all classes and conditions. As such they were central to the development of the new, devout, modern Irish Catholic culture.[16]

It also occurred at a time when significant changes were taking place in education in Ireland. In October 1831 Lord Stanley, the Chief Secretary to Ireland, wrote to the Lord Lieutenant outlining the government plan regarding a system of national education for Ireland. This became known as the Stanley Letter.[17] The main aims of the proposed system were to afford 'a combined literary and separate religious education ... for the poorer classes of the community' and 'to unite in one system children of different creeds'.[18] To achieve this, the Letter proposed that a government-appointed Board of Commissioners be created, which should have representations from the Established Church, the Catholic Church and the Presbyterian Church. The Board would have control over schools built by or placed under its auspices. It would also have control over all the books to be used in the schools and the funds voted annually by Parliament. Stanley proposed that the schools be kept open for four or five days a week for literary instruction, whilst separate religious instruction could take place on the remaining one or two days and either before or after school hours on the school days. A system of inspection was also proposed to ensure that regulations were enforced. The Commissioners drew up a set of rules to operate the proposed system, which, in subsequent years, were altered and adapted under pressure from the different religious bodies. This manipulation by the Churches was compounded by the failure of the Board to implement the scheme as it was intended from the outset. The result was a system of national education that was denominational in practice, over which the local patrons, and by extension the Churches, had a significant degree of control.[19]

With the exception of the Ursulines, all of the convents in Ireland in the first four decades of the nineteenth-century had been founded in the country or had been operating here from the middle of the seventeenth-century. During this period the work of nuns was directed overwhelmingly towards the poor and was distinguished by a non-specialized approach. In 1820 only 10 per cent of convents catered for the middle and upper classes, rising to 14 per cent by 1840. The introduction of congregations from abroad during the period from 1840 to the mid 1860s brought greater involvement by the women religious in the education of girls whose families could afford to pay for their education, and in various kinds of custodial care. In 1864 just over 11 per cent of convents ran asylums for orphans and a sizeable majority of them, 84 per cent, operated schools of various kinds.[20] More than anything else nuns were educators, and the most important social effects achieved by them were through the systems of schools they created. During the early years of the nineteenth-century nuns had little impact on public education in Ireland. In 1824 there were 46 schools attached to 'nunneries' as compared to 9,352 hedge schools and 1,727 schools connected with the various Protestant education societies.[21] Once the National System of Education was established in 1831 some of the earliest applications for assistance from the Commissioners came from convent schools, with 26 of them connecting to the System by April 1837.[22] By 1853, the first year in which figures were compiled on convent and monastic schools as a specific group, 99 convent schools had joined the System. This rose to 111 in 1857, 132 in 1864, and 145 in 1870.[23] The returns of the *Special Report on Convent Schools* listed 129 schools attached to various orders of nuns that had connected to it by

1863. These schools catered for 68,000 children in infant, female and industrial schools. The figures also show that over 77 per cent of the convent schools operating within the System were run by the Sisters of Mercy and the Presentation Sisters, both of which were strongly committed to working with the children of the poor.[24]

To establish some degree of independence from the state, nuns refused to take the state examinations for classification as salaried teachers.[25] As a result they were paid on a capitation basis per pupil. In 1850 this was increased from £10 to £20 for each 100 children on the roll.[26] By 1874, the average cost to the state per nun in the system was £13, one-third the cost per lay teacher at £37.[27] In assessing the competence of convent schools, the inspectors' comments on the observance of regulations, quality of teachers and the effect of the school on a locality point to the favourable nature of the *Special Report*. In general they stated that the Board's rules were 'very well observed'. One report stated that in relation to the attainments, method of teaching and organizing skill of the teachers, the Sisters 'appear to be thoroughly qualified as regards attainments, and they exhibit much skill and judgement in the regulation of the classes. They employ the improved modes of teaching with earnestness and intelligence.'[28] Finally, in relation to the general impact of convent schools on education in the local area one inspector recorded that:

> Were it not for this school several of the ordinary female schools of my district would be very ill off for competent teachers. Not to mention the many teachers appointed from this school before it came under my superintendence, I am able to state, of my own knowledge, that within the last three or four years six of my best teachers were appointed from among its monitresses.[29]

This positive view had been expressed ten years earlier by Maurice Cross, then Secretary of the National Board, when he said that 'Convent schools present, generally, the best specimen of education that Ireland can produce.'[30] The decision by the government in 1883 to give state support to denominational training colleges confirmed the prominent position of nuns in elementary education.[31] This decision also represented an admission of failure regarding the provision of trained teachers for the system. By funding the training college they established in Baggot Street in 1877, the authorities gave the Sisters of Mercy control over the main avenue of access to the teaching profession at primary level for Catholic women. This in turn formalized the profound impact nuns had on education, both directly through their own schools and indirectly through the training of women teachers for all Catholic schools in the National System.

In addition to this focus on elementary education, secondary schools for Catholic girls were also established by the religious orders of nuns including the Dominicans, the St Louis, the Sacred Heart, the Ursulines and the

Faithful Companions of Jesus.[32] The Intermediate Education (Ireland) Act of 1878, which provided grants to male and female students on an equal basis, also played an important role in making higher education available to women.[33] However, second-level education was in the main confined to girls of the middle classes whose parents could afford the fees and who could spare a daughter from the need to find employment. For the vast majority, education beyond primary level was unusual.[34]

The Presentation Order

The Presentation Sisters were founded by Nano Nagle in Cork City in December 1775 and have been involved in the education of girls in Ireland for over 240 years. The congregation was the first of the modern Irish religious institutes for women to be established, and from its inception was dedicated to the religious, literary and industrial instruction of the children of the poor, most particularly their daughters. The Order was founded by Nagle in an effort to ensure the continuation and permanence of the work in which she had been engaged since the mid 1750s.[35] By 1830, the Presentation network incorporated twenty-eight convents and schools, and over the course of the nineteenth and twentieth centuries the Institute developed to become one of the biggest providers of education to Catholic girls in Ireland.[36] In contrast to other Irish congregations of women religious – such as the Sisters of Charity, the Sisters of Mercy and the Holy Faith – the Presentation Order confined its mission to education, and did not begin to engage in other types of work until the later decades of the twentieth-century. Although this concentration on education reduced Nagle's original vision to a single mission, it defined the congregation as a teaching order, and its members as both women religious and educators specifically.

Nano Nagle was born in 1718 in Ballygriffin, County Cork, the eldest of Garret and Ann Nagle's seven children. The Nagles were a wealthy Roman Catholic family whose ancestry has been traced back to the Norman invasion of Ireland in 1169. Having completed her education abroad, Nagle lived in Paris for a number of years before returning to Ireland. Following the deaths of her parents and one of her sisters, she moved back to the family home in Ballygriffin at some point after 1749.[37] The poverty, ignorance and superstition of the poor people living around her, and how these conditions affected them, had a significant impact upon Nagle and she resolved to dedicate her resources to the poor.[38] Overwhelmed by the hopelessness of the situation, she returned to the Continent to enter the religious life but did not reach the stage of final profession. This was a time of spiritual torment for her, which culminated in the advice of her director to return to Ireland to instruct Irish children.[39] In one of her letters to the first Irish Ursuline, Nagle confided that 'Nothing would have made me come home but the decision of the clergyman that I should run a great risk of salvation if I did not follow the inspiration.'[40]

Nagle opened her first school on the south side of Cork City, in a little cabin in Cove Lane (now Douglas Street) near her brother's residence sometime around 1755. The schoolhouse was a rented mud cabin that had two earthen-floored rooms, a garret and a thatched roof.[41] This was quickly followed by a second school on the north side of the city, and within eighteen months she was catering for about 400 children. Originally, Nagle's intention was to cater for girls only, but at the insistence of her family she obtained another cabin in Cove Lane in which forty boys were taught by a master whose salary she paid. Her work expanded to such a degree that by 1769 she had opened seven schools: five for girls and two for boys.[42] Nagle did not confine herself to working with the children in the schools. After the hours at the schools were finished, she visited and tended the sick, the aged and the poor in their homes and in the city's infirmaries before she returned home.[43] Her first attempt to secure permanence for this work led to the successful foundation of the Ursuline Order in Ireland in 1771. However, the Ursulines' observance of their Rule of Enclosure meant that of the three schools in Cove Lane, they could only work in the one that lay within that enclosure. The Sisters taught in this girls' school every day, supplementing Nagle's programme with needlework. The Cork Ursulines opened a boarding school for the daughters of the merchant classes in January 1772, and a steady increase in the numbers of both religious and pupils led the community to move from this campus to Blackrock in 1825. Although she was a regular visitor to the convent and spent time in the religious instruction of the boarders every Saturday, Nagle did not become a member of the community. Instead, she remained in her cottage at the gates of the convent. Faced with the continuing need to secure the future of her work she established a new religious society, one that was devoted exclusively to the poor. Calling her new congregation the Sisters of the Charitable Instruction of the Sacred Heart of Jesus, she began her novitiate along with three companions on Christmas Eve 1775, and professed final vows in June 1777.[44]

Nagle's death in 1784 marked the beginning of a difficult period for the fledgling congregation and the small community struggled to survive. Illness and death, the embezzlement of funds, and the scarcity and insecurity of new members reduced the small community almost to the point of closure. The remaining years of the eighteenth-century saw the Sisters work towards canonical recognition in conjunction with Francis Moylan, then bishop of Cork. During this process, they changed the name of the Institute to the Sisters of the Presentation of the Blessed Virgin Mary, compiled and adopted Rules and Constitutions, and began to observe the Rule of Enclosure. By 1800 five new Presentation convents were established in Killarney (1793), George's Hill Dublin (1794), Waterford (1798), North Presentation in Cork City (1799) and Kilkenny (1800). These five houses became known as the Primary Foundations and played a significant role in the growth and development of the Order.[45] Final papal approval was granted in 1805 and with it came the status of religious order and the profession of solemn vows. By their observance of enclosure and the profession of solemn vows, the Sisters narrowed the focus of their mission from a wider engagement with welfare concerns and placed the education of girls at its centre. Over the course of the nineteenth-century the Presentation Order developed its network of convents throughout the country, opening fifty-four between 1807 and 1900.[46]

Rules and Constitutions, and the Presentation Directory

Nagle's vision of education centred on the quality of life, the quality of society and the relationship of people with God. Her schools acted as a vehicle to service this vision. In turn, the supernatural basis of Roman Catholic education formed an integral part of the ethos of the schools of the Presentation Sisters. A system of education that did not include the hope of eternal happiness and reduced education to the mundane transactions of this world proved problematic for her successors.[47] The Rules and Constitutions adopted by the Sisters in 1793 were based on those of the Ursulines and, with some necessary changes to accommodate the adoption of enclosure and solemn vows at the time of final approval, remained the basic document of the Sisters as the Institute grew throughout the nineteenth-century.[48] As prescribed by them, teaching was a coordinated act of love of God. The opening paragraph stated clearly that:

> The principal end of this Religious Institute is the instruction of poor girls in the principles of Religion and Christian Piety. In undertaking this very arduous, but most meritorious task, the Sisters, whom God is graciously pleased to call to this state of perfection, will encourage themselves and animate their zeal by the example of their Divine Master.[49]

It was 'a duty incumbent on the Sisters to teach the children the Catechism daily' and to teach them 'to offer themselves up to God from the first use of Reason, when they awake in the morning, to raise up their hearts to him'.[50] The first and second chapters of the *Constitutions* detail the purpose of the Institute and the place of the schools, before they describe the vows, enclosure and other aspects of religious life, whilst the second part outlines the administrative structures and governance of the Institute as a religious entity. The Sisters, therefore, were identified as women religious/school mistresses/school managers from the first.[51] This synthesis of roles means that attempting to separate them is, in many respects, an artificial exercise. Women who joined the Presentation Order were nuns: nuns who opened, organized and taught schools that cultivated the tender minds of children, instructing them in the duties of religion. In so doing the Sisters were 'associated to the functions of those blessed spirits, whom God has appointed Guardian Angels to watch over and direct them in the ways of their eternal salvation'.[52]

As a result of a conscious attempt at promoting a sense of shared history and tradition among the new foundations of the nineteenth-century, the *Presentation Directory*, and its companion the *Ceremonial*, were published in 1850.[53] Isabella McLoughlin, one of the foundresses of the Kilkenny convent, began work on the project in response to requests for a record of both the history and customs of the Institute. McLoughlin died in 1838 without finishing her work and responsibility for completing the task was undertaken by the South Presentation Convent in its role as mother-house. Each new house of the Order, both in Ireland and abroad, received a copy of the publications, which influenced the pattern of the Sisters' daily lives for many years. Raphael Consedine points out that where the *Directory* interpreted the *Constitutions* it could claim to be an expression of what had been in the Order from its very foundation. However, the detailed sections covering every aspect of the Sisters' lives were the result of a gradual process of accumulation, mostly from Ursuline sources. Notwithstanding this, the *Directory* acts as a valuable source on the practices and customs of the Sisters in their schools during the nineteenth-century.[54]

Management

The Presentation mission of education became the basis on which its network of convents and schools evolved, and establishing a Presentation Convent School was an integral part of this process. From the establishment of the Primary Foundations a growing awareness of their mission developed among the Catholic population. This led to approaches to individual Presentation communities requesting that they establish convents in towns and villages specifically because they would also open a school in the locality. The convents in Galway (1815), Limerick (1837) and Clondalkin (1857) were all established in response to direct requests to the communities in Kilkenny, South Presentation and Carlow respectively.[55] Upon their arrival in any new location, all Presentation communities opened their schools as soon as was practically possible. In some instances the new communities took over the running of schools that were already in existence, whilst in other situations the schools that the Sisters opened were new enterprises in themselves. The small group of women that opened the convent in Galway moved into a house in Kirwan's Lane where they took over the running of the existing poor school that was operating there. They also assumed responsibility for the care of thirty poor children who boarded and lodged on the premises.[56] The Limerick foundation took over the school operated by Catherine Maria King, the convent's foundress, and the founding Sisters in Clondalkin assumed control of the girls' national school that had been closed in their favour.[57] Equally the Thurles (1817), Wexford (1818) and Millstreet (1840) communities all opened new schools when they established their convents in the towns.[58]

When a new foundation of the Order was first established the communities were housed in various types of buildings. Some were accommodated in local houses that were available to the founders, whilst other communities were provided with purpose-built convents. The house in Kirwan's Lane, Galway was a private dwelling not designed to accommodate the members of a convent community, let alone the growing numbers of children under their care. In 1816 they moved, with the children, to a house on the Green.[59] In March 1819 they moved a second time to their final home in the western suburbs of the city.[60] Sisters Francis Cormack and Augustine Power opened the Thurles convent in July 1817 in a small house in Stradavoher where the two women marked out their enclosure and opened their school.[61] Not surprisingly the small house proved entirely unsuited to their work, interfering with both the observance of their Rule and the effective operation of the school. On the advice of friends the Sisters offered to buy the house and schools of the Christian Brothers. The Brothers agreed, selling the property for £1,000 and moving to a small house until their new monastery and schools were built.[62] In November 1817 the Thurles community moved to their new home, which required many alterations to make it comfortable. However, the schools attached to it were fine and spacious, and the facility of hearing Mass in the parish chapel compensated for the difficulties presented by the house.[63] In contrast, the groups of women that established the foundations in Wexford and Clondalkin moved into purpose-built convents.[64] In both instances the work had been carried out with the help of bequests from former parishioners, of £1,600 and £2,000 respectively, for the specific purpose of building the convents.

Schoolhouses

According to the *Constitutions* the schools were to be 'situated as conveniently to the convent as the great end of the Institute shall admit of'.[65] In practice, however, the original schoolhouses in which the women opened their first schools represented quite a variety. As we have seen, Nano Nagle opened her first school in a rented mud cabin that had two earthen-floored rooms and a thatched roof. Similarly, when she first opened her school in George's Hill in 1766, Teresa Mulally rented the back room on the top floor of a three-storeyed house in Mary's Lane in Dublin.[66] When they started the Sisters in Galway, Thurles and Wexford, all conducted their schools in rooms in the convent houses, whereas the convents in Limerick, Millstreet and Clondalkin had separate school buildings adjacent to their convents. Comparing the situations in Wexford and Clondalkin gives some idea of the different scenarios. As the only school in Wexford run by religious, the Presentation Convent School attracted large numbers of children and adults when it opened in 1818. In addition to the children of the town, it also catered for children from the orphanage that had been opened by the Talbot family.[67] The *Second Report of the Commissioners of Irish Education Inquiry* (1824) describes the schoolroom used by the community in Wexford as a good room attached to the convent, which catered for between 120 and 180 pupils.[68] By 1834, when the school connected to the National System of Education, this space was described by Reverend Mother Baptist Frayne as a lime-and-stone building located under the convent chapel, consisting of three rooms – one measuring thirty-four feet long by thirty-three feet wide; the second measured eighteen feet long by ten feet wide; and the third, located above the second, with the same dimensions.[69] On its entry to the National System thirty-four years later the newly completed schoolhouse in Clondalkin was described as one of the buildings of the Presentation Convent which was devoted to the purposes of the school. It was a two-storeyed, neo-Gothic building, in excellent repair, constructed from limestone and mortar with a slate roof. It was connected to the convent by means of a corridor. There were two schoolrooms, a classroom, and a closet for keeping books and supplies. The junior and senior rooms were 36 feet long, 19 feet 6 inches wide and 14 feet high. They had floors, plastered walls, windows that opened and fires. There were seven desks 8 feet 4 inches long, fifteen forms 7 feet 6 inches long, sitting room for eighty pupils and desks for forty.[70]

Whatever type of school accommodation the various convents started with they all improved, altered and expanded it to address the needs of the developing school communities. In January 1862, forty-four years after the convent was established, the community in Wexford opened a new school building separate from the convent, to which they added a new infant school and lavatory in 1869.[71] In August 1876 two new schoolrooms were opened by the bishop of Ferns to cater for the infant boys and a new work-room was added for industrial training.[72] The Sisters in Clondalkin also developed their school accommodation. In 1864, they increased the length of each room by 8 feet, moving the school stairs into a section of the room occupied by the original Benefit School of the convent. They also added a new music room, a fire-place and a much needed cloakroom at this point.[73] In 1870 the Sisters opened an extension to the original school to house their Benefit School, which was built at the same time as an extension to the convent itself. These improvements, additions and extensions were carried out to cater for the increasing numbers of children that attended the schools throughout the nineteenth-century and continued into the twentieth-century.

School organization

In terms of school organization, the successful operation of the convents and their schools depended on the combined endeavour of all members. That these women lived and worked together in community required organization, coordination and management from the earliest days of the Institute onwards. Unless they were unable to do so through ill health or infirmity, all of the Sisters in the convent communities worked in the schools. Although the Applications to the Commissioners of National Education recorded those in attendance in the school as the Ladies of the Presentation Convent in general, in relation to the Presentation Convent Wexford Baptist Frayne clarified that 'The School is under the direction of the Nuns exclusively'.[74] The Application from Thurles contains the following details:

> The persons engaged in the Teaching & conduct of the School are the Ladies of The Presentation Convent of Thurles. Twelve in number all equal to the duties of the School, their ages ranging from twenty to fifty, one being over fifty but vigorous. The Lady Superioress at present upon whom chiefly the general superintendence of the School duties lay[?] is Mrs Eliza Greene.[75]

Apart from the nuns who were listed as the managers of the schools, the Salary Books of the Commissioners do not name any of the Sisters who taught in the schools individually. Under the columns entitled 'Teacher' and 'Classification' they are included in the term 'Nuns'. In contrast, details on all of the monitresses and workmistresses sanctioned and paid by the Board were included in these files.[76]

The model of governance outlined in the *Constitutions* prescribed the way in which individual communities were to be organized and how they were to operate.[77] The schools were to be 'proportioned to the number of Religious capable of attending without overcharging or too much distressing themselves'. The Sisters were to attend the schools 'with all zeal, charity, humility, purity of intention and confidence in God' and to 'undertake the charge, and chearfully [*sic*] submit to every labor and inconveniency annexed thereto, taking Jesus Christ … for their Model and Companion'. Having praised God and Our Lady they were to salute with all reverence and devotion the Guardian Angels of the children. On completion of the Devotion to the Passion of Christ they were to 'endeavour to inspire the poor Children [*sic*] with the greatest Reverence and Devotion to their Guardian Angels'.[78] In each school the pupils were to be divided into classes of ten or twelve depending on the number, with one of the more sedate among them to be appointed as a superintendent of each class. A school register was to be kept that recorded the names and ages of the children upon entrance to the school, the date on which they were received into the school, their addresses, and their parents' names and occupations. The schools were to be kept as clean and airy as possible and the Mother Superior or Assistant was to visit them at least once a fortnight.[79]

The *Directory* brought further detail to the work of the Sisters. Its outline for the duties of the Superioress with regard to the schools included daily superintendence of the schools to ensure their smooth running, the careful supervision of all the mistresses, overseeing general school discipline, the appointment and direction of the monitresses, and the regulation of equipment and supplies.[80] Regulations for the mistresses stated that they were to show great respect for and deference to the Mother Superior, following any orders she gave. They were also to support and assist one another in their work. Each mistress had to take her turn in charge of the care of the school for a week at a time. This mainly involved opening the door at a particular hour each morning to let the children in, saying the morning and evening prayers, reading the evening lectures, signalling the changes in duties throughout the day and dismissing the children when all the devotions were concluded. Punctuality was considered essential and when engaged in their work in school they were not to allow their attention to be distracted by useless conversations or work that was not directly pertinent to the act of instructing the children. Sisters were not to converse with one another whilst in school; any necessary communication regarding the improvement of the children was to be deferred to a more appropriate time.[81] To avoid the frustration of her efforts, each mistress was to ensure that strict silence was observed in her class during school hours. Children were to be encouraged to learn through patience, indulgence and charity with the occasional use of presents and rewards. They were to be disciplined through gentle admonishment, and physical punishment or harsh treatment was not countenanced. Serious transgressions on the part of the children were dealt with by the Mother Superior.[82]

The archives for the Presentation Convent Terenure, Dublin, contain a document which describes a system of rewards and penalties that was operated by the Sisters when the convent was located in Richmond Road, Dublin between 1820 and 1866. Designed as a poster and entitled *Richmond Free Schools, Presentation Convent*, it also outlines the timetable and rules of the schools. The system of rewards and penalties centred on merit tickets. Credits were rewarded with merit tickets and debits were punished by their withdrawal. A directive in the 'Rewards' section reads: 'To the child most distinguished for neatness, regular attendance and good conduct – 200 tickets'. In the 'Penalties' section it noted: 'Being out of school without permission – 2 tickets. Going home without leave – 10 tickets. Quarrelling, ill-temper or any other misconduct – 10 tickets'.[83] Mistresses were not to engage in worldly news or idle conversation with the children; neither were they to receive any presents from them. On occasion, they were to meet with the parents or guardians of the children to discuss their progress and behaviour in school and at home. The overall conduct of the mistresses with the children was to be characterized by sweetness, prudence and maternal indulgence.[84]

Curriculum

The secular subjects at the heart of the curriculum in Presentation schools were reflective of contemporary attitudes regarding the appropriate subjects for the education of girls. The *Directory* outlined the purpose of these subjects, and the particular importance of needlework:

> As the poor cannot receive a more precious inheritance, than a spirit of economy and industry, particular attention shall be paid to instil it into the minds of the children. That pernicious propensity to talk and idleness, should as much as possible, be banished from amongst them. Besides, therefore, the more serious and to them, less interesting studies of Reading, Writing, Arithmetic, Geography, and Grammar, they should be carefully instructed in all sorts of needle-work, as being the means by which they may in after life, obtain more securely a decent livelihood. To the poor, this is certainly, the most essential acquirement which they can obtain; and it should therefore be to every Presentation Religious, one of the chief objects of her care and attention.[85]

In reading, the children were only allowed to read books that would inculcate the practice of virtue and devotion, whilst the reading of books for amusement was forbidden. Bringing into school books that could lead to the destruction of pious and prudent sentiments in the minds of others was viewed as a most punishable offence.[86] In writing, the children were taught to hold the pen properly to begin with, and having learned this were instructed in the exact formation of the letters. Writing on slates took place first and the progression to paper occurred when they had mastered the combinations of letters. They were not taught to write in small hand until they could form a good, bold large hand. Finally, to write freely from dictation, children were taught to write in a running hand with speed and precision.[87] Arithmetic was described as 'one of the most important branches of profane knowledge' and, when properly taught, was viewed as an excellent way of strengthening the mind and preparing it for the acquisition of any other kind of knowledge. Knowledge of tables and notations was deemed absolutely necessary for acquiring any facility in arithmetic. After knitting, children were taught to hem and sew, and how to mark out on canvas or coarse linen. When they had advanced from this level they were taught to cut out and arrange the work for themselves, with particular attention paid to finishing. Instruction in needlework was done for the hour between twelve and one o'clock every day.[88]

Religious instruction

Whilst the secular curriculum taught by the Sisters conformed to generally accepted ideals regarding education both inside and outside the National System, the programme of religious instruction was entirely that of the Presentation Order. The *Constitutions* nominated the education of poor girls in 'the principles of Religion and Christian Piety' as the central characteristic of the Institute, and over fifty years later the *Directory* detailed how this could be done in the day-to-day life of their schools.[89] The *Directory* explained the central role of Christian Doctrine in their schools:

> Although much time must be employed in teaching the poor children to read, write and work, Presentation Nuns, must nevertheless remember, that the Christian doctrine, decency, cleanliness, and correctness of manner, are the chief and most necessary points to be attended to ...

They were to be taught:

> to treat their parents with the utmost respect and affection ... practice great civility and charity in their communication with each other, and great submission and politeness, in their intercourse with Religious.... to renew frequently during the day, the consecration of themselves to God, which they make in the morning.... No age is too young to be taught how to subdue their passions and evil inclinations, or to make them acquainted with that failing which is most predominant in them.[90]

The programme that was devised was based on *The Rudiments of Faith* by Cardinal Robert Bellarmine and the *Douai Catechism*, which was not entirely suited to the instruction of children.[91] The *Constitutions* addressed this by clarifying that the Sisters were to explain the Catechism to the children 'briefly and simply, adapting their language to the age and capacity of the children ... cautious not to propose any thing abstruse, that might embarrass themselves or the children'.[92] The *Directory* went further, recommending 'great simplicity, prudence, and caution ... lest anything be advanced extending beyond the capacities of the children'.[93] In practice the Sisters were to devote half an hour every day to teaching the Catechism exclusively, keeping simply to the text and without introducing any discussion or questions that would only serve to confuse the children. Curiosity on the part of the pupils was to be carefully repressed at this stage. It was necessary to teach them to listen to divine things with great respect and to submit to the truths of the faith. Once the children were capable of reflection, they were instructed in the duties that attended conversion to God. This included morning prayer, honouring and respecting their parents and superiors, a daily examination of conscience, and a thorough confession. Instruction would lead them to an abhorrence of sin and an awareness of the punishment that was the consequence of its commission. Cleanliness was an important part of this process and it was to be insisted upon from an early age. Preparation for the sacraments of confession and communion began when the children were well versed in these aspects of the Catechism.[94]

For confession, instruction was in the three parts of penance – contrition, confession and satisfaction. The importance of a full confession was impressed upon the children. They were taught how to examine their consciences according to order, on the Commandments and on the seven deadly sins. They were also taught how to confess their sins properly, distinguishing three kinds of sins: sins against God; sins against the neighbour; and sins against the self in thoughts, words and works. They were instructed in reciting an act of contrition for their sins and the formation of resolutions of amendment. Children who had not made their communion were to receive confession at least once a month or more often if recommended by their confessor.[95] Those who were being prepared for first communion received particular instruction every day, with frequent attendance at confession included as part of the preparation. When the children were considered ready, a day was appointed and arrangements were made to hold the ceremony. Prior to this the parent of each child was seen and enquiries were made as to her conduct at home. This information contributed to the decision as to whether or not she was ready to receive communion. A week before the communion day the preparation became more intensive with instruction concentrating on piety and devotion.[96] Two days before the ceremony, the girls were withdrawn from the school for the final part of their preparation which included attending Mass each day, reciting the rosary and other devotions. On the eve of the communion, they received absolution and were instructed in how to receive the host with reverence and decency. If sufficient funds were available, a breakfast was provided for the communicants and each child received a prayer book in which her name was inscribed and the date of her first communion.[97] The girls were kept separate from the other pupils for the rest of the day and allowed home from school an hour earlier than usual.[98] Preparation for confirmation followed the same routine as that for communion. The children were instructed in the nature of the sacrament, why it was instituted, its matter and form, its effects, the meaning of the ceremonies used in its administration, why the bishop conferred it, the dispositions that were necessary to receive it worthily, and why it could not be repeated.[99] How this preparation for the sacraments translated into the life of an individual school can be seen in the case of Clondalkin. Instruction was given both during school hours and, on occasion, in the evenings. Whilst children received first communion every year, confirmation took place every three to four years with all the children, and some adults, from Clondalkin and the surrounding districts being confirmed together.[100]

In addition to this, the children were taught to recite specific prayers at various times of the day. At nine o'clock the children knelt for morning prayers, which were led by the teacher. These included Acts of Adoration, Faith, Hope, Charity and Thanksgiving; a prayer offering and directing intentions; and an invocation of the Blessed Virgin and Saints, the Pater, Ave, Gloria Patri, Credo, the Angelus Domini, and adoration of the Blessed Sacrament which was repeated three times.[101] They were to bless themselves before and after the Catechism and at the striking of the clock when they were also to say a Hail Mary. From 11.45 a.m. they were to make an examination of conscience since the evening before, whilst continuing to work. At noon they recited the Acts of Faith, Hope and Charity and the adoration of the Blessed Sacrament three times with the teacher.[102] Evening prayers were said from 2.45 until 3.00 p.m. whilst the children were dressed for home, and prayers included a lecture, read by the Sister from *Challenor's Meditations* or another suitable book. The Rosary was said at this time one day in the week.[103]

Conclusion

The Presentation Order was the first of the modern congregations of women religious to be established in Ireland, and over the course of the nineteenth-century secured its position within the sphere of Irish Catholic education. Based on the work of Nano Nagle among the poor of Cork City, its institution was the result of her strength of purpose and her conviction as to the necessity and value of this work. The women who inherited the emerging congregation shared her deep spirituality and dedication to the service of God, and developed an organizational structure that facilitated the realization of this mission. They identified the instruction of poor girls as the defining aspect of the Institute, and made it clear that its members expressed and developed their relationship with God by teaching the 'Principles of Religion and Christian Piety' to the children who came to their schools. This strong educational identity became a type of calling card for the Order, opening the way for Irish Catholics to approach the Sisters to open convents and schools in their towns and villages, which in turn provided the impetus for the development of a Presentation network throughout the country.

The teaching staff of the schools comprised the Sisters of the various convents who assisted by the pupils they appointed and trained as monitors, and occasionally lay staff who were employed as workmistresses. For the Presentation religious, the instruction of poor children was seen as a divine function, and the rewards for the successful fulfilment of this vocation lay beyond this life. The decision by the Sisters to remain outside the system of teacher classification was rooted in this belief of divine calling and the inappropriateness of assessment by a purely secular system. The qualifications and experience of the Sisters who conducted the schools on joining the National System were accepted by the Commissioners without question. Equally, they were generally assessed as being in possession of 'very superior acquirements' to operate and manage the schools under their direction. Although some women who were trained teachers entered the convents, most of the nuns received their training within the convent or school.

The evolution, implementation and recording of the various organizational routines and practices ensured the consolidation of the Order as both a religious and an educational entity, enabling the Sisters to underline the character of their congregation. The successful development of the Institute demonstrates that Presentation Sisters were women religious dedicated to the mission of education, who opened schools that endured, grew and thrived across the nineteenth-century, continuing into the twentieth-century. Their success within the highly restricted and paternalistic environments of the Irish Catholic Church and National Education is testament to their skills as educational administrators and managers, in addition to their skills as negotiators, property developers, financial and business managers, and diplomats. All of these skills were deployed in their work as educators.

Notes

1 An Act for the relief of His Majesty's Subjects Professing the Popish Religion, 17 and 18 Geo. III, c. 49; James Kelly, 'Nineteenth-Century Catholicism', in Seán Duffy (ed.), *Atlas of Irish History* (Dublin: Gill and Macmillan, 2000), 86–7.
2 Tony Fahey, 'Nuns in the Catholic Church in Ireland in the Nineteenth Century', in Mary Cullen (ed.), *Girls Don't Do Honours: Irish Women in Education in the Nineteenth and Twentieth Centuries* (Dublin: WEB Press, 1987), 7–30 (9).
3 Tom O'Donoghue, *Come Follow Me and Forsake Temptation: Catholic Schooling and the Recruitment and Retention of Teachers for Religious Teaching Orders, 1922–1965* (New York: Peter Lang, 2004), 21–2.
4 Deirdre Raftery, 'The "Mission" of Nuns in Female Education in Ireland, c. 1850–1950', *Pedagogica historica*, 48:2 (2012), 299–313 (299–300).
5 Rebecca Rogers, 'Reconsidering the Role of Religious Orders in Modern French Women's Education', *Vitae scholasticae*, 10:1–2 (1992), 43–51; Elizabeth M. Smyth (ed.), *Changing Habits: Women's Religious Orders in Canada* (Montreal: Novalis Publications, 2007); Bart Hellinckx, Frank Simon and Marc Depaepe, *The Forgotten Contribution of the Teaching Sisters: A Historiographical Essay on the Educational Work of Catholic Women Religious in the 19th and 20th Centuries* (Leuven: Leuven University Press, 2009).
6 Fahey, 'Nuns in the Catholic Church'; Caitríona Clear, *Nuns in Nineteenth-Century Ireland* (Dublin: Gill and Macmillan, 1987); Caitríona Clear, 'The Limits of Female Autonomy: Nuns in Nineteenth-Century Ireland', in Maria Luddy and Cliona Murphy (eds), *Women Surviving: Studies in Irish Women's History in the Nineteenth and Twentieth Centuries* (Dublin: Poolbeg Press, 1989), 21–34.
7 Mary Peckham Magray, *The Transforming Power of the Nuns: Women, Religion, and Cultural Change in Ireland 1750–1900* (Oxford: Oxford University Press, 1985).
8 Maria Luddy, 'Foreword', in Margaret H. Preston, *Charitable Words: Women, Philanthropy, and the Language of Charity in Nineteenth-Century Dublin* (Westport, CT and London: Praeger, 2004); Rosemary Raughter, 'A Natural Tenderness: The Ideal and Reality of Eighteenth-Century Female Philanthropy', in Maryann Gialanella Valiulis and Mary O'Dowd (eds), *Women and Irish History: Essays in Honour of Margaret MacCurtain* (Dublin: Wolfhound Press, 1997); Rosemary Raughter, 'Pious Occupations: Female Activism and the Catholic Revival in Eighteenth-Century Ireland', in Rosemary Raughter (ed.), *Religious Women and Their History: Breaking the Silence* (Dublin: Irish Academic Press, 2005), 25–49.
9 Suellen Hoy, 'The Journey Out: The Recruitment and Emigration of Irish Religious Women to the United States, 1812–1914', *Journal of Women's History*, 6:4/7:1 (Winter/Spring 1995), 64–98.

10 Máire M. Kealy, *Dominican Education in Ireland, 1820-1930* (Dublin: Irish Academic Press, 2007).
11 The Presentation Convent archives included are: South Presentation Cork; George's Hill Dublin; Presentation Convent Thurles; Presentation Convent Wexford; Presentation Convent Galway; Presentation Convent Limerick; Presentation Convent Millstreet, Cork; and Presentation Convent Clondalkin, Dublin.
12 Clear, *Nuns in Nineteenth-Century Ireland*, 36–44; Fahey, 'Nuns in the Catholic Church', 7–10; Margaret MacCurtain, 'Godly Burden: Catholic Sisterhoods in Twentieth-Century Ireland', in Anthony Bradley and Maryann Gialanella Valiulis (eds), *Gender and Sexuality in Modern Ireland* (Amherst: University of Massachusetts Press, 1997), 245–55.
13 Maria Luddy, *Women and Philanthropy in Nineteenth-Century Ireland* (Cambridge: Cambridge University Press, 2004), 24.
14 Fahey, 'Nuns in the Catholic Church', 10–11.
15 Peckham Magray, *The Transforming Power of the Nuns*, 9.
16 Ibid., 128–9; see also Clear, *Nuns in Nineteenth-Century Ireland*, 160.
17 The Stanley Letter, in *Royal Commission of Inquiry into Primary Education (Ireland)*, Vol. I, Part I, *Report of the Commissioners: With an Appendix*, Sessional Papers 6 (Dublin: HMSO, 1870), 22–6.
18 Ibid., 23–4 (emphasis in original).
19 Donald H. Akenson, *The Irish Education Experiment: The National System of Education in the Nineteenth Century* (London: Routledge and Kegan Paul, 1970). See also Norman Atkinson, *Irish Education: A History of Educational Institutions* (Dublin: Allen Figgis, 1969); John Coolahan, *Irish Education: History and Structure* (Dublin: Institute of Public Administration, 1981); Áine Hyland and Kenneth Milne (eds), *Irish Educational Documents*, 3 vols, Vol. I (Dublin: CICE, 1987).
20 Clear, *Nuns in Nineteenth-Century Ireland*, 103–4.
21 British Parliamentary Papers (BPP), *Second Report of the Commissioners of Education Inquiry (Abstract of Returns in 1824, from the Protestant and Roman Catholic Clergy in Ireland, of the State of Education in Their Respective Parishes)*, 12 (1826–7), XII.1, 6–18.
22 James Kavanagh, *Mixed Education: The Catholic Case Stated; or, Principles, Working, and Results of the System of National Education: With Suggestions for the Settlement of the Education Question. Most Respectfully Dedicated to the Catholic Archbishops and Bishops of Ireland* (Dublin: John Mullany, 1859), 233. See also Akenson, *The Irish Education Experiment*; Atkinson, *Irish Education*; Coolahan, *Irish Education*.
23 BPP, *Appendix to Twentieth Report ... for the Year 1853* (1834), H.C. 1854, XXX, pt. i, 319; BPP, *Appendix to Twenty-fourth Report..., for the year 1857*, (2456–1), H.C. 1859, VII, 252–255; BPP, *Appendix to Thirty first Report..., for the year 1864*, (3496), H.C. 1865, XIX, 262–265; *Appendix to Thirty-seventh Report..., for the year 1870*, 656–659.
24 BPP, *Special Report made to the Commissioners of National Education on Convent Schools in Connection with the Board*, H.C. 1864 (405), XLVI.63.
25 Fahey, 'Nuns in the Catholic Church', 20.
26 Kavanagh, *Mixed Education*, 234–5; BPP, *Appendix to the Twenty-second Report..., for the year 1855*, 381.
27 Fahey, 'Nuns in the Catholic Church', 20.
28 Ibid., 50 and 69.
29 Ibid., 45.

30 Kavanagh, *Mixed Education*, 242.
31 Coolahan, *Irish Education*, 32.
32 Anne V. O'Connor, 'The Revolution in Girls' Secondary Education in Ireland 1860–1910', in Cullen, *Girls Don't Do Honours*, 31–54.
33 Under the terms of this act a Board of Commissioners was to be appointed to devise and administer a system of examinations on the results of which fees would be paid to managers of schools which fulfilled the Board's regulations. Successful pupils would receive prizes, exhibitions and certificates.
34 Maria Luddy, *Women in Ireland, 1800–1918: A Documentary History* (Cork: Cork University Press, 1995), 90. Figures for the 1901 intermediate examinations show about 2,000 girls presenting for exams as against nearly 6,000 boys. See David Fitzpatrick, '"A Share of the Honeycomb": Education, Emigration and Irishwomen', in Mary Daly and David Dickson (eds), *The Origins of Popular Literacy in Ireland: Language Change and Educational Development 1700–1920* (Dublin: Trinity College and University College, 1990), 167–89 (172).
35 For a comprehensive examination of the history of the Presentation Sisters see William Hutch, *Nano Nagle: Her Life, Her Labours and Their Fruits* (Dublin: McGlashan and Gill, 1875); and T. J. Walsh, *Nano Nagle and the Presentation Sisters* (Dublin: M. H. Gill and Son, 1959). For studies of the history of the congregation from within its membership, see M. Raphael Consedine, PBVM, *Listening Journey: A Study of the Spirit and Ideals of Nano Nagle and the Presentation Sisters* (Elsternwick, VIC: Congregation of the Presentation of the Blessed Virgin Mary, 1983); Sr Mary Pius O'Farrell, *Nano Nagle: Woman of the Gospel* (Cork: Cork Publishing, 1996); Sr Mary Pius O'Farrell, *Breaking of Morn: Nano Nagle (1718–1784) and Francis Moylan (1735–1815). A Book of Documents* (Cork: Cork Publishing, 2001).
36 'Conspectus', in Hutch, *Nano Nagle* (insert); in Ireland, Presentation convents accounted for 55 per cent of all convents in 1840. By 1900, Presentation and Mercy congregations together made up 58 per cent of all Irish convents. Clear, *Nuns in Nineteenth-Century Ireland*, 52.
37 Walsh, *Nano Nagle*, 23–42; O'Farrell, *Woman of the Gospel*, 30–62. Ballygriffin is a townland situated between Mallow and Fermoy in the north of the county.
38 Mother Clare Callaghan to Bishop Coppinger, autograph letter (AL), n.d., in Walsh, *Nano Nagle*, 382.
39 Walsh, *Nano Nagle*, 43; Consedine, *Listening Journey*, 27.
40 Nano Nagle to Miss Fitzsimons, AL, 17 July 1769, in Walsh, *Nano Nagle*, 344–7. After her death in 1784, Thomas Roche, the administrator of her estate, removed all of Nano Nagle's personal and family papers from the convent. Later attempts at recovering these papers proved unsuccessful. All that has survived is a collection of her letters, sixteen complete and a fragment of another. The sixteen complete letters are reproduced in the appendices of Walsh, *Nano Nagle*, 344–67.
41 Walsh, *Nano Nagle*, 44–7.
42 Nano Nagle to Miss Fitzsimons, 17 July 1769, 345.
43 Walsh, *Nano Nagle*, 50; Consedine, *Listening Journey*, 51; O'Farrell, *Woman of the Gospel*, 93–4.
44 Walsh, *Nano Nagle*, 85–100.
45 Ibid., 146–59; Consedine, *Listening Journey*, 121–45. With the opening of the North Presentation Convent, the house in Cove Lane became known as South Presentation Convent.
46 Conspectus, in Hutch, *Nano Nagle*; M. Raphael Consedine, *Nano Nagle Seminars July–August 1984* (Cork: Nano Nagle House, Douglas Street, 1984), 38–41; 'Presentation Development Chart', in Walsh, *Nano Nagle* (insert). Seven

convents were established overseas between 1856 and 1866, seven between 1867 and 1874, and thirty-two between 1875 and 1900.
47 O'Farrell, *Woman of the Gospel*, 262.
48 Consedine, *Listening Journey*, 173. Later modifications of the Constitutions were made by the various Congregations of the Presentation Sisters in view of local circumstances, and changing ecclesiastical practice left core passages untouched. Early in the twentieth century, developments in canon law made revision necessary, but many Congregations found ways to retain much of the original document, sometimes in their Directories.
49 *Rules and Constitutions of the Sisters of the Congregation of the Charitable Instruction 1793*, in Consedine, *Listening Journey*, 406–26.
50 Ibid.
51 Consedine, *Listening Journey*, 176.
52 Ibid., 406.
53 *A Directory for the Religious of the Presentation Order According to the Practices of the Parent House, Founded in the Year 1775 by the Venerable Mother Nano Nagle, in Douglas Street, Cork* (Cork: Wm Hurley, 1850); *A Ceremonial for the Use of the Nuns of the Presentation Order in Which the Various Ceremonies and Practices of Devotion Are Set Forth as Observed in the South Presentation Convent Cork* (Cork: Wm Hurley, 1850).
54 Consedine, *Listening Journey*, 211–52.
55 Edmund Ffrench, Warden of Galway and its District, to Mrs McLoughlin, Presentation Convent Kilkenny, 17 October 1815, quoted in Hutch, *Nano Nagle*, 180–18; Presentation Convent Limerick (hereafter PCL), MS Annals, 3 and 4; Presentation Convent Clondalkin (hereafter PCC), MS Annals, Vol. I, 1–12.
56 Presentation Convent Galway (hereafter PCG), Annals 3 and 4, quoted in Margaret C. Scully, 'Galway Schooling and the Presentation Sisters: An Account of the Work of a Religious Body in the Practice of Education (1815–1873)' (M.Ed. thesis, University College Cork, National University of Ireland, 1973), 10–11.
57 PCL, MS Annals, 2 and 3; PCC, MS Annals, Vol. I, 1–12.
58 Presentation Convent Thurles (hereafter PCT), MS Annals, 1–3; Presentation Convent Wexford (hereafter PCWx), MS Annals; Hutch, *Nano Nagle*, 373–5.
59 Hutch, *Nano Nagle*, 184; PCG, Annals, in Scully, 'Galway Schooling', 13. The Green is now known as Eyre Square.
60 Hutch, *Nano Nagle*, 184; Scully, 'Galway Schooling', 13.
61 PCT, MS Annals, 2 and 3; Maria Luddy, 'Presentation Convents in County Tipperary, 1806–1900', *Tipperary Historical Journal* (1992), 84–95 (85). Luddy describes the house in Stradavoher as a thatched cottage.
62 PCT, MS Annals, 3–5. The Christian Brothers had opened a school for the boys of the town near the cathedral a year before the arrival of the Sisters. After the move to their smaller quarters the archbishop paid their rent of £17 per annum in favour of the nuns.
63 Ibid., 5.
64 PCWx, MS Annals; PCC, MS Annals, Vol. I, 1–12.
65 Consedine, *Listening Journey*, 407.
66 George's Hill Archives Dublin (hereafter GHAD), GHAD/H/1 (1), MS Annals.
67 PCWx, MS Annals, 1.
68 BPP, *Appendix to Second Report of the Commissioners of Irish Education Inquiry*, 94–5.
69 National Archives of Ireland (hereafter NAI), ED 1/92, MS no. 116, Applications. The second room was listed as being 'the under floor of the house (lately orphanage?) to the large schoolroom'.

70 NAI, ED 1/29, MS no. 174, Applications.
71 PCWx, MS Annals, 1859–63,1867 and 1869.
72 Ibid., 1876 and 1882.
73 PCC, MS Annals, Vol. II, 67–70.
74 NAI, ED 1/92, MS no. 116, Applications.
75 NAI, ED 1/82, MS no. 32, Applications.
76 NAI, ED 4, Salary Books. The details kept on the monitresses included names, dates of appointment, classification, dates of promotion, amounts paid to them and, occasionally, dates of resignation.
77 *Rules and Constitutions*, in Consedine, *Listening Journey*, 406–20.
78 Ibid., 407.
79 Ibid., 407–8.
80 *A Directory for the Religious of the Presentation Directory*, 14–17.
81 Ibid., 21–9.
82 Ibid.
83 *Bicentenary Vista: Presentation Convents Dublin* (Drogheda: Drogheda Printers, 1976), 16.
84 *Presentation Directory*, 21–9.
85 Ibid., 20.
86 Ibid., 24–5.
87 Ibid., 41–2.
88 Ibid., 45–53.
89 *Rules and Constitutions*, Chapter 1, quoted in Consedine, *Listening Journey*, 406.
90 *Presentation Directory*, 17–20.
91 Consedine, *Listening Journey*, 226–7. Consedine explains that in the letter accompanying the *Decretum laudis* of 1791 Bellarmine's work was recommended as the basis for teaching Christian doctrine.
92 *Rules and Constitutions*, Chapter 1, quoted in Consedine, *Listening Journey*, 406.
93 *Presentation Directory*, 30.
94 Ibid., 18–20 and 29–32. The nuns were advised that to prepare themselves for giving general instructions in or explaining the Catechism, they should occasionally read over *The Poor Man's Catechism*, *The Catechism of the Council of Trent*, *The Sincere Christian*, *The Duties of a Christian*, *Familiar Instructions* or any other approved book of instruction.
95 *Presentation Directory*, 33–6.
96 Ibid., 36–7.
97 South Presentation Convent Cork Archive, copy of *Communion Certificate of Annie Sullivan*.
98 *Presentation Directory*, 37–9.
99 Ibid., 40.
100 PCC, MS Annals, Vol. I, 46; Vol. II, 70–4, 116–18 and 164–5. Girls and boys who had left school to work before being confirmed received instruction separately in the infant and the senior schools from 6.00 to 8.00 p.m. each evening in the weeks before the confirmation day and, when necessary, during the Sunday school. Along with the Sisters, the priests of the parish also instructed the working girls and boys in preparation for confirmation.
101 *Presentation Directory*, 51–2.
102 Ibid., 53.
103 Ibid., 53–4.

Chapter 6

Sisters and the creation of American Catholic identities

Margaret Susan Thompson

By the late nineteenth century, one of the primary fears of the US Catholic hierarchy was the 'leakage' of believers from the fold: the loss of Catholic identity through neglect, apathy, or – in an era of revived nativism and xenophobia – proselytism and apostasy. From a twenty-first-century perspective, the first response of the bishops to this perceived crisis seems unsurprising, if not inevitable: at the Third Plenary Council of Baltimore (1884) they declared the 'absolute necessity' for a Catholic school in every parish. This was reinforced by the pronouncement that it was the 'obligation of pastors to establish them' where they did not already exist, and of a parallel obligation for parents to enroll their children whenever possible. Traditionally, this has been cited as evidence of the prelates' concern for educating their rapidly expanding flocks, in a nation where at least some formal schooling was becoming the norm for most children, and where the public schools not infrequently reflected an unapologetically Protestant (and sometimes blatantly nativist and anti-Catholic) world-view.[1] But it seems just as legitimate to regard this as acknowledgement, however inexplicit, of the effectiveness of what teaching Sisters were already doing.

This chapter is based upon extensive research in the archives of over six dozen women's congregations throughout the United States, as well as in the published histories and primary source materials for about 200 others. These represent over half the apostolic communities present in the United States prior to 1917, including nearly all of those with more than 100 members, as well as those active within the nineteenth century. To give some indication of the scope of ministerial involvement by American women religious, consider that, as of 1884, at least 256 active communities of Sisters had been established in the United States; most were engaged in teaching as a significant if not exclusive apostolate.[2] By 1917, the number had grown to at least 422. Table 6.1 provides an overview of the origins of these communities, and demonstrates the range of founding experiences they represent.

Even some communities founded in the United States were intended from the outset to work solely with particular ethnic or language populations, and so may have resembled communities founded outside the country more than those typically understood to be 'American'. Examples of these include the Sisters of St Cyril and Methodius (Slovak), the Sisters of St Casimir (Lithuanian), and the Franciscan Sisters of St Joseph and the similarly named Sisters of St Joseph of the Third Order of St Francis (both Polish). Among those of European or Canadian origin, the major languages (other than English) that they initially spoke included French, German and Polish, with smatterings of Italian, Spanish and Dutch also evident. As shall be demonstrated, different communities contended with the disparate demands of adaptation, assimilation and cultural separatism in various and sometimes contradictory ways. While not all responses to ministry, even the teaching ministry, in the new nation can be included in an analysis of this brevity, it is hoped that the range of experiences that are presented indicate not only the diversity of experiences that Sisters in the USA underwent, but also the complexity both of American religious life and of American Catholicism.

It is not the purpose of this chapter to provide either a broad overview of what teaching Sisters did, or even of how effectively they implemented the stated objective to staunch the 'leakage' among immigrant and ethnic populations.[3] Instead, the intention is more limited but nonetheless fundamental to analysis of the contributions of teaching Sisters to the education of the multi-cultural American Catholic population. It is to present evidence of the difficulty and complexity that Sisters themselves confronted in facing ethnocentrism and related controversies within their own ranks, as religious congregations themselves negotiated the tensions between cultural retention and assimilation. While the present discussion will be necessarily suggestive and episodic rather than comprehensive, its purpose is to identify a variety of the responses that Sisters came up with, as well as to locate the emergence of what might be regarded as a 'third way' – that of identity *integration*.

Ethnic diversity in American Catholicism and American women's religious life

The Catholic Church in what is now the United States has been ethnically diverse since its beginning, and this is reflected in the linguistic and cultural identities of its early women's religious orders. Of the first twenty apostolic communities that persisted (all established by 1845), for instance, eight were English-speaking from the outset, while eleven were French (including three founded primarily by African Americans or Afro-Caribbean women) and one (the Ohio Sisters of the Precious Blood) spoke German. In the remaining fifteen years before the Civil War, most new foundations consisted of offshoots from those already in America, although French Canadian and German foundations became increasingly prominent.[4] For present purposes, it is helpful to consider three categories of congregations, and how they responded to the cultural and linguistic tensions of ethnicity. In the end, it will be possible to

Table 6.1 Founding and 1917 status of apostolic American women's orders, 1727–1917.*

	1	2	3	4	5	6	7	8	**Row Total**
1727–1810	1	—	—	2	—	—	—	—	3
1811–1820	4	—	1	1	—	—	—	—	6
1821–1830	4	—	—	1	—	—	—	—	5
1831–1840	1	2	1	4	—	—	—	—	8
1841–1850	4	5	4	8	3	—	—	1	25
1851–1860	5	9	9	12	14	9	—	—	58
1861–1870	5	8	7	6	8	19	—	—	53
1871–1880	6	7	14	12	7	22	1	—	69
1881–1890	8	2	15	5	5	22	2	1	60
1891–1900	5	4	16	3	5	8	1	—	42
1901–1910	15	2	32	2	3	6	—	—	60
1911–1917	5	1	23	3	—	3	—	1	36
Column Total	**63**	**40**	**122**	**59**	**45**	**89**	**4**	**3**	**425**

1. Indigenous community, originally founded in the U.S.
2. Independent community, originally founded as a branch of an indigenous U.S. congregation.
3. Founded outside the U.S., & remained part of an international congregation.
4. Founded outside the U.S., & became independent in the U.S.
5. Offshoot from a U.S. foundation of a foreign order; became an independent U.S congregation.
6. Independent offshoot of an independent U.S. congregation with foreign antecedents.
7. Subsequent U.S. foundation of a foreign order; remained part of an international congregation.
8. U.S. Foundation that became part of an international congregation.

*An earlier version of this table originally appeared in Thompson, "Cultural Conundrum," 229; the one here has been updated following the discovery of additional communities. Principal sources consulted include: Elinor Tong Dehey, *Religious Orders of Women in the United States*, rev. ed. (Hammond, IN: W. B. Conkey, 1930); Joan M. Lexau, *Convent Life: Roman Catholic Religious Orders for Women in North America* (New York: Dial Press, 1964), pp. 209-387 ("Index of Orders"); and Evangeline Thomas, *Women Religious History Sources: A Guide to Repositories in the United States* (New York: R. R. Bowker, 1983), pp. 169-76 ("Table of U.S. Founding Dates").

arrive at some preliminary and suggestive ideas about their contributions to the emergence of a distinctly *American* Catholic identity.

The first category consisted of communities in which English was the 'community language' from the outset, and in which English was expected to be the primary if not exclusive language of ministry, as well.[5] Mother Seton's Sisters of Charity and its subsequent offshoots are of this type, as are many if not all other indigenous US foundations such as the Sisters of Loretto, the Sisters of Charity of Nazareth, the Dominicans of St Catharine and St Mary-of-the-Springs, the Sisters of Charity of Our Lady of Mercy (OLM, South Carolina), Iowa's Sisters of Charity of the Blessed Virgin Mary (BVM, Iowa), and the Sisters of Mercy. In the case of the OLMs, BVMs, and Mercys, an overwhelming proportion of their first-generation members were Irish-born, though only the Mercys came to the USA as vowed religious.[6] The others drew their members largely from British stock in New York and Maryland (or, in the case of the Kentucky communities, from families who migrated to the 'Holy Land' from old Maryland families).[7] Rightly or wrongly, these communities became regarded by many in the American Church, including the preponderance of its early prelates, as what Sisters were 'supposed' to be. This normative understanding of American Sisters as English-speaking would have persistent and significant consequences.

The second category consisted of communities comprising Sisters who spoke languages other than English (in the early years, primarily French; in later years, more commonly German and Polish), and who anticipated that they would continue to minister to populations who spoke the same language. This was certainly true of the first congregations in New Orleans: the Ursulines, who arrived from France in 1727, and the native-born women of colour who formed the Sisters of the Holy Family in 1842. Similarly, the Religious of the Sacred Heart who settled first in Missouri (1818) and the Afro-Caribbean Oblate Sisters of Providence (Baltimore, 1829) understood that they would be working primarily with francophone Catholics, whether from the Old World, Canada, Louisiana or San Domingue; so did Louisiana's Sisters of Our Lady of Mount Carmel, among others.[8] In such cases, French remained both the house language and the language of ministry for many years after their establishment in the USA. And those who spoke other languages but who aspired to enter such communities were expected to learn the new tongue. For example, Esther Sammon was born in Ireland in 1843, came to New York as a child in 1850, and determined to enter the Brooklyn (later Amityville) Dominicans, entering as a teenager and taking vows in 1873. In order to do so, she had to learn German, which she did, and with which, after several years, she acquired a 'passing ease'. Not until almost 1880, after a number of other non-German candidates had joined, did the Mother General have the Rule translated into English. By that time, Sister Sammon, now Mother Mary Ann, had begun an orphanage in the small town of Blauvelt, staffed primarily by others like herself who were native English speakers. And largely because of the difficulties in bridging the language barrier and its cultural concomitants, the Blauvelt community became autonomous in 1890.[9]

The third category began in ways similar to the second group, with a first language other than English that, in at least some cases, was presumed to be an advantage for their prospective ministry. Thus, when Father Louis Gillet invited US-born but French-speaking Theresa Maxis Duchemin to leave Baltimore's Oblate Sisters of Providence and help him found a new congregation in Michigan, just over the Canadian border, it was her linguistic capacity that made her attractive. Arriving with another former Oblate, and joined by one and then another francophone woman from the vicinity, the founding Sisters, Servants of the Immaculate Heart of Mary (IHM), did not begin to use English as their house language for a number of years, and Theresa never became fluent.[10] But other communities, although not

English-speaking upon arrival, appreciated from the outset that they would need to learn the native language and to learn it well enough to use it, almost immediately, in their work. These groups would have to adapt quickly not only to English but, in subsequent years, to the languages of other immigrant groups who came to settle in the areas where they began to minister.

For some communities, such as the IHMs and the Oblates from whom two of their founding members had come, the need to learn English was not immediately anticipated. But as more and more of those who sought their services in schools were not French speakers, the Sisters began to appreciate that their communities' own survival might depend upon adaptation. One practical way to do this was to admit women who were English-speaking or bilingual into their own ranks, and to assign them to teach the other members of the community. Thus, the first 'inculturation' ministry in such congregations might be among the Sisters themselves.

Three examples are illustrative. The first American candidate admitted to the Sisters of St Joseph, who travelled from France to Caskaskia, Illinois and then to St Louis in 1836, was a young woman of Irish-American identity named Ann Eliza Dillon who began to teach the immigrant Sisters English as soon as they arrived, and who entered the community herself a year later. As a cradle Catholic and native English speaker, she brought both piety and familiarity with the language increasingly spoken by the surrounding population. Although she died tragically soon after her profession (which she made in English), she established a pattern whereby others like her would be welcomed into the CSJ novitiate and quickly came to predominate. Within less than half a dozen years of their settlement in the USA, French was no longer the congregation's normative language.[11]

The Sisters of Notre Dame de Namur (SND), whose first band arrived in Cincinnati in 1840, were somewhat more prepared for a setting in which few spoke French. Because of the Napoleonic wars, their community had already moved its Mother-House from France to Belgium and, even when the group had only a handful of members, its Constitution declared that the Sisters would converse and minister in the language of the people with whom they were missioned. Thus, as the first band travelled over the Atlantic, the difficulties of their journey were tempered by the absurdity of trying to hold recreation in their soon-to-be everyday tongue. Although only one of the original missionaries knew any English when the group left Belgium, all began 'in great good humor' to speak it nearly full-time as soon as they got to Cincinnati in 1840. Within weeks, they were writing home about the entertainment this inspired at recreation, the laughable struggles of Sister Xavier (who served as portress – doorkeeper) – and the admission of their first postulant, who 'is Irish but nevertheless speaks English very well'. Importantly, this postulant decided to join their ranks rather than those of other Sisters she was aware of because the SNDs seemed more 'American' with their absence of Lay Sisters! Another of the early English-speaking entrants was also an

Irish-American, Susan McGroarty (entered in 1846) – who, as Sister Julia, would be the founder of Washington, DC's Trinity College for women.[12]

Finally, consider the French Sisters of the Holy Cross, five of whom came to Indiana in 1843. Initially speaking no English, they found it difficult to prepare themselves for the teaching to which they aspired, since those who sought their services wanted lessons presented in the language of the land. Ten years later, a young woman auspiciously came to visit her brother, a Holy Cross seminarian, on her way to join the Sisters of Mercy in Chicago. An alumna of Visitation Academy in Washington, then perhaps the most renowned Catholic women's school in the country, Eliza Gillespie came from an Ohio family prominent in both the military and politics. She became instantly convinced that God was calling her to stay with this community, which she entered, soon becoming its first American Superior, Mother Mary Angela. Her talent as teacher, leader, and Americanizer transformed what might have remained a community of ill-equipped housekeepers and struggling primary teachers into the cosmopolitan congregation that eventually offered the first graduate programme in Catholic theology open to American women.[13]

Cultural eclecticism and resistance in American congregations

Many congregations became culturally eclectic almost as inadvertently as the Sisters of the Holy Cross. As pastors learned of their skills as teachers, they often invited Sisters to open new parish schools or to teach in ones previously conducted by lay teachers – often considered unreliable and usually desirous of higher salaries than their vowed counterparts! Over time, these invitations came increasingly from so-called 'national parishes' or mixed ones, whose clergy and members displayed various ethnicities, almost by definition non-English-speaking. While such pastors, and their parishioners, might well have preferred Sisters who shared their heritage, these were not always available. Thus, the Holy Cross Sisters' nearest conventual neighbours, the Sisters of Providence, who settled near Terre Haute, Indiana, in 1840, found themselves in an environment where most of the clergy, like themselves, were francophone; however, the population at large was mainly English- or German-speaking. This, an early annalist noted, was 'a circumstance which was to prove problematic in the future'. So the Providence nuns, like their neighbours, inevitably welcomed women of disparate ethnicities into their ranks; indeed, Mother Mary Cecilia Bailly – the woman who would replace the founding Superior, Mother (now Saint) Théodore Guérin, in 1856 – was the daughter of a Native American mother.[14]

In other cases, 'American' Sisters – generally meaning English-speaking, whatever the origin of their community – were the only available option. As young women came in contact with these orders, they were often inspired to seek admission. For the most part, they were welcomed *if* they could merge easily into the extant community culture, which meant sacrificing not only their native languages but also customary prayers, devotions, cuisine and other elements of their ethnicity. The so-called 'melting pot' was one in which the cultural identity of the 'other' was expected to disappear, rather than to transform in any way that to which it was added. This was not something that always dissipated over time, unfortunately; it persisted well into the mid-to-late twentieth-century. As late as the 1980s, in Brooklyn, New York, Mercy Camille D'Arienzo could reminisce about how awkward it was to be the only Italian American in her community – a situation she found almost as anachronistic as the contemporaneous Sister Thea Bowman's as the only African American in the Franciscans of Perpetual Adoration. While subsequent sociological modellers proposed replacing the melting-pot metaphor with a 'stew' or salad bowl – in which the various components remained distinct and perhaps even added new flavour to the whole – this was not always descriptive of how religious communities responded to the challenge of diversity. Although within a Catholic context it did not take long for the transformation to occur that Noel Ignatiev notably described in his book entitled *How the Irish Became White*, even the often-disparaged immigrants from Erin were not so welcoming to the 'others' they encountered.[15]

Other responses were possible, of course, and occurred with some frequency. Many communities of disparate national origin evolved easily and relatively comfortably into multi-ethnic conglomerates. The historian of the American Province of Franciscan Missionaries of the Sacred Heart, for example, described the intentionally international nature of their first US foundation this way:

> In this miniature assembly of four Sisters representing four different nationalities, there was no absence of variety; French was taught by Rev. Mother M. Gertrude, Italian by Sister M. Pelligrina whose musical accents were duly appreciated by her enthusiastic compatriots, Sister M. Constantia conducted the class in German, and Miss Mary Dobbins, the first American postulant, who had entered on December 23, 1865, presided over the class in English.

Similarly, within a decade of their arrival from Bavaria in 1850, the School Sisters of Notre Dame contained Irish, French and Polish members, as well as the predominant German speakers; Mother Caroline Friess, the American Vicar (Superior) saw this as a great boon to the congregation's growth, as she could provide variously fluent teachers to schools for different nationalities – and, whenever possible, put the Sisters under a Superior of the appropriate ethnicity.[16]

The same could not be said, however, for her Milwaukee neighbours, the also-German School Sisters of St Francis. While they admitted women from the increasing numbers of Polish parishes they served, the policy seemed to be to turn them disproportionately into 'housekeepers' regardless of their intellectual gifts,[17] and to appoint German Superiors (and enforce the use of the German language for prayer and recreation) regardless of the ethnicity of the parish. As a result, in 1901, roughly a quarter-century after the community's establishment in Wisconsin, the vast majority of its Polish members – with the encouragement of several priests and the bishop of Green Bay – 'eloped' and formed their own autonomous congregation, the Sisters of St Joseph of the Third Order of St Francis (SSJ-TOSF).[18] A similar breakoff group, the 'Polish Franciscan School Sisters' of St Louis, Missouri, were established contemporaneously by Archbishop John J. Kain as a separate ethnic community comprising former members of the German Franciscans of Joliet, Illinois.[19] Franciscans, to be sure, weren't the only order to face such fissures. French and Irish members of the predominantly German Dominicans of Racine, Wisconsin broke away in 1880 to form a small congregation of Franciscans in Green Bay. And the Blauvelt congregation was not the only Irish departure from the New York Dominicans; it was primarily Irish members who staffed the Midwestern missions which later established autonomy in Grand Rapids and Adrian, Michigan.[20]

Cultural chauvinism and ethnic exclusivism

Many communities retained determinedly ethnic identities long after it was appropriate or even practical. The Franciscan Sisters of Philadelphia, for instance, were founded around 1850, but remained proudly German until the turn of the twentieth-century, and not without the encouragement of the hierarchy. As late as 1872, authoritarian Archbishop James Wood decreed that only German Sisters should be admitted and that, if a non-German identified only as 'Miss Irene' were accepted into the novitiate, 'I have reason to believe you will regret it.'[21] And consider the memoir of Sister Salesia Walter, who entered the community in 1896:

> The German language was used entirely then, morning and night prayers, stations, rosary, meditation were all in German. We English speaking novices must even accuse ourselves in chapter in German. In order to do this, we went to the German novices, to ask how to say things and did they have fun at our expense in telling us what to say. One novice said 'nicht' before everything she said in German. Sister Aloysia said to her, 'You have told us everything you did not do, now tell us the things you did do.' Another novice said something about jumping over a broom stick. This being so far-fetched, Sister Aloysia asked her who had told her to say that. When the novice told her, a German conversation followed between that novice and Sister Aloysia and we knew that the novice was being taken to task for it, so the fun ceased. All our instructions were

also given in German, then translated into English as everyone in the Novitiate could speak English. We learned to say the office by being told to listen to how the old professed Sisters said it and imitate them. We stopped using the German language during the war with Germany when the officials forbade its use in common.[22]

Similarly, the Stella Niagara Franciscans, near Buffalo, New York were a province of an international and multi-ethnic congregation, but their US province remained entirely and deliberately German until 1928, a decade *after* the Great War. According to their annalist:

> all American aspirants who were of English, Irish, French, Polish or Italian extraction, had to become bilingual as all prayers were said, and all retreats were given in German. To insure practice in the official tongue, German was spoken in recreations three days a week and every day during Lent and Advent.[23]

Language, apparently, while enforced, was also recognized as a penitential matter – and not only, one might suspect, in this particular order.

Not all orders remained homogeneous, but that didn't mean they became melting pots, either. Recreation must have been painful in the numerous communities that continued to print prayer manuals, Constitutions and customaries in more than one tongue, or to conduct disparate retreats based upon language proficiency. As late as 1930, the Racine Dominicans offered both German and English retreats, and they were not unique. At least they, however, did not segregate different nationalities by rank, as the School Sisters of St Francis did – or the Chicago Sisters of Mercy, who assigned the first two German women to seek admission to the Lay Sister ranks.[24] A century later, when Lay Sisters were becoming nearly impossible to attract in the egalitarian USA, the Religious of the Sacred Heart decided to recruit women from Latin America solely for the purpose of filling that class.[25] So perhaps it is not surprising that, well into modern times, at least some congregations decided to avoid the 'diversity' issue entirely by remaining monolithic; the Buffalo Province of the Felicians, a Polish congregation, for instance, did not admit their first non-Polish applicant until well after the Second World War, more than half a century after the province was established, and seventy-five years after the community came to America.[26]

Ethnic exclusivity was, of course, more common in the nineteenth-century. Consider what happened to the German-speaking Dominican Sisters who were sent from Brooklyn, New York to Mission San José, California in 1876. Their new bishop was originally Spanish, and most of the women who sought to enter under their Superior, Pia Backes, were unquestionably Irish. Officially still under the jurisdiction of the Mother House in New York, Mother Pia was repeatedly frustrated by criticism from her superiors that too much of their teaching was conducted in English, that the needs of the (relatively few) German Catholics should come first and that no more than 10 per cent of the postulants she accepted were to be of Irish heritage. None of this was feasible, all of it was frustrating and, by the 1890s, they had become autonomous.[27] Today, as for over a century, the Mission San José Dominicans show little indication of their Germanic roots, but pride themselves on the diversity of their membership and their ministries.

Implications for Americanization and American religious life

So what were the implications of all this for Sisters' religious lives and ministries? Like those they served, these women religious were themselves products of cultures and circumstances that left them torn between determination to remain faithful to their heritages and their simultaneous desires to become fully and acceptably 'American'. But what did either of these competing desires actually *mean*? For the Sisters and for those with whom they worked, ethnicity and faith were often inextricably connected. To remain Catholic in the heterogeneous and religiously pluralistic setting that was America was for many synonymous with remaining German, or Polish, or French, or Lithuanian, or Italian, or even Irish. In extreme cases, an inability to reconcile Americanization and cultural fidelity might result in the establishment of new religious communities, such as the SSJ-TOSFs already mentioned; or the similarly titled but completely distinct Polish American Franciscan Sisters of St Joseph; or the emergence of entirely new hyphenate-American congregations defined solely by their ethnicity: the Lithuanian Sisters of St Casimir, the Slavic Sisters of St Cyril and Methodius, or the Mexican American Missionary Catechists of Divine Providence.[28] Under such auspices, ethnically distinct populations were educated in schools that tried to combine cultural retention with often exuberant American celebrations of holidays such as 4 July and George Washington's birthday. Concerning Columbus Day, for instance, the first band of British Franciscan Sisters reported gleefully, shortly after their arrival in Baltimore: 'Columbus celebration! 400th Anniversary of discovery of America!!! Meat allowed … Great excitement all day. House & garden illuminated. Grand torch light procession in the evening. Sisters all crazy!'[29] Similar messages appeared in the house diaries and correspondence of most immigrant communities, as well as references to the opportunity such occasions offered for training their students (and, not incidentally, themselves) in nationalistic observance.

This ministry, and its concomitant determined patriotism, meanwhile, did not occur in a vacuum; Sisters, even more than those they served (because they often were under attack as some of the most visible agents of this so-called 'alien' religion), were well aware of the frequently recurring threats of suspicion and nativism that characterized so much of the experience of American Catholics. Therefore, service that overrode or transcended such prejudices not only permitted Sisters to live in peace, but also undermined the antipathies of their more xenophobic neighbours. As these women nursed during epidemics and wars, many outside the Church came to know Catholics and to appreciate them – if not as Catholics, then as humane and self-sacrificing people who often were willing to risk their lives in helping others: even potentially hostile strangers.[30] It was not uncommon for Sisters to volunteer as nurses even if this were not one of their communities' established ministries. Thus, during the American Civil War, orders like Holy Cross – who prior to this time had never nursed – provided Sisters to serve not only on land but on the waters of the Mississippi River, thereby earning them official recognition as the first US Navy nurses.[31] Shortly after their arrival in San Francisco, Sisters of Mercy from Kinsale offered their services to nurse during a virulent cholera epidemic. The local *Daily News* reported the consequences this way:

> a more horrible and ghastly sight we have seldom witnessed. In the midst of this scene of sorrow, pain, anguish, and danger were ministering angels who disregarded everything to aid their distressed fellow creatures. The Sisters of Mercy, rightly named, whose convent is opposite the hospital, as soon as they learned the state of things, hurried to offer their services. They did not stop to inquire whether the poor sufferers were Protestants or Catholics, American or foreigners, but with the noblest devotion applied themselves to their relief. One Sister might be seen bathing the limbs of a sufferer; another chafing the extremities; a third applying the remedies; while others with pitying faces were calming the fears of those supposed to be dying. The idea of danger never seems to have occurred to these noble women; they heeded nothing of the kind. If the lives of any of the unfortunates be saved they will owe their preservation to those noble ladies.

As a result, the Mercy annalist wrote, the archbishop offered the Sisters his 'highest appreciation. He considered them the chief factor in restoring religious harmony in San Francisco. And it may be said that Know-Nothingism did not again dare to raise its head, in the old way, in that fair city.'[32] Similarly, when a tornado devastated much of Rochester, Minnesota, some of the local Franciscan teaching Sisters offered both themselves and their convent in aid of their many injured neighbours. Even without training, their efforts so impressed a father and his two sons who were local physicians that they persuaded the community to open a permanent hospital in the city; it became St Marys Hospital, the first piece of what is now a clinic named after those doctors: the internationally renowned Mayo Clinic, where St Marys and the founding contribution of the Franciscans remain a centrepiece.[33]

Schools also served to undermine prejudices and to prepare more welcoming settings into which Catholics could be assimilated into American society. It was almost always the case, particularly in small and newly settled towns, that parochial schools and academies enrolled at least some non-Catholic students, thereby providing high-quality and accessible education that would not otherwise have been available. Sisters were often the only people in a community who offered training in the arts and in music – requests by founding teachers for pianos to be provided (generally by funds from their Mother-Houses and not by local citizens or pastors) were not a matter of seeking luxury but a recognition that being able to offer lessons would result not only in revenue but in appreciation. As Mother Rose Lynch, then Superior of the Dominican Sisters of Columbus, Ohio, declared in 1850:

> A Protestant girl educated in a Catholic Academy sees with her own eyes, what Catholics are, what their genuine doctrines are, and what morals they practice. When she finishes her education, she may not yet be a Catholic, but she is no longer a Protestant, she does not protest any longer against the Catholic Faith and morals. She will never be persuaded that Catholics are idolatrous and vicious; and not infrequently when she will hear the Catholic abused, the memory of the life of the Sisters, who withdraw themselves from the pleasures of the world to give themselves to mortification, to prayer, and to take care of the Motherless, will prompt her to defend the Catholic Religion against the attacks, of even, her nearest connexions.[34]

Thus, by undermining the prejudices of others, teaching Sisters could lessen the antipathy of formerly (or potentially) suspicious neighbours, thereby making it easier for other Catholics to gain acceptance or at least tolerance in an otherwise unwelcoming environment.

Of course, the primary mission of these Sisters was inevitably to the Catholic population. By offering social services and education to their fellow believers, Sisters themselves gave priority to 'saving souls' – but realized that many of those with whom they worked had more practical motives in mind. Consider this explanation in 1862 from Milwaukee's Bishop John Martin Henni to Mother Benedicta Bauer, founder of the Dominicans of Racine, Wisconsin, explaining why even in the 'German school' it was necessary to offer instruction in English (and to have Sister-teachers qualified to provide it):

> Often a Catholic school is not supported when a free school is near by. In your circumstances I can in no wise take it amiss when you wish to give up the poorly attended school particularly since you have only one Sister qualified to teach English, and she can supply in the German school what otherwise would be missing. The English language should be taught also in the German school, especially to the boys. Otherwise they are forced

sooner or later to go to English schools in order to acquaint themselves with the language of the land, as is customary and proper. If you had a sufficient number of English-speaking teachers, I would strongly insist that the parish school should remain in progress, but as matters stand now, I cannot require it of Rev. Gibson or the parish, in view of the debts on the church. Meanwhile I desire above all that your Order train teacher-candidates in both languages as well as possible, and then with God's help you will succeed even in the parish of St Patrick.[35]

And this, of course, returns to the overriding Catholic concern to staunch immigrants' 'leakage' from the faith. Thus, what this chapter has attempted to suggest is that Sisters were recognized as the most successful ministers in the Catholic Church in achieving this – but that, at the same time they were proving their worth to the bishops who would acknowledge their centrality so forcefully in 1884, they were struggling with powerful challenges in their own communities. Before they could serve the multi-ethnic, multi-cultural population that characterized American Catholicism – and characterized it more complexly rather than less as time went on – they would have to decide how to respond to its challenges within their own ranks. What did 'sisterhood', or community, or American, *mean* under such circumstances?

Answers to this question were complex and exceedingly varied. But it can be argued that the diversity of answers meant that tensions between cultural retention and assimilation – while central to American Catholic culture from the outset – would never achieve complete resolution. There are *types*, not *a* type, of American Catholic identity, and awareness of and, indeed, comfort with such heterogeneity may be the first step towards any meaningful or comprehensive understanding. So, for now, it may be helpful to consider two potentially promising conceptual frameworks. The first comes from Claudette LaVerdiere's new spiritual biography of Mary Joseph (Mollie) Rogers, founder of the Maryknoll Missionary Sisters. It took nearly three-quarters of a century, LaVerdiere writes, before a community that from the outset had included Europeans and Hispanics, African Americans and Asians, was able to make a conscious turn at its 1978 General Assembly from assimilation to *integration*.

> They had learned that when a new candidate enters, regardless of her culture, everybody has to change, to adapt, not only the new person. Ideally everyone moves over to make a welcoming space. Life in community necessitates doing this over and over again.[36]

The other, perhaps both more challenging and more potentially holistic, approach is from Diana Eck, head of Harvard's Pluralism Project, and is articulated in her profoundly evocative book, *A New Religious America*. Eck argues that Americans need to move beyond a dichotomy between exclusion and assimilation, to one of pluralism, which she defines as the opportunity in America to 'come and be yourself ... a oneness [that] is shaped by the encounter of the many'. She sees pluralism as moving beyond the melting pot and the stew and the salad to a symphony: 'sounding not unison, but harmony, with all the distinctive tones of our many cultures'. It is, she says, 'engagement with, not abdication of, differences and particularities'. Pluralism, she concludes, 'is premised not on a reductive relativism but on the significance of an engagement with real difference'.[37]

Conclusion

Some women religious in the United States understood pluralism in this way implicitly, even in the nineteenth-century. Others still resist this perspective today. But until scholars acknowledge and grapple with Sisters' struggles to comprehend individual, communal and multi-cultural identity, it is impossible to appreciate fully both the challenges and the possibilities of their ministries. To put this another way, the first classrooms that American teaching Sisters had to enter were not in their schools, but in their convents. And their first students were not the children, but themselves.

Notes

1 The term 'leakage' derives primarily from the very influential Gerald Shaughnessy, *Has the Immigrant Kept the Faith? A Study of Immigration and Catholic Growth in the United States, 1790–1920* (New York: Macmillan, 1925). See also Hugh J. Nolan (ed.), *Pastoral Letters of the United States Catholic Bishops*, 6 vols, Vol. I (Washington: National Conference of Catholic Bishops, 1984): 224–5; Margaret Susan Thompson, 'Cultural Conundrum: Sisters, Ethnicity, and the Adaptation of American Catholicism', *Mid-America*, 74 (1992), 205–30; J. A. Burns, *The Growth and Development of the Catholic School System in the United States* (New York: Benziger Brothers, 1912); JoEllen McNergney Vinyard, *For Faith and Fortune: The Education of Catholic Immigrants in Detroit, 1805–1925* (Champaign: University of Illinois Press, 1988).
2 List of US congregations compiled by and in possession of the author. An abbreviated version can be found in Thompson, 'Cultural Conundrum'; see also Table 6.1 above.
3 Other aspects of this topic are explored in Margaret Susan Thompson, 'Adaptation and Professionalisation: Challenges for Teaching Sisters in a Pluralistic Nineteenth-Century America', *Paedagogica historica*, 49:4 (2013): 454–70.
4 Thompson, 'Cultural Conundrum'; see also Barbara Misner, *Highly Respectable and Accomplished Ladies: Catholic Women Religious in America, 1790–1850* (New York: Garland, 1988).
5 'Community language' is not a formal term, but it generally is understood to refer to the language in which vernacular prayer occurred, and in which other activities such as recreation, spiritual reading and retreats were carried out.
6 Mother Anne Francis Campbell, 'Bishop England's Sisterhood [Sisters of Our Lady of Mercy], 1829–1929' (Ph.D. thesis, St Louis University, 1968);

Mary Teresa Austin Carroll, *Leaves from the Annals of the Sisters of Mercy*, 4 vols, Vol. III (New York: P. O'Shea, 1888); Ann M. Harrington, *Creating Community: Mary Frances Clarke and Her Companions* (Dubuque, IA: Sisters of Charity of the Blessed Virgin Mary, 2004).

7 Clyde F. Crews, *An American Holy Land: A History of the Archdiocese of Louisville* (Wilmington, DE: M. Glazier, 1987).

8 Jane Frances Heaney, *A Century of Pioneering: A History of the Ursulines in New Orleans, 1727–1827* (New Orleans: privately printed, 1993); Mary Francis Borgia Hart, *Violets in the King's Garden: A History of the Sisters of the Holy Family* (New Orleans: privately printed, 1976); Mother Shawn Copeland, *The Subversive Power of Love: The Vision of Henriette Delille* (Mahwah, NJ: Paulist Press, 2009); Louise Callan, *The Society of the Sacred Heart in North America* (New York: Longmans, Green, 1927); Diane Batts Morrow, *Persons of Color and Religious at the Same Time: The Oblate Sisters of Providence, 1829–1860* (Chapel Hill: University of North Carolina Press, 2011); Margaret Gannon, *Paths of Daring, Deeds of Hope: Letters by and about Mother Theresa Maxis Duchemin* (Scranton, PA: privately printed, 1992); Charles E. Nolan, 'Carmelite Dreams, Creole Perspectives: The Sisters of Mount Carmel of Louisiana, 1833–1903' (Ph.D. thesis, Gregorian University, Rome, 1970).

9 Bernardita Gillis and Timothy Cunningham (eds), *Here We Shall Be* (Blauvelt, NY: privately printed, 1977); Mother Philomena Yonker and Mother Wilhelmina Huston, *The Story of a Century: A Brief History of the Sisters of St Dominic of Blauvelt, New York* (Blauvelt, NY: privately printed, 1975).

10 Gannon, *Paths of Daring*; Marita-Constance Supan, 'Dangerous Memory: Mother M. Theresa Maxis Duchemin and the Michigan Congregation of the Sisters, IHM', in *Building Sisterhood: A Feminist History of the Sisters, Servants of the Immaculate Heart of Mary, Monroe, Michigan* (Syracuse, NY: Syracuse University Press, 1997), 31–67; Gilbert Ahr Enderle, *I Desire to Be Everywhere: Louis Florent Gillet, Frontier Missionary, Founder, and Contemplative Monk* (Baltimore: privately printed, 2012), 153–217.

11 Sister Mary Francis Joseph [Ann Eliza Dillon] to Bishop Joseph Rosati, 22 March 38, Archives of the Sisters of St Joseph of Carondelet, St Louis, Missouri; Mary Lucida Savage, *The Congregation of Saint Joseph of Carondelet* (St Louis: B. Herder, 1923), 50–60; Dolorita Marie Dougherty, Helen Angela Hurley, Emily Joseph, St Claire Coyne *et al.*, *Sisters of St Joseph of Carondelet* (St Louis: B. Herder, 1966), 6–67.

12 Helen Louise Nugent, *Sister Louise, American Foundress* (New York: Benziger Brothers, 1931), 130–1, 60–1, 77, 83–4, 251–2; Helen Louise Nugent, *Sister Julia* (New York: Benziger Brothers, 1928); Angela Elizabeth Keenan, *Three against the Wind. The Founding of Trinity College, Washington, DC* (Westminster, MD: Christian Classics, 1973). For discussions of class and lay Sisters, see Margaret Susan Thompson, 'Sisterhood and Power: Class, Culture, and Ethnicity in the American Convent', *Colby Library Quarterly*, 25 (September 1989): 149–75; Phil Kilroy, *The Society of the Sacred Heart in Nineteenth-Century France, 1800–1865* (Cork: Cork University Press, 2012), 9–84.

13 Anna Shannon McAllister, *Flame in the Wilderness: Life and Letters of Mother Angela Gillespie, CSC, 1824–1887* (Paterson, NJ: St Anthony Guild Press, 1944); Mother Georgina Costin, *Priceless Spirit: A History of the Sisters of the Holy Cross, 1841–1893* (Notre Dame: University of Notre Dame Press, 1994). On Visitation Academy, see George Parsons Lathrop and Rose Hawthorne Lathrop, *A Story of Courage: Annals of the Georgetown Convent of the Visitation of the Blessed Virgin Mary* (Cambridge, MA: Riverside Press, 1894); on the School of Sacred Theology,

see Gail Porter Mandell, *Madeleva: A Biography* (Albany: State University of New York Press, 1997), 183–9.
14 Mary Carol Schroeder, 'The Catholic Church in the Diocese of Vincennes, 1847–1877' (Ph.D. thesis, Catholic University of America, 1946), 1; Mary Borromeo Brown, *History of the Sisters of Providence of Saint Mary-of-the-Woods, Indiana, 1806–1856* (New York: Benziger Brothers, 1949).
15 Camille D'Arienzo, 'My Pact with Camillus', in Ann Patrick Ware (ed.), *Midwives of the Future: American Sisters Tell Their Story* (Kansas City, MO: Leaven Press, 1985), 22–36; Charlene Smith and John Feister, *Thea's Song: The Life of Thea Bowman* (Maryknoll: Orbis Books, 2012); Noel Ignatiev, *How the Irish Became White* (New York: Routledge, 1995).
16 Mother Cherubim Duffy, *Franciscan Missionary Sisters of the Sacred Heart in the United States, 1865–1926* (Peekskill, NY: privately printed, 1927), 18; Barbara Brumleve and Marjorie Myers (eds), *Mother Mary Caroline Friess: Correspondence and Other Documents*, Resource Publication no. 35 (Elm Grove, WI: SSND Heritage Research, 1985); Judith Best, *Sturdy Roots: An Educational Resource for Studying the Heritage and Spirit of the School Sisters of Notre Dame*, DVD (St Louis: privately produced, 2005); identities of multi-ethnic members and Superiors in the Profession Book and Provincial Annals, SSND Archives, Milwaukee, WI, and Baltimore, MD.
17 The congregation never had formal 'choir/lay' distinctions in the United States (though its German precursor did) – but, nonetheless, stratified attitudes and de facto distinctions seem to have remained part of at least some of the community's cultural sub-text. Thus, although its still-standard history was published after the Second Vatican Council, and although its author was a trained scholar who later left the congregation and identified herself as an anti-patriarchal (and post-Christian) feminist, the book was unaccountably entitled *He Sent Two*, a reference to the pair of women officially recognized as its founders: Sisters Alexia and Alfons. However, there actually were three, including Sister Clara; Clara, though, was a lay Sister – and, thus, never acknowledged as a 'true' founder. Mother Francis Borgia [Rothluebber], *He Sent Two: The Story of the Beginning of the School Sisters of St Francis* (Milwaukee: Bruce Publishing Company, 1986), 28, 44, 54, 78; for more on Francis Rothluebber, see her 'The Power of Dialogue,' in Ware, *Midwives of the Future*, 117–28.
18 Josephine Marie Peplinski, *A Fitting Response: The History of the Sisters of St Joseph of the Third Order of St Francis*, 2 vols, Vol. I, *The Founding* (South Bend, IN: privately printed, 1982), esp. 91–162. Transcribed memoirs by many of the founding Sisters recounting the separation (compiled in the 1930s, translated from Polish to English in the 1970s by Peplinski) can be found in the SSJ-TOSF Archives, Stevens Point, Wisconsin.
19 'Polish Franciscan School Sisters', in *The Catholic Church in the United States of America: Undertaken to Celebrate the Golden Jubilee of His Holiness, Pope Pius X*, 3 vols, Vol. II, *Religious Communities of Women* (New York: Catholic Editing Company, 1914), 211–12.
20 Louise Hunt, *A History of the Sisters of St Francis of the Holy Cross, 1868–1995* (Green Bay, WI: privately printed, n.d.); Mona Schwind, *Period Pieces: An Account of the Grand Rapids Dominicans, 1853–1966* (Grand Rapids, MI: privately printed, 1991); Mary Philip Ryan, *Amid the Alien Corn* (St Charles, IL: Jones Wood Press, 1967).
21 Archbishop James Wood to Mother M. Agnes, 28 February 1872, Archives of the Franciscan Sisters of Philadelphia, Aston, Pennsylvania. No 'Miss Irene'

was listed in the investiture records anywhere near the time in question, so she was either rejected or left before she would have been admitted to the novitiate.
22 Mary Salesia [Walter], 'Some Memoirs of My Years in the Franciscan Community' (typescript, n.d., but written after a 1956 fire, according to internal evidence), 15–16, Archives of the Philadelphia Franciscan Sisters.
23 Georgia Dunn, *Towers of Monabaur* (Derby, NY: St Paul Publications, 1971), 97.
24 Carroll, *Leaves from the Annals*, Vol. III, 99.
25 Margaret Susan Thompson, *'To Serve the People of God': Nineteenth-Century Sisters and the Creation of an American Religious Life*, Cushwa Center for the Study of American Catholicism (University of Notre Dame) Working Paper Series 18, no. 2 ([Notre Dame, IN: Cushaw Center, 1987), 10: interview with Mother Odeide Mouton, RSCJ, Grand Coteau, Louisiana, 27 February 1986.
26 Thompson, 'Sisterhood and Power', 160: interview with Sister Suzanne Marie Kush (former Buffalo, NY Felician Vocation Director), 9 January 1987.
27 Mother Seraphina Staimer (Brooklyn) to Mother Pia Backes, 22 January 1880, 10 and 26 June 1882, Mission San José Dominican Archives; Pia Backes, *Her Days Unfolded*, trans. Bernardina Michel (St Benedict, OR: Benedictine Press, 1953), 6–22; Mary Thomas Lillis, *Seed and Growth: The Story of the Dominican Sisters of Mission San José* (Fremont, CA: privately printed, 2012), 93–122.
28 Peplinski, *A Fitting Response*; Mary Emmeline Glica, 'The History of the Franciscan Sisters of St Joseph: 1897–1960' (M.A. thesis, St Bonaventure University, 1964); Mary Emerentia Petraslek, *A Brief History of the Sisters of SS Cyril and Methodius, Told in Five Decades, 1909–1959* (Danville, PA: privately printed, 1959); Mother Leona Naujokas, *History of the Foundation of the Sisters of Saint Casimir* (Chicago: privately printed, 1940); Mary Paul Valdez, *History of the Missionary Catechists of Divine Providence* (San Antonio: Archdiocese of San Antonio, 1978).
29 House diary, 21 October 1892, Franciscan Sisters of Baltimore Archives.
30 From a secular perspective, see Charles E. Rosenberg, *The Cholera Years: The United States in 1832, 1849, and 1866* (Chicago: University of Chicago Press, 1962), 64, 95, 139–40; see also Ursula Stepsis and Dolores Liptak (eds), *Pioneer Healers: The History of Women Religious in American Health Care* (New York: Crossroad, 1989), 39–85; Barbra Mann Wall, *Unlikely Entrepreneurs: Catholic Sisters and the Hospital Marketplace, 1865–1925* (Columbus: Ohio State University Press, 2005), 74–101; Mary Denis Maher, *To Bind up the Wounds of War: Catholic Sister Nurses in the US Civil War* (Westport, CT: Greenwood Press, 1989).
31 Costin, *Priceless Spirit*, 181–94; Maher, *To Bind up the Wounds of War*; Ellen Ryan Jolly, *Nuns of the Battlefield* (Providence: Providence Visitor Press, 1927)
32 Carroll, *Leaves from the Annals*, Vol. III, 482–3.
33 Mary Francis Ann Hayes, 'Years of Beginning: A History of the Sisters of the Third Order Regular of Saint Francis of the Congregation of Our Lady of Lourdes, Rochester, Minnesota, 1877–1902' (M.A. thesis, Catholic University of America, 1956), 37–8; Ellen Whelan, *The Sisters' Story: Saint Marys Hospital–Mayo Clinic, 1889–1939* (Rochester, MN: Mayo Foundation for Education and Research, 2002).
34 Mother M. Rose Lynch to the Society for the Propagation of the Faith, Paris, 12 March 1850, Archives of the Dominican Sisters of St Mary of the Springs, Columbus, Ohio.
35 John Martin Henni to Benedicta Bauer, 8 November 1862, Archives of the Dominican Sisters of Racine, Wisconsin.

36 Claudette LaVerdiere, *On the Threshold of the Future: The Life and Spirituality of Mother Mary Joseph Rogers, Founder of the Maryknoll Sisters* (Maryknoll, NY: Orbis Books, 2011), 85.
37 Diana L. Eck, *A New Religious America: How a 'Christian Country' Has Become the World's Most Religiously Diverse Nation* (San Francisco: HarperCollins, 2001), 70–1.

Chapter 7

'Have your children got leave to speak?'

The teacher training of New Zealand Dominican Sisters, 1871–1965

Jenny Collins

Introduction

An exploration of the teacher training of Dominican Sisters engages with key 'global' issues facing Catholic women religious as they worked to establish their identity as educators; to improve the socio-economic and educational opportunities of their pupils; and to protect their congregational autonomy against encroachment by ecclesiastical and state authorities in New World countries such as Canada, Australia, the United States and New Zealand. This chapter is the result of a study undertaken in 2013 in Ireland and New Zealand that explored the contribution of Catholic Sisters to the development of the New Zealand education system. It utilizes convent and other archival sources to highlight some of the complexities that underpinned the education of New Zealand Dominican Sisters in the years between 1871 and 1965. It explores a number of transitions that re-shaped congregational identity and the training of new members of the order. While the education of new recruits was initially designed to maintain the religious and cultural values brought with the Sisters from Ireland, by the 1930s Dominican Sister-teachers were adopting pedagogical innovations and implementing state models of teacher training while modifying them to maintain their own independence. At the same time the limited autonomy allowed Sisters in the pioneering years had been replaced by more detailed guidelines for behaviour and the performance of rituals. An examination of the oral histories of eight Dominican Sisters[1] who taught in their order's primary and secondary schools in the years from 1931 to 1965 highlights the challenges of life at the chalk face and key developments in teacher training in the highly regulated 1930s and 1940s. Increased secondary rolls and the integration of Catholics into the mainstream of New Zealand society that took place in the 1950s presented a broader challenge to Catholic teaching religious. In response Dominican Sister-teachers began to take part in community-based professional development and to move from an 'apprenticeship' model based on religious formation to a professional model of teacher training that incorporated state expertise while protecting congregational autonomy.

An historical overview

Before examining the training of Dominican Sister-teachers, the following will consider some of the historical influences that helped to shape the development of the Catholic education system and the teacher training of Catholic Sisters.[2] The nineteenth-century Catholic Church, suspicious of the 'secular' values implicit in state education, and distrustful of Catholic parents who they believed lacked both the time and the capacity to teach the correct religious values,[3] encouraged the movement of 'active' religious orders into the field of education, particularly in English-speaking countries such as England and Wales, Australia, the USA, and New Zealand.[4] The Church responded to what it saw as a 'hostile world' by creating an education system that would ensure the transmission of faith and the reproduction of Catholic cultural and spiritual values. The 'Irish' teaching orders that came to New Zealand in the latter part of the nineteenth-century were the foundation on which that education system was built.[5] Teaching orders such as the Sisters of Mercy, the Sisters of St Joseph, the Christian Brothers and the Marist Brothers worked to provide a basic primary school education for the largely working-class 'Irish' Catholic population, while orders such as the Religious of the Sacred Heart, the Dominican Sisters and the Society of Mary also offered a secondary education for the educational advancement and social mobility of the select few.[6]

Complex relations between diocesan and pontifical orders and the episcopal authorities in each diocese shaped the Catholic education system in New Zealand. Diocesan-based orders such as the Mercy Sisters provided the 'shock troops' that established the parish-based elementary education system in all four dioceses.[7] Subject to the authority of the bishop they were able to provide a quick response to diocesan-based educational needs but suffered from a certain insularity and inflexibility in regard to national educational needs. The pontifical orders such as the Dominican Sisters retained a greater independence and a closer contact with international educational developments, but their educational interests frequently crossed diocesan boundaries and they in their turn were shaped by particular cultural and pedagogical traditions and by the requirements of their own internationally based authorities.[8]

When the 1877 Education Act made primary schooling free, compulsory and 'secular', and abolished state aid to denominations schools in New Zealand, the Catholic Church saw the development of a system of parochial schools as crucial to its survival. Young Catholic women were encouraged to join teaching orders to staff these schools. By 1900, when each parish had a primary school, maintained by donations, school fees and the efforts of the teachers, seven out of eight religious were working in the field of education and the overwhelming majority of these were Irish in origin.[9] The success of the nineteenth-century Catholic educational mission to transmit the faith and provide a basic primary education to the children of the Irish-Catholic immigrants depended largely on the efforts of these Irish religious, in particular the Sisters who staffed and ran the majority of Catholic schools.[10] For them, as for the Dominican Sisters, teaching was a vocation rather than a career. They worked to ensure the success of the Church's educational mission: the reproduction of religious values and the social and economic advancement of Catholic pupils through access to and success in the state examination system.[11]

Dominican connections with education go back to the order's beginning in the thirteenth-century. Founded to teach the Gospel and combat heresy, the order has a strong scholastic tradition, with links to university cities such as Paris, Bologna, Montpellier and Oxford, and produced many leading theologians and philosophers.[12] While the friars became involved in preaching, teaching and mission work, the focus of the nuns' work was teaching. In the case of the New Zealand Dominican Sisters, Dominican tradition was interwoven with a strong Irish influence. In 1871, the Sisters brought this cultural and scholastic background with them to Otago.[13] The work of education was clearly articulated in their Constitutions.

> The official work of the Congregation of the New Zealand Dominican Sisters is to maintain and teach schools of all grades, both for boarders and day-scholars; as well as Training Colleges, Hostels and other institutions for the promotion of education and instruction, according to the law and mind of the Holy Catholic Church.[14]

In New Zealand, the Dominican Sisters[15] initially established primary and secondary schools in the provinces of Otago and Southland, including three secondary colleges for girls: St Dominic's Dunedin in 1871, St Catherine's Invercargill in 1882, and Teschemakers near Oamaru in 1912. In 1931, at the request of Bishop Liston, and to meet the needs of the burgeoning Catholic population in the north, they expanded into the Auckland province establishing primary schools in Helensville and Northcote. In 1944 they set up a school for the deaf in Wellington, which transferred to Feilding in 1952. St Dominic's Northcote expanded and became a registered secondary school in 1952.[16]

Teacher training in the early years

Until the end of the nineteenth-century, the Sisters continued to draw on their Irish experiences for the teacher training of their Sisters. Letters back to Sion Hill, Dublin written by the ten founder Sisters include references to the 'monitorial system' then in use in their 'poor schools' in Ireland, and questions about curriculum and textbooks to be used in classrooms. The challenges they faced included isolation, delays in communication with their Mother-House, the difficulty of getting teaching resources, and the urgent need for teaching Sisters for the rapidly expanding schools around Otago and Southland. Mother Gabriel Gill, the first prioress, took a direct role in the training of teacher Sisters. In the early 1870s and 1880s she accompanied Sisters as they set up new schools in parishes around Otago and Southland and supervised the system of training for new recruits as they joined the order. Pressures on the Sisters in these years included the shortage of suitably qualified recruits,[17] and the need to utilize lay Sisters and pupil-teachers to meet the demands of rapidly expanding numbers in the primary schools.[18] Letters indicate the use of both lay Sisters and pupil-teachers in the primary schools in the 'missions' and highlight Gabriel Gill's disquiet over the use of these 'non experts': 'Whether we can send a Sister next week to replace S. M. Hyacinth [a lay Sister] or not, you will have to withdraw the Lay Sister from the School.'[19] Concerned to ensure consistency of practice, Gabriel Gill prepared a series of lectures that included specific guidelines for the behaviour of teachers and their relations with pupils. These 'lectures' were probably delivered on Saturdays, or during the school holidays or the summer break when the Sisters gathered for their Chapter. Trainee teachers were expected to exercise discipline over students, preferring the 'vigilant eye' rather than corporal punishment.[20] They were encouraged to maintain their distance from their pupils and to avoid close relations with them and with 'seculars'.[21] The importance of forming the character and morals of Sister-teachers was paramount:

> All who embrace the profession of educating youth must first endeavor to form their own characters, with a view to the great end they have proposed to themselves – otherwise their book learning will avail but little – they will have no control over the minds, manners or lives of those entrusted to their care.[22]

As in Ireland, a Mistress of Schools was appointed to supervise the training of teachers, the habits and dispositions of children, and the quality of the lessons. She had oversight of the junior teachers (including pupil-teachers and lay Sisters) and was expected to 'point out defects in a Sisterly manner to the faulty Sister'. She was expected to watch over children's behaviour in order to 'correct faults and form the heart of each child individually to the practice of virtue'.[23] While the main aim of schooling was a religious one, to 'curb the passions and cultivat[e] the budding virtues of God's own little ones' teachers were told to encourage 'the progress of the children in secular knowledge'.[24] The Mistress of Schools was expected to visit each class daily and to hear the Home Lessons at least three times in the week 'so that every child may feel that the Nuns do not throw the weight of their teaching on the Pupil Teachers and that the Mistress may know exactly how each child is progressing'.[25] While the Mistress of Schools held no spiritual jurisdiction over her trainee Sisters, she was expected to report any problems to her Superiors and to the Chapter.

The training of twentieth-century Dominican Sisters

The training of a new Dominican recruit[26] focussed on religious formation and teacher training. Young women who entered the Dominican Sisters in the years from 1871 until 1965 engaged in a life of teaching and prayer underpinned by notions of sacrifice and self-effacement. According to the Rule, relations among Sisters were to be marked by charity and compassion.[27] From their arrival in 1871 until the Second Vatican Council (1962–5),[28] the New Zealand Dominican congregation, like many religious orders, was internally stratified into two classes of members: the choir Sisters and lay Sisters. Although they were bound by the same vows, the two classes differed in their responsibilities and their rights. The religious habit worn by the Sisters included 'a white tunic; a white scapular for the Choir Sisters, a black scapular for the Lay Sisters; and a black cappa'.[29] Postulants wore a black dress and bonnet, and when they became Novices they wore a white veil, which was changed to a black one after profession.[30] The primary function of choir Sisters, the main focus of this discussion, was 'to seek and provide for the salvation of souls by the uninterrupted ministry of teaching and preaching'.[31] They were given a voice in Chapter and were allowed to vote for the election of the Mother Superior and her counsellors. The lay Sisters on the other hand were not obliged to be present at the Divine Office, 'save at the Salve Procession after Compline, and at the weekly Libera'.[32] Their main duties were domestic. They managed the daily operations of the community, thus freeing the choir Sisters to undertake the educational mission of the order.

By 1931, the profile of Sisters in the Dominican Community represented a continuum of age and experience, from postulants who were exploring their suitability for religious life, to elderly women who had spent their lives as religious.[33] The presence of women from different generations helped to maintain the institutional memory of the order. Through the process of their initiation into the community they passed on the customs and traditions they themselves had been given to the new recruits. Elizabeth M. Smyth suggests that such an institutional memory also had a physical manifestation in the form of the mother-house residence that attested to the stability of the community.[34] The Dominican Sisters had established their mother-house at St Dominic's Priory in Dunedin and it was to this place that the new recruits came to begin their religious and teaching formation. Although the professed Sisters frequently moved from 'mission to mission' to teach in different schools, they came and went from a central home.[35] Smyth suggests that in this way Catholic Sisters had a structure of community stability to support them. It was this structure that also preserved traditional ways of religious formation and teacher training, as will be examined in the following.[36]

Religious formation

After taking the traditional vows of poverty, chastity and obedience, a newly professed Sister would prostrate herself before the altar. There, arms outstretched, she symbolically 'died to the world' and was 'born anew into Christ'.[37] It was the culmination of a formation process that had begun when a young woman entered the convent as a postulant, and which intensified at her clothing in the religious habit and the adoption of a new name. Most Constitutions and customaries explicitly forbade the keeping of memorabilia from – or even verbal references to – members' former lives; even contact and communication with families and friends were severely restricted or prohibited.[38] The reasons for this deliberate stripping away of identity were various. Margaret Thompson suggests that at least one of them was the fostering of a Christian communal ideal that traced its roots back to scripture: a society in which there 'does not exist among you Jew or Greek, slave or free, male or female; all are one in Christ Jesus'.[39] She points out, however, that it was rare for that ideal to reach fruition. Instead, both unintentionally and by design, religious orders mirrored the secular world in which they functioned, and from which their all-too-human membership was drawn. Among other things, religious life reflected the class and ethnic tensions that characterized society, particularly the patterns of culture and society brought to New Zealand by the Sisters and by working-class Irish Catholics.[40]

By 1933, when the Dominicans had established themselves as a separate congregation, they had largely worked through the challenges facing them as missionary pioneers in a raw colonial environment. They lived in a more regulated environment with clear guidelines for the performance of rituals such as the Divine Office. The Sisters were expected to arrive promptly and together. It took years for a new choir Sister to learn to take part in the Office and she was expected to exercise self-discipline. One of the most important means of preserving discipline and regulating the behaviour of the community was the Chapter of Faults, which was held weekly.

> At Chapter the Sisters shall speak only to accuse themselves or to proclaim others, or to answer the Superior's questions. They shall not speak afterwards of what has taken place at Chapter in a manner either disrespectful to authority or injurious to charity.[41]

The process of socialization, the vows of the Sisters and the normative force of vocation were underpinned by daily scheduling in the convent. The early missionary years in the congregation, which had allowed for flexibility and a certain individuality to occur, had been replaced by a period of consolidation and conservatism, and a switch in emphasis from the individual to the group.[42] When a young woman entered the convent she would have six to eight months as a postulant, and if she decided to go on she entered the

Normae, or canonical year. During this time the Sister wore a white veil. She didn't teach but concentrated on religious formation, learning the Rule and the Constitutions of the order and accompanying the fully professed Sisters to the chapel for the prayer times.

The correct formation of a novice, essential for the Dominican tradition, placed a high value on a search for 'truth' through prayer and contemplation.[43] This formation was seen as an important part of her teacher training, as a Sister was prepared for her role in the classroom. Sisters training to be primary teachers also studied for their Teacher's Certificate by correspondence.

Developments in teacher training

The question of the role of congregations such as the Dominicans in the formation of their members as teachers is one with international implications. Whilst teaching orders such as the Dominican Sisters worked to ensure a continuity of religious values via the religious formation of their members and an in-house apprenticeship system of teacher training, they were also concerned to ensure that the professional qualifications of their teachers were equivalent to the those in the state system. Until the end of the nineteenth-century the Catholic education system had its own curriculum and its own inspectors, and relied on an apprenticeship system of teacher training within each religious order. After 1895 with the arrival of state inspection the focus shifted to the acquisition of state qualifications, particularly for primary teachers in Catholic schools. From the 1920s onwards the teacher training of New Zealand Catholic teachers was focussed on state certification. In an attempt to encourage the large number of unqualified teachers (both Catholic and state) to work towards the Teacher's Certificate, the Department of Education set up a correspondence programme. The majority of Catholic teachers, including Dominican Sisters, sat their 'Teacher's C' – a state qualification – whether or not they went on to teach in their orders' primary or secondary schools.[44] State certification enabled Catholic teachers to achieve a basic standard of professional qualification and claim the equivalence of Catholic primary schools with those of the state system.

The 1930s and 1940s also heralded a number of other teaching and pedagogical developments for Catholic teachers generally and for the Dominican Sisters in particular. Mother Reginald Quilter and Sister Dominica McKay contributed papers to the first Conference for Catholic Teachers, held in Wellington in 1931. Mother Reginald was appointed to the Executive.[45] Two young Sisters, St Joan Terry and Aquin Lister, were trained as Montessori teachers in Christchurch before establishing Montessori classrooms in Dunedin and Oamaru:

> About this time a Montessori school, full equipped, was opened in Dunedin and Oamaru, the building called Lourdes in Oamaru being

enlarged and renovated to suit the new requirements. Sisters M. St Joan and Aquin respectively were in charge.[46]

The initiative seems to have been relatively short-lived, but for years afterwards a classroom at St Joseph's Primary School was known as the Montessori classroom.[47] In 1943 two Sisters, Stanislaus Gavin and Rose Nobel-Campbell, travelled to Waratah, New South Wales to be trained in the teaching of the deaf at the Dominican School for Deaf Girls: 'There the two Sisters spent eight months observing methods of teaching and familiarising themselves with the work that lay ahead of them. State schools in New South Wales were also visited.'[48] A school for the deaf was set up in Wellington in 1944; in 1952 it moved to Feilding.

'Have your children got leave to speak?' Learning to teach in a primary classroom

After a year as a novice Sisters who elected to go on with religious life made their first profession. Many began their apprenticeship as a teacher in a primary classroom. A Sister-teacher's day was tightly scheduled and highly regulated, beginning with the Office, personal prayer, duties and then school. A Sister who entered in 1947 recalled arising at 5.30 a.m., attending Chapel at 6 and reciting the Office until 6.30, followed by thirty minutes' silent prayer.

> At seven o'clock we had Mass and at half past seven or twenty to eight we would go to breakfast. At eight o'clock you would shoot up and make your bed or do whatever you had to do and then go to school at half past eight. That went right on till four o'clock and then you would have a lecture.[49]

For a beginning primary teacher there was considerable support, with an experienced teacher available to oversee a new teacher's progress. Classrooms were often divided between two classes. This meant that the children had to work quietly. It was a challenge for a new teacher:

> I can remember having Standard One and Two on one side of the room and another Sister must have had Standard Three and Four. There was a curtain between the two classes. Of course I didn't have the control she had. She'd pull aside the curtain and she would say, 'Have your children got leave to speak?' ... That was a common expression with nuns . . this was a convent expression.... Because they would all be gassing away, you know.

In the 1930s and 1940s the Sisters did most of their training in the classroom under the supervision of a senior Sister. Later they studied for their Teacher's Certificate by correspondence. The supervising teacher or Mistress of Schools helped the new teacher prepare lesson plans, checked the workbooks and maintained a watching brief on the discipline in the classroom. A Sister who entered in 1936 remembered the influence of a Sister Elizabeth White on her development as a teacher.

> Yes, I started teaching part-time but only under the supervision of a much older teacher, a teacher who was highly trained and highly skilled. ... One Sister, Sister Elizabeth, the old Sister Elizabeth, taught at one end of the classroom and we taught at the top end. You didn't take senior classes at that stage. In our day anyone who entered taught first in primary school. You had to do that. It was part of your training so that you would know how to get discipline as you gradually went up the school.

There were some advantages in being new. A Sister who entered in 1941 recalled that the children saw the young postulants as a bit of a novelty. Being rather sporty she enjoyed teaching netball, tennis, and later all the rugby at St Thomas' Academy in Oamaru.

> But of course the children loved the postulant because you were in a little black bonnet and black veil and you were young. I was always very fond of sport being part of a big family who played sport ... I took all the sport of the day because I had played netball, which was basketball then, and played cricket with my brothers in primary and secondary school. And I played tennis of course. ... When we went from the novitiate we went into the Juniorate at Oamaru where we were further trained as teachers and did exams. I took all the rugby. I always took the St Thomas' Academy for rugby.[50]

Most new teachers encountered initial difficulties with classroom discipline. Sister Clare Timpany recalled that some of the children made life difficult for her.

> These children could be a bit naughty with postulants because they knew we were in training. So they were sizing me up. ... On days when I had them by myself I would be keeping them quiet and saying 'Now not a sound before three minutes', and then I'd time them using my watch.

Sometimes a Sister's enthusiasm for teaching got away on her and she forgot about the need to moderate her voice. In the following situation Sister Clare is told about the loudness of her teaching (at the end of the day), when the Sisters gather for recreation (and social talking is permitted).

> We were outside and we were walking up and down at recreation and I was all enthusiastic about teaching. I had been teaching the clock to Standard One and I was telling them about it. My voice must have been too loud. And a voice from the back, Sister Colman, who was walking up with someone else behind me, her voice came through, 'Yes and I think they'd be able to hear you down at the Post Office.' ... In other words I was teaching too loudly. She was next door and probably she couldn't take her class because of the noise I was making teaching my class.

Remembering this occasion at a distance of more than sixty years Sister Clare tells it as an allegory of a new, enthusiastic teacher learning to moderate her behaviour in the face of the codes of behaviour expected of a Dominican Sister-teacher. There is a sense here too that she was also negotiating the limits of the behaviour allowed to a new recruit to religious life. As in many of the interview accounts of early years in the convent, humour and self-deprecation helped her to learn the ropes in the classroom and to 'fit in' to life as a Dominican Sister.

Two of the Sisters who entered in the 1930s recalled teaching in the Montessori classroom at St Joseph's. One Sister spent some time teaching in the Montessori and primary classes after she entered in 1937. However, her advanced piano teaching qualifications meant that she was destined for a role as music teacher – an important source of income for the convent.

> As a postulant I was taking Standard Three and Four classes up in St Joseph's as it was at the time ... as a postulant you were still able to do things such as teaching (piano) and during that year I had done my Teachers' LTCL while I was still at school ... I loved teaching and I came across to the children. When I was in the Montessori [classroom] teaching them numbers and things like that I made use of the piano.

Sister Imelda Windle (who entered in 1933), found herself working with Sister St Joan Terry, who had been trained in the Montessori method in Christchurch and had taught her the previous year when she had been in the fifth form.

> When I went up to the classroom, there was my teacher and she was in charge of the Montessori – what did I think? She's been demoted....[51] She had not; she had gone to Christchurch with another Sister to learn the whole Montessori system. The five-year-olds were there and also Standard One [in the Montessori classroom]. On the 7th of October I was put in charge – you see – even though I lacked the qualifications. I had the experience and the expertise of somebody else in the classroom.

There is an interesting narrative here that is replicated in several of the Sisters' stories. I have already described the hierarchy within the convent that was based on the system of choir Sister and lay Sister – an inheritance of the class-based system that the Dominican Sisters brought from Ireland. An additional academic hierarchy within the convent is suggested here – one based on the Sister's education and her position as a primary or secondary teacher. The secondary teacher, particularly one who had received a university education had more status, was more likely to wield authority, to influence the running of convent affairs and to become prioress general.[52]

'Talk about ignorance is bliss': first experiences of secondary teaching

From the 1920s onwards, there was a re-definition of the original nineteenth-century educational mission of creating and maintaining a separate elementary Catholic school system in New Zealand. Catholic secondary schools, initially advocated as a way of protecting Catholic pupils from the 'evil influence' of state secondary schools, were increasingly seen as a means of promoting Catholic citizenship and social and economic mobility 'now that higher education is no longer the privilege of the wealthy'.[53] Faced with the rapidly expanding secondary rolls in the years after the Second World War, religious orders such as the Dominican Sisters faced an urgent need for more qualified secondary teachers. Sisters who showed academic potential were selected to undertake university studies. Of the eight Sisters interviewed, two had a university education when they entered; four Sisters went on to undertake university qualifications, moving to secondary teaching later. Sister Vincent McCarthy had done a commercial course before entering but she was encouraged into a degree while she was still in the novitiate.

> So I entered in 1936 and then during the novitiate they decided that I should go and do a B.A. degree, so I started studying then. I did all my degree extramurally and I forgot to say, when I left school, before I got a job I went to Rossbothman's Business College, for one year, and I got junior and senior government exams. For a wee while I was teaching commercial at St Dominic's; I think it was only for one year.

Like many of the Sisters of the time Vincent was expected to teach a range of subjects. Sisters who already had degrees were expected to learn to teach on the job.

> You didn't get any help at all. What did they say … it was 'feet forward!' In those days you see it was sort of laid down, but a while later you had to have a degree before you could teach.

A key shortage of qualified science teachers among the Dominican Sisters until the mid 1930s meant that unqualified Sisters taught science in addition to their other subjects. Sister Maria McDonald, who had hated science at school, found she had to work to 'keep ahead' of the students.[54] She recalls a particular occasion when her lack of knowledge had some unforeseen consequences.

> I remember once – talk about ignorance is bliss. We made laughing gas one day and of course they all sniffed it but that's all right because I didn't stop them, I didn't know any better. So anyway I went up to have my lunch and the Sister, it was Sister David, was on duty.[55] She came along to me and said the girls were behaving disgracefully in the dining room. They were all laughing, they were my room too. The two tables were laughing their heads off and they wouldn't stop no matter what she said .... Anyway I went down to school myself in the afternoon after lunch and you know I was only down there for about quarter of an hour and I suddenly felt myself go weak and I laughed and I laughed and I laughed and we all laughed together.

Sister Winefride Morris was the first qualified science teacher in the Dominican Sisters.[56] When she entered in 1934 she discovered that little had changed since her own school days. The 1931 inspection report had outlined the problem: 'the subject throughout the school should, if possible, be placed in the hands of one teacher with special scientific training'.[57] At first Sister Winefride found herself teaching in a science room down in the basement of the convent, which the inspectors had described as 'depressing'.[58]

> The science room ... was down underneath the parlour way down in the depths of the convent below road level. They used to teach commercial in there, typing, and I often used to have to remove the typewriters to the back bench before I could start teaching. It was very outmoded apparatus; they must have bought that fifty years previously, fairly old-fashioned stuff and chemicals that were most dangerous.... Science didn't have such an important place in the school in those days ... I had the seniors twice a week when they sat what was called home science for University Entrance.

Secondary teachers found themselves joining the other trainees in giving demonstration lessons for primary classes, as Sister Winefride recalled:

> We had class education, making up lesson plans and all the rest of it, for primary as well. Sister Marie Therese used to take us on Sundays ... I had to teach social studies and I hadn't done anything like that before except history in school. Now I was teaching English too. I wasn't actually teaching the primary but we all had to go and do these lessons and then

give demonstration lessons.... The notice would go up that Sister so and so was teaching a class in the Study Hall and anyone who was free was invited to attend. We'd go and this whole row of retired Sisters would be sitting around.

In this delightful story it is possible to sense the community of Sisters watching the new recruit to see 'how she is doing'. After this initial period of training, which was generally spent at the Mother-House in St Dominic's priory, Sisters took temporary vows and some spent time at the Juniorate in Oamaru where they received further training and did exams.

Towards a 'professional model' of teacher training

In a situation where Catholic religious were not admitted into state training colleges,[59] Catholic bishops established a Catholic training college at Loreto Hall, Auckland in 1950, as a way of protecting Catholic 'principles and aims' while promoting professional standards, including the preparation of Catholic teachers for state primary certification.[60] Loreto Hall, run by the Religious of the Sacred Heart, was modelled on Sacred Heart training colleges in Europe, the British Isles, North and South America, the East, and Australia.[61] A New Zealand Sister, Patricia Mackle, undertook postgraduate training at Edinburgh University and Craiglockhart before taking up the role of principal.[62] Although their overall numbers tended to be relatively small, the students attending the training college came from a wide range of teaching orders.[63] On completing the two-year course, a graduate was awarded a 'Loreto Hall Training College Certificate' based on 'a record of her teaching ability ... in the internal term examinations and in the external State C[ertificate] Examination'.[64] For the first ten years of its existence the students at Loreto Hall were female members of religious orders but by the early 1960s lay women were admitted. Loreto Hall was accredited as a training college in 1963. Until then students sat the state certification examination as correspondence students. In the years of its operation (1950–85), Loreto Hall trained 787 Catholic teachers, the majority (228 religious and 211 lay teachers) being trained for the Auckland diocese. In the 1970s male students, first Marist Brothers, then lay men, were admitted to Loreto Hall.[65]

Only one of the eight Sisters interviewed attended Loreto Hall. Sister Clare remembered the innovative 'modern teaching methods' she learned at Loreto Hall, methods she later practised in the primary classroom:

> I did everything I could, class management, the methods of teaching and everything ... then I went to Helensville for one year as a class teacher... in a country place I had all the time and the enthusiasm and I worked hard.

However, the Dominican Sisters, like a number of religious congregations, had reservations about sending all their Sisters to undertake the two-year course at Loreto Hall.[66]

First, many were reluctant to surrender their trainees to other influences during the crucial years of their formation. Second, at a time of increased demands for secondary credentialling the focus of Loreto Hall remained on primary certification. Third, religious orders were mindful of the costs, and protective of their own autonomy. As a result, most continued to train the majority of their own recruits. In a practice not unlike the sending of religious for training at state colleges, the Dominican Sisters sent individuals such as Sister Clare to be trained at Loreto Hall, after which they utilized her expertise to set up their own teacher training facilities. In Sister Clare's case she was being prepared to 'go to Dunedin, to Dominican Hall [to run] a mini training college'.

While Loreto Hall was, at most, a partial solution to the teacher credentialling crisis facing Catholic schools, the integration of Catholics into the mainstream of New Zealand society that took place in the 1950s presented a broader challenge to Catholic religious to adapt their approach to religious life and teacher training. Crucially for the purposes of this chapter, there was a growing expectation not only for higher standards of teacher training among Catholic religious, but also that ongoing professional development should keep pace with developments in pedagogy and the increased specialization taking place in secondary education. By the late 1950s, as the restrictions on religious life eased, Dominican Sister-teachers began to develop contacts with their peers in state schools. Sisters recalled taking part in community activities such as 'Education Week' and participating in state-run refresher courses. Sisters began to join and lead professional associations, as one recalled.

> When I came to the priory I was secretary to the Otago Maths Science Association in Dunedin, which always included several members of the university staff and heads of science of various schools. One of the teachers would pick me up and take me along to the meeting.

Concluding thoughts

This chapter has examined the intense process of formation that prepared a new member of the Dominican congregation for her life as a Catholic Sister-teacher in the years from 1871 to 1965. Issues such as authority and power relations are evident in religious formation and teacher training practices that prepared Sisters to transmit the Catholic faith and to reproduce Catholic cultural and religious practices. While these were key to the formation of congregational identity and the success of the educational mission of the order, the intense process of socialization into convent life also stripped away the identity and autonomy of an individual Sister. While the teacher training of Dominican Sisters was designed to protect the academic integrity of their schools and to ensure that pupils received an education that would enable their social, economic and educational advancement, a new recruit was also subject to a religious formation process, a highly regulated life in a convent community, and practices of work and prayer designed to reproduce these values in their pupils.

Key transitions occurred. In the early years the spiritual and teacher formation of Sisters was designed to maintain the religious and cultural values brought from Ireland. Sisters faced the challenges of isolation, delays in communication with their Mother-House, the difficulty of getting teaching resources, and the urgent need for teaching Sisters for the rapidly expanding schools around Otago and Southland. However, by 1933, the early missionary years in the congregation, which had allowed for flexibility and a certain individuality to occur, had been replaced by a period of consolidation, conservatism and a switch in emphasis from the individual to the group. Whilst teaching orders such as the Dominican Sisters worked for a continuity of religious values via the religious formation of their members and an in-house apprenticeship system of teacher training, they now strove to ensure that the professional qualifications of their teachers were equivalent to the those in the state system. Dominican Sisters sat their 'Teacher's C' – to ensure a basic standard of professional qualifications and the equivalence of Dominican primary schools with those of the state system. The 1930s and 1940s also included a number of other teaching and pedagogical developments including attendance at Catholic teacher conferences, the establishment of two Montessori schools and a school for the deaf, and the foundation of primary and secondary schools in Auckland.

Oral accounts of the Sister-teachers who entered religious life in the years 1931 to 1959 illuminate a tightly scheduled life in the hierarchical world of the convent and the role of a senior Sister as supervisor and support. Primary Sister-teachers studied for their Teacher's Certificate by correspondence and those who showed academic potential were selected to undertake university studies to provide qualified teachers for the rapidly expanding secondary schools. Concerns about the cost, and fear of the loss of congregational autonomy during the crucial years of a teacher's formation, meant that only limited numbers of Sisters attended the Catholic Training College at Loreto Hall after it was established in 1950. By the early 1960s Dominican Sister-teachers, like other Catholic religious, began to take part in state-run professional development and refresher courses as a way of raising the standards of teaching in Catholic schools and of protecting the integrity of the Catholic educational mission. By 1965 the concept of teacher training via an apprenticeship system was replaced by the notion of a professionally educated, state-certificated teacher. This development took place at a time when the Second Vatican Council was signalling a sea change in the Catholic Church: a time when teaching religious were asked to reconsider their role and function. But that story is beyond the scope of this chapter.

Notes

1 The oral history interviews were undertaken in convents around New Zealand in the early 2000s as part of masters and Ph.D. thesis research; Jenny Collins, 'Hidden Lives: The Teaching and Religious Lives of Eight Dominican Sisters, 1931–1961' (M.Ed. thesis, Massey University, 2001); Jenny Collins, 'For the Common Good? The Catholic Educational Mission, 1945–1965' (Ph.D. thesis, Massey University, 2006).
2 'Teacher training' in New Zealand generally refers to the formal and informal 'pre-service' teacher training. 'Professional development' generally refers to teacher education after certification or qualification.
3 See *New Zealand Tablet* (6 April 1922), 19; ibid. (14 July 1921), 21.
4 Tom O'Donoghue, *Come Follow Me and Forsake Temptation: Catholic Schooling and the Recruitment and Retention of Teachers for Religious Teaching Orders, 1922–1965* (New York: Peter Lang, 2004).
5 D. H. Akenson, *Half the World from Home: Perspectives on the Irish in New Zealand* (Wellington: Victoria University Press, 1990).
6 The Society of Mary, a missionary order of priests founded in Lyons, France at the end of the nineteenth-century, ran secondary schools for boys. The Marist Brothers had – at Rome's insistence – separated from the Society of Mary in 1852 to run primary schools for boys. In New Zealand they also ran a secondary college. P Graystone, *A Short History of the Society of Mary 1854–1993* (Rome: Society of Mary, 1998); J. P. Kane, 'The Marist Brothers in New Zealand Education 1917–1967' (Dip.Ed. project, Massey University, 1977).
7 By the 1890s there were four dioceses: Auckland, Wellington, Christchurch and Dunedin. These were divided into a number of parishes, each run by a diocesan priest whose duty it was to establish a local parish primary school and arrange (through the bishop) for a religious order to come and staff the school.
8 Collins, 'For the Common Good?'.
9 E. R. Simmons, *A Brief History of the Catholic Church in New Zealand* (Auckland: Catholic Publications Centre, 1978). By 1900, there were 65 Brothers, and 626 nuns in New Zealand.
10 Jenny Collins, 'Schooling for Faith, Citizenship and Social Mobility: Catholic Secondary Education in New Zealand, 1924–1944', *Journal of Educational Administration and History*, 37:2 (2005), 157–72. At most, the Brothers and priests constituted only one-seventh of the numbers of Catholic Sisters.
11 Jenny Collins, 'From "Apprentice" to "Professional": The Training of New Zealand Catholic Teachers, 1945–1965', *History of Education Review*, 34:2 (2005), 27–40.
12 Famous Dominicans scholars include Thomas Aquinas and Catherine of Siena.
13 For a detailed history of the Dominican Sisters in Ireland and New Zealand see Collins, Jenny, (2013), ""To the very antipodes": Nineteenth-century Dominican Sister teachers in Ireland and New Zealand". *Paedagogica Historica* no. 49 (4): 494–512.
14 *Constitutions of the New Zealand Dominican Sisters under the Protection of Our Lady of the Most Holy Rosary and of St Catherine of Sienna, 1933*, 32, Auckland Catholic Diocesan Archives (hereafter ACDA).
15 Within this paper, I use the term 'religious' interchangeably with 'nun' and 'Sister', although historically the terms had different meanings. Nuns took solemn

vows and lived an enclosed monastic existence while Sisters took simple vows and undertook apostolic works in the community.
16 Augustine McCarthy, *Star in the South* (Dunedin: St Dominic's Priory, 1970). As the result of building difficulties and the proximity of a new road, the Northcote primary school transferred to Blockhouse Bay in 1962 and the secondary to Henderson in 1967.
17 Most of the early recruits came from working-class Irish immigrant families. They completed a basic education at the parish school and entered as Lay Sisters. Their main role was to provide domestic services to the convent and they were not required to bring a dowry. In comparison Choir Sisters completed a college education and were expected to supply a dowry.
18 Pupil-teachers were usually girls who had completed their education in a Dominican school.
19 Sister Peter Jordan to Mother Gabriel Gill, Easter Sunday (28 March) 1880, Archives of the New Zealand Dominican Sisters (hereafter ANZDS), GH3/3/11. However, by 1894 Gabriel Gill is chiding Sister Bertrand McLaughlin, the 'local Superior' at Oamaru, for using lay Sisters as teachers at Oamaru without permission. Mother Gabriel to Mother Bertrand McLaughlin, 21 September 1894, ANZDS, GH/1/15. Sister Peter Jordan, a lay Sister (one of the ten founder Sisters), taught catechism to junior classes in Invercargill in the 1880s.
20 The avoidance of corporal punishment is an ongoing theme in the lectures.
21 Mother Gabriel Gill, 'Qualities of Good Teachers', *c.* 1870s, GH1/4/3, ANZDS. Gabriel Gill (1837–1905) was the Founder Prioress of the New Zealand Dominican Sisters.
22 Ibid.
23 Mother Gabriel Gill, 'Mistress of Schools', *c.* 1870s, GH1/4/6, ANZDS.
24 Ibid.
25 Ibid.
26 The Sisters themselves used the term 'recruit' widely. In a letter to Sion Hill, Sister Rose Cantwell refers to her delight at the arrival of 'the long-wished for recruits': Sister Mary Rose to Mother Clare, 23 January 1881, GH3/4/1, ANZDS.
27 'The Sisters shall ... avoid with utmost care, in their conversation, manners, and conduct, everything that would disturb or diminish mutual charity; and with patience bear the defects of others.' *Constitutions*, 25–6, ANZDS.
28 The Second Vatican Council was convened to bring the Catholic Church into the modern world. It asked all religious communities to go back to their founding documents and consider their role in a changing world.
29 The black 'cappa' is the black cloak worn by all Dominicans.
30 *Constitutions*, 24–5, ANZDS.
31 Ibid.
32 The Salve procession was made daily after Compline. The weekly Libera was sung for deceased Sisters.
33 This profile has now changed. With the decrease in the number of new recruits, the Dominican Sisters, like many religious orders, have now a preponderance of middle-aged and elderly Sisters.
34 Elizabeth M. Smyth, 'Writing Teaches Us Our Mysteries: Women Religious Recording and Writing History', in *Creating Historical Memory: English-Canadian Women and the Work of History*, ed. Alison Prentice and Beverly Boutillier (Vancouver: University of British Columbia, 1997), 101–28.
35 Collins, '"To the Very Antipodes" Teachers in Ireland and New Zealand', *Paedagogica historica*, 49:4 (2013), 494–512.
36 Smyth, 'Writing Teaches Us Our Mysteries'.
37 The quotes are drawn from the New Testament: Colossians 2:20; 1 Peter 1:23.

38 Margaret Susan Thompson, 'Sisterhood and Power: Class, Culture, and Ethnicity in the American Convent', *Colby Library Quarterly*, 25 (September 1989), 149–75.
39 Galatians 3:28.
40 Thompson, 'Sisterhood and Power'. Smyth, 'Writing Teaches Us Our Mysteries'.
41 *Constitutions*, 31, ACDA.
42 Collins, 'To the Very Antipodes'. In 1917 the Code of Canon Law introduced detailed regulations for religious orders.
43 *Veritas* (truth) is one of the Dominican mottoes.
44 Each order trained its own teachers via an apprenticeship system. For further discussion of this topic see Collins, 'To the Very Antipodes'.
45 *Annals 1931*, GH6/3/13, ANZDS.
46 *Annals 1930*, GH3/6/12, ANZDS. St Joan Terry was a newly professed thirty-year-old at the time. She taught Latin and English in the late 1960s. Named after St Joan of Arc, she was a formidable personality: a strict disciplinarian with a flair for the dramatic performance. We called her 'the battle-axe'. However, I still remember her passionate teaching of Shakespeare (the censored version) with great fondness.
47 This was known as the Montessori classroom when I was at St Dominic's in the 1960s.
48 Collins, 'From "Apprentice to Professional"'.
49 These and the following oral accounts are from interviews undertaken as part of an M.Ed. degree taken in 2001; Collins, 'Hidden Lives'. In order to protect the privacy of Sisters who have requested it, some names are withheld.
50 St Thomas' was a boys' preparatory school. The boys went on to St Kevin's College, which was run by the Christian Brothers Order.
51 The implication being that she had somehow been demoted, as she had become a primary teacher after previously being a secondary teacher.
52 A glance at the list of prioresses, sub-prioresses, and (after 1934) prioresses general and vicaresses general would seem to support this assertion.
53 *New Zealand Tablet* (3 May 1923), 4.
54 Sister Maria McDonald was known as Sister Attracta before a post-Vatican II ruling allowed Sisters to return to their given name if they wished.
55 Mother David Stark went on to become prioress general from 1957 to 1969.
56 Sister Winefride had completed a diploma of home science at the University of Otago before entering.
57 J. I. Hetherington, in *Inspection Report on St Dominic's College, 1931*, Hocken Library, University of Otago (hereafter HL).
58 E. Caradus, in ibid.
59 McCarthy, *Star in the South*.
60 'Meeting of Principals and Head Teachers Held at Loreto Hall Saturday 20 February 1960', Sisters of the Sacred Heart Archives (hereafter SSHA).
61 The Society invited two Scottish Sisters of the Sacred Heart, Kathleen Adamson and Josephine Welsh, to set up the new venture.
62 Anon., 'Loreto Hall 1950–1985: Dream and Reality and Memory', n.d., SSHA.
63 In 1954 there were twenty-two trainees from eight religious orders; 'Survey 1954', SSHA.
64 Ibid. For a more detailed consideration of Loreto Hall see Collins, 'From "Apprentice" to "Professional"'.
65 Loreto Hall closed in 1985, after which Catholic teachers trained in state teachers' colleges; anon., 'Loreto Hall 1950–1985'.
66 See A. H. W. Harte, *The Training of Teachers in New Zealand from Its Origins until 1948* (Christchurch: Simson and Williams, 1972).

Chapter 8

Great changes, increased demands
Education, teacher training and the Irish Presentation Sisters

Louise O'Reilly

> Great changes in the system of education were looming in front, new ideas were beginning to take possession [of] the minds of our people, criticism of religious Orders was becoming more intense and more vocal, and increased demands were being made on ... intellectual and educational resources.[1]

Introduction

The Presentation Order was founded in 1775 by Nano Nagle in Cork, as an active congregation of Sisters to teach and care for the poor. In 1805, a change in the Rule and Constitution declared the Sisters as an order with solemn vows and a strict Rule of Enclosure. The latter restricted the Sisters' apostolate, which became confined to education. During the nineteenth-century, the order experienced rapid expansion. By the beginning of the twentieth-century, the structure of the order had completely changed from its founding days and consisted of autonomous houses throughout Ireland and abroad. This structure prohibited contact among convents, led to isolation between Sisters and restricted the progression of their apostolate, education.

Changes in education in Ireland began in the nineteenth-century. These changes saw the introduction of a non-denominational system of education under the National Education Board, which was established in 1831. The Board offered financial assistance to those schools which came under the new system. Seeing them as a way forward for Catholic schools, the bishops in Ireland encouraged religious teaching orders, such as the Presentation Order, to come under the Board. Although an advantage financially, it also meant that the rules of the Board had to be adhered to. By the twentieth-century, one of these rules included the official training of teachers in schools that were attached to the National Education Board. This also required nuns to become officially trained teachers in convent schools.

Education and the structures of the Presentation Order are the focus of this study, which draws on archival sources. This traces the question of the structures and status of the order, which, under the 1805 Rule and Constitution, had become an enclosed order: structurally, each house was autonomous. By the twentieth-century this structure posed problems for the order both in religious life and in their apostolate, education. Legislation introduced by Rome and implemented by bishops at the synods of 1900 and 1927, held in St Patrick's College, Maynooth, County Kildare saw the beginning of change, to which the Sisters had to adhere. The Presentation Sisters were faced with a dilemma: how to hold onto structures that were in place since the 1805, and continue to retain their leading role as teachers within the world of education in Ireland.

Education in Ireland at the start of the nineteenth-century

In 1800, education for the majority of the Irish population was devised by the Established Church of Ireland, who believed 'that the education of the poor was the key to the pacification of the Catholic population and the peaceful integration of the country into the Union'.[2] The charter schools were an example of one such school system that was state-funded. However, it was a system unacceptable to Catholics and encouraged an alternative unofficial system of education, known as hedge schools, which rose during the latter half of the eighteenth-century. Irene Whelan argues that the 'phenomenal growth of the hedge-school system in the late eighteenth-century' seems to have led to the belief 'that popular education would have to be re-directed into channels controlled by the existing establishment'.[3] Bible societies, which were founded in Ireland in 1808, became a channel used by the Established Church to control the education of the lower classes. This reached its peak during what became known as the 'Bible war' of 1824–5. A debate on education developed between members of Protestant Bible societies and Catholic clergy and gentry. Catholics presented their case at meetings of the Bible societies held in 1824–5, and later petitioned the House of Commons in 1825. This was an opportunity for Catholics to seek support and funds for an education that would suit the needs of the Catholic population.

In 1825, a commission was set up to enquire into the state of education in Ireland. Its findings were a significant factor in directing the future of Irish education. The conclusion was 'that schools should be established for the purpose of giving to children of all religious persuasions such useful instruction as they may severally be capable and desirous of receiving'.[4] The founding of the National Education Board in 1831 following on the 1825 commission of enquiry marks a watershed in the development of education in Ireland. It placed financial support within the reach of all schools which fulfilled its criteria for recognition. Bible society schools targeting Catholics did not of course disappear, as publicized by the Catholic activist Margaret

Aylward, in the 1850s and 1860s, but they were eclipsed by this entirely new, centrally funded but locally managed system.[5] The focus of the new system of the National Education Board was to develop a non-denominational national school system in Ireland. The option of associating with the new Board was given to schools run by religious orders. Those who chose to go 'under the Board' had to abide by the rules and regulations of the Board; in return they received state funds for teaching and building and were subjected to regular inspection.

Education and the Presentation Order, 1805–1900

The Presentation Sisters were a religious order dedicated solely to teaching. From 1805 to 1900 there was continuous expansion of the order throughout Ireland. By 1840, 'the Presentation Order alone accounted for 55% of all convents in Ireland'.[6] This expansion was to meet the urgent need for Catholic schools that had developed in early-nineteenth-century Ireland where education was always open to proselytizing agencies. 'The final approbation of the first Irish religious foundation wholly dedicated to the education of youth was a providential happening in view of new educational trends.'[7] The development of a national education system in Ireland by the National Board would cater for all religious denominations and move away from the proselytizing activities which 'had plagued previous bodies'.[8] The bishops recommended that the Presentation Order associate with the Board as the 'clergy [wanted to] avail themselves of this ascendancy, and [were] more anxious, merely on religious grounds, that education should be in the hands of religious than of lay teachers'.[9]

By 1864, there were forty Presentation schools registered with the National Education Board.[10] The Powis report of 1868 described the conditions and teaching within convent schools. A topic of discussion was the subject of enclosure. According to one commissioner:

> In regard to the moral as distinct from the religious influence of convents, it seems not improbable that the spectacle of women who, as in the case of the Presentation nuns and the Poor Clares, have taken perpetual vows of enclosure and devote themselves exclusively to the work of education, has an attractive power, which by its singularity, places the convent schools in a position of superiority over ordinary national schools.[11]

This report referred to the canonical status of enclosure as enhancing the position of Presentation nuns, as it was felt that, 'vows of enclosure probably convey to the minds of the mass of people, an idea of devotedness to their undertaking ... greater than is ascribed to the most moral and most assiduous of ordinary teachers'.[12] However, this view changes somewhat as the report progresses. A debate emerged over the topic of enclosure, where 'A former witness in his evidence drew a distinction in regard to the qualifications possessed by religious ladies; he drew a distinction between different Orders.'[13] This observation referred to the standard of teaching. It suggests that cloistered orders such as the Presentation nuns were less qualified than those that were uncloistered, such as the Mercy Sisters. The debate concluded:

> Some of the best schools are conducted by the Presentation Nuns ... the Presentation Nuns are cloistered nuns, and as the Sisters of Mercy go about, and see a great deal of the world, they perhaps have more sharpness and knowledge of things than the others.[14]

In addition to the difference of canonical status among teaching orders, it was also pointed out that religious such as the Mercy Sisters, 'undergo a special training for teaching'.[15] The Sisters of Mercy underwent teacher training, in the Baggot Street training college, run by their own congregation. The Presentation nuns had no formal training for teaching and would not venture into this until the twentieth-century. However, the lack of training in teaching orders was observed in the commissioners' report: 'the teachers are not really teachers in the strict sense of the word; they have never been trained to teach'.[16] The report objects to the belief that as nuns were members of a religious order they did not have to be formally trained: 'there is too much of the feeling that the religious habit and profession brings with it the power, as it does the willingness to teach others'.[17] Seemingly, one commissioner suggested that nuns should be tested on their ability to teach, but 'the idea [was] repulsive in the extreme to all the nuns' and it was also repulsive to 'the Irish mind of submitting nuns to such a test'.[18]

The lack of training of nuns of the Presentation Order did not diminish their role as the leading teaching order in Ireland in the nineteenth-century. Although most Sisters did not hold teaching qualifications, they were involved in the monitorial system. This system allowed large groups of pupils to be taught by a small teaching force. The teacher oversaw the work of monitors/pupil-teachers, which in effect was a type of teacher training.[19] Table 8.1 lists the number of monitors that were employed in Presentation schools connected with the National Board of Education in 1863. This was a substantial number, reflecting both the competence of the Sisters and the very large numbers of pupils. The special reports carried out in 1864 by the commissioners regarding convent schools also stated that attendance in the schools of the Presentation Order was impressively high. It was also noted on the Presentation convent inspection report for Enniscorthy, County Wexford that 'formerly there was a large female school in the town' but that 'on the establishment of the present one [Presentation convent] it immediately began to fall away and in a short time ceased altogether'.[20] Evidently the schools of the Presentation Order had become so popular that they began to eclipse the local schools.

Changes in Church legislation

The introduction of new legislation from Rome in 1900 relating to religious institutes of women marked the beginning of change for the Presentation Order. The first of these documents, *Conditae a Christo*, promulgated by Leo XIII on 8 December 1900, was said to be 'one of the key documents relating to congregations of simple vows'.[21] This Constitution defined the two types of religious institutes with simple vows: those which were diocesan and those of pontifical right. The aim of this clarification was to ensure that 'the authority of the superiors of congregations and the authority of the bishops should be of complete accord'.[22] It was followed shortly after by the papal document, *Perpensis*, 3 May 1902. This document renewed Leo XIII's earlier decree, but it also 'indicated that the vows of the Presentation were simple'.[23]

This clarification of the juridical status of the Presentation Sisters meant that legislation introduced from 1900 to 1918 was relevant to the congregation, whose status had now become one of pontifical right with simple vows. However, the Presentation Sisters did not seem to recognize this change and continued as a religious institute with solemn vows, observing the Rule of Enclosure, 'for a few years after Vatican II'.[24] It was the bishops who initiated change within the Presentation Congregation in the form of diocesan amalgamation. It became a topic of discussion at the plenary synods held in St Patrick's College, Maynooth, County Kildare in 1900 and 1927.

The Irish episcopal decrees on religious life and education, 1900–1927

From 1900 onwards, in addition to the legislation introduced by Rome, there were also new decrees issued by bishops at the plenary synod of St Patrick's College. The first of these synods was held in 1900, which 'produced five hundred and twenty-five decrees over forty-five different titles'.[25] Among the topics legislated for, two were to have a substantial effect on women religious in Ireland. These included education and in particular a document on 'nuns'. According to the decrees relating to the latter it stated:

> where houses ... of Sisters or of nuns, just like the Sisters of Mercy or the Presentation Nuns [are] in one diocese [and are] now separated, [they should] merge under the same superioress [and] together unite [in the] diocese or per province.[26]

The tradition of autonomous houses, separate from each other, long established in the Presentation Order (and in some other congregations) was set to be disturbed.

The advice to unite was interlinked with the question of education. It was decreed that 'nuns who direct schools must be trained to teach properly, and to achieve this purpose institutions are to be erected by each community for the formation of their subjects'.[27] In the case of the Presentation Congregation, each convent was separate; there was no common novitiate to train new Sisters in religious life and no training given to teach. Again, this move by the bishops put pressure on religious teaching congregations to amalgamate and strengthen their position in education. In addition, schools under the care of nuns were not 'to be placed under the Commissioners of National Education, except with the express permission of the ordinary'.[28] The Catholic clergy hoped to retain full control of convent schools, although this instruction was to change later as convent schools had to be under the National Education Board to receive funding.

In 1927 the plenary synod of Maynooth was held, at which it was suggested that:

> the statutes produced by the synod show a great change upon what we find in the Maynooth plenary synod of 1900 ... mainly because of the influence of the 1917 code. The 1927 synod produced four hundred and sixty-two decrees spread over forty-nine titles.[29]

However, once again the issue of 'nuns and Sisters' was highlighted at the synod. The decree of the 1900 synod regarding union between convents such as those of the Presentation Sisters was renewed, as was the instruction to set up institutions specifically for the purpose of training all new Sisters both in religious life and as educators. Regarding the latter, the decree stated that 'the committee of bishops already set up will take care that this decree about junior Sisters is brought into effect'.[30] Both the 1900 and 1927 synods were concerned with 'uniting' women religious institutes at diocesan level; this, it was hoped, would strengthen their position in the field of education.

Bishops and education in early-twentieth-century Ireland

In the early-twentieth-century changes within the education system in Ireland became of great concern to the bishops. Changes introduced by the National Education Board were believed to adversely affect the position of the Church in the world of education. The bishops believed that the long-running education question was based on 'two systems of education, resting on principles opposed to one another, [striving] for the mastery, and whether there had been a question of founding a university or a village school, the same vital issues were at stake'.[31] The bishops knew it rested with teachers within Catholic schools to promote the principles of the Church.

> In many respects the office of teacher is allied to that of a priest, and is almost sacred in the nature of the work for which it is instituted ... the interests of religion must come first in their thoughts.[32]

Table 8.1 Number of monitors in Presentation schools in 1863

County	School	No. of monitors	Total no. of pupils enrolled in 1863
Cork	Doneraile	8	405
Cork	Midleton	10	834
Cork	Fermoy	9	572
Cork	Mill Street	4	446
Cork	Youghal	6	715
Cork	St Finbar's	9	2,575
Kerry	Killarney	7	352
Kerry	Dingle	4	567
Kerry	Tralee	11	735
Kerry	Milltown	3	374
Kerry	Cahirciveen	3	602
Kerry	Listowel	5	818
Kerry	Castleisland	3	579
Tipperary	Cashel	9	644
Tipperary	Thurles	9	512
Tipperary	Carrick-on-Shannon	4	355
Tipperary	Fethard	5	359
Carlow	Carlow	12	728
Carlow	Bagnalstown	4	297
Dublin	Richmond	6	354
Dublin	Clondalkin	4	413
Dublin	George's Hill	19	1,128
Kildare	Kildare	6	260

Source: Return of name and locality of convent and monastic schools in connection with Commissioners of National Education in Ireland, 1864, 4–30, H.C., 1864 (400).

However, the schools were staffed by lay teachers as well as religious and it seems that in 'recent years their organization [had] manifested a painfully un-Catholic spirit'.[33] The Irish National Teachers' Organisation had been set up at the end of the nineteenth century, its first congress held in 1868 as a 'reaction to the teachers' depressed state'.[34] The Organisation promoted the interests of national teachers, which included salaries and pensions for teachers.[35] However, the Organisation's

> campaign to secure protection against summary dismissal and a right to due process in disputes with the managers, encountered a much longer period of agitation, litigation, Episcopal admonitions and pastorals and an ecclesiastical ban on INTO in two of the ecclesiastical provinces of the country.[36]

The Teachers' Organisation was seen by the bishops as a threat to their position as managers. An official joint pastoral by the bishops, 'The Management of Catholic Schools', in June 1898, offered a 'defence of the clerical managerial system, describing those who would weaken it as enemies of the Catholic Church'.[37]

From 1900, the National Education Board began to introduce changes, known as the New Programme, into the school system in Ireland. These changes, although seen by some as an improvement, were also seen as a threat to the existing system, both internally in relation to nuns as teachers and externally in relation to management by the bishops. This sparked off a controversy between the hierarchy and the National Education Board. The first related to a New Programme, which was revised in 1904. This programme was said to have been 'a marked success and has resulted in a distinct improvement in the character imparted to Irish children'.[38] However, it was pointed out that the teachers in these schools, 'do not possess the education or the trained intelligence necessary to enable them to utilise fully the opportunities afforded them by the comparative freedom of the new system'.[39] This criticism was directed at all teachers in the national schools, including convent schools. The reaction to it was defensive and the newspapers at the time were inundated with articles relating to this topic. The subject of nuns as teachers, in particular, came to the fore. It was felt that 'everyone knows … these ladies as they are untrained'.[40] This criticism of nuns was refuted by a local priest, who in reply to this comment stated 'the nuns do receive a training' and insisted that 'before the introduction of the new programme, higher results were secured by the nuns' schools'.[41] It was felt that qualified or 'certified' teachers were crucial to the success of the new, revised programme.[42] The New Programme course consisted of 'having separate programmes [subjects] for schools under three or more certified teachers'.[43]

The National Education Board also introduced new rules and regulations regarding the qualifications of teaching staff in national schools, which identified those who were eligible for appointment. The rules stipulated that 'persons who have been trained in a recognised training college' and those 'already recognised as certified National teachers' were suitable candidates for teaching in national schools.[44] These two rules were among many concerning the appointment of national teachers, whether qualified persons or those eligible as certified assistants – that is, those who had undertaken a period of training. However, the rules also stated that when 'a person of any of these classes … cannot be found to fill an occurring vacancy, the Commissioners will be prepared to consider an application for the recognition of an uncertified candidate'.[45] This was only on the condition 'that the candidate shall immediately pass an examination for a provisional certificate'.[46] This increased insistence that teachers should have attended a training college, have taken exams and hold a certificate for teaching meant that many nuns would not be recognized as qualified to teach in their own 'convent national schools'. This resulted in the movement by the bishops to encourage training for both existing and prospective members of religious teaching congregations.

The subject of teacher qualifications was an important issue for the bishops. As managers of convent national schools, they were responsible for the implementation of the National Education Board's directives. According to the rules and regulations of the Board, 'the commissioners also reserve to themselves the power of withdrawing the recognition of a patron or of a local manager if he shall fail to observe the rules of the Board'.[47] The rules also stated that recognition would be withdrawn 'if it shall appear to them that the educational interests of the district require it'.[48] It was the managers of schools who had the 'right of appointing the teachers', but this was also 'subject to the approval of the Board, as to the character and qualifications'.[49] The failure of nuns in convent schools to hold certificates for teaching, or to be able (at the very least) to demonstrate that they were in the process of acquiring such a qualification, placed the bishops in an uncomfortable position, vis-à-vis the body which funded these schools.

The debate was carried out in the national newspapers, with numerous persons contributing. One article titled 'The Bishop's Pronouncement' stated the position of the bishops clearly: 'No scheme which is based on the idea of depriving the Catholic pastors of this country of absolute control of the parochial primary schools will ever be approved by the people.'[50] The debate became known as the 'managerial question' and was believed to be the beginning of a more 'secular and materialistic system of education'.[51] It threatened to diminish the power of the bishops, who felt that 'the danger of a revolutionary change in the administration of Irish Education' was imminent.[52]

The issue of trained teachers and the management of the schools motivated the bishops to encourage change within teaching congregations such as the Presentation Sisters. The first step was to provide teacher training for nuns, which would then place convent schools on a par with secular national schools and also keep them in line with the rules and regulations of the National Education Board. If this was successful, it would secure the bishops' control over parochial schools.

Reaction of bishops to changes in education

In a move to resolving the crisis around the lack of teaching qualifications among nuns, the bishops appointed a subcommittee to look at the issue. A form of centralization within religious institutes of women was proposed. According to a memorandum 'On the Training of Nuns as Teachers in Primary Schools', which was adopted by the bishops at Maynooth in 1913, the concern was how this training could be carried out. It seems that 'various means of doing so [had] been suggested to the standing committee'.[53] Among these it was felt that the most ideal situation would be a training college under the care of nuns, which would be on the lines of training colleges for lay teachers.[54] However, it was felt that this presented too many difficulties: 'even if the nuns of the various Orders could be induced to study in the same college, which is doubtful', there was also the issue that 'convents could ill spare nuns for a two years course of training'.[55] The conclusion that was reached was that nuns had to have qualifications to teach in primary schools; this was the single solution, the 'only qualification that will ultimately satisfy the people and protect the nuns' schools from hostile criticism'.[56] These suitable qualifications included 'a) a Diploma of the National Board or b) a Diploma in teaching of the National University, or c) a Certificate such as the Commissioners of National Education agreed to give to the Sisters of Charity'.[57] It was suggested that to achieve these qualifications 'perhaps the best plan (as a temporary expedient at least) to adopt would be to set up a small training school in each convent'.[58]

Most religious institutes consisted of several convents within each diocese. For example, in the case of the Presentation Sisters in the diocese of Kerry, there were ten houses, as was the case in the diocese of Kildare and Leighlin. If each house was to have its own training college, it would mean that there would be twenty training colleges between the Kerry and Kildare and Leighlin dioceses. The impracticability of this was self-evident. Financially, this option was too costly, and numerically, the number of Sisters was different in each house. For a small group of Sisters, the strain on resources would be too great. However, the bishops did suggest that:

> A valuable adjunct to this local training school would be the establishment of a central noviceship where the novices of the same Order in a diocese or group of dioceses would be gathered into one central house to go through the ordinary course of Religious training and at the same time obtain under competent teachers the education which would fit them afterwards to take their places in schools.[59]

The suggestion of setting up a central noviceship had now become a solution to this problem.

> We cannot conclude without expressing the opinion that the moderate programme we have sketched out cannot be satisfactorily accomplished except in a central noviceship, and we therefore recommend that where it is at all feasible such a noviceship should with the authority of the Holy See be set up.[60]

Case study of the Presentation Congregation

The changes legislated by Rome in 1900 affected the position of the congregation. As noted above, in 1910 it had been clarified by Rome that the congregation was to be recognized as one with simple vows and of pontifical right. Despite such an authoritative statement on their status, the

Presentation Sisters themselves never recognized the official canon law status and continued to hold on to traditions, such as observing the strict Rule of Enclosure, up to the conclusion of the Second Vatican Council, in 1965.

In Ireland the episcopal decrees relating to women religious issued at the synods of St Patrick's College, Maynooth also had a major effect on the congregation. The move by the bishops to encourage religious institutes of women to amalgamate arose from concerns regarding changes in education. The Presentation Sisters' main apostolate was teaching. If teacher qualifications were not gained or the changes proposed by the bishops introduced, it was believed they would 'retire into the background, and yield to others, more qualified'.[61] In the early-twentieth-century, this precipitated change within the Presentation Congregation in Ireland. Sources reveal that change first came in the form of diocesan amalgamation, which included setting up a central novitiate. The bishops put forward their case directly and unequivocally: 'if the nuns are to keep their place in the schools, they must be trained and certified', and 'the bishops think it is absolutely essential [to] have amalgamation of the different houses of each Order in each diocese'.[62] One of these early amalgamations involved ten houses of the Presentation Sisters forming one diocesan group in Kerry in 1927. The bishop of Kerry, Charles O'Sullivan, who had initiated this move, wrote to each Presentation house in his diocese pointing out his concerns regarding the position of nuns in education: 'I may further state that should any convent not fall in with this arrangement [amalgamation] I will feel bound not to admit any postulant to that convent unless she holds a higher diploma.'[63] The bishop was demanding full amalgamation in 1921; this did not occur within the Kerry diocese until 1927. It is evident from his speech at the official promulgation of the Kerry amalgamation that the changing world of education was behind this move. He pointed out that changes in education could have serious repercussions on the Presentation Congregation. He stated that:

> for many years past those of us who were more closely in contact with the progress of the world and with the current of events in our country saw, very clearly grave difficulties and dangers ahead, some of which threatened the very existence of your Order here.[64]

The fear of extinction was also echoed by other diocesan bishops and the urgency of the situation is reflected in their correspondence. Bishop William Codd of the diocese of Ferns, in his endeavours to unite Presentation houses in his diocese, wrote to the Sacred Congregation in Rome about his fears. He believed that the independent house in Enniscorthy would fail to exist without some form of amalgamation: 'The isolation of the Enniscorthy community has to be ended, if the community is to survive, and if their schools are to continue under the charge of teachers of the Congregation.'[65] His solution was 'the urgent need of union', and he 'strongly approve[d] of the effort to bring it about at once'.[66] According to Bishop O'Sullivan, it was

> Those who were interested ... who were concerned for the continuance of your magnificent work among the poor of our diocese [who] were genuinely alarmed. We were forced to the conclusion that drastic changes were necessary and that a big forward step was vitally essential if you were to continue successfully the work intended by your foundress or indeed, even to survive as [a] teaching Order in Kerry.[67]

The survival of the Presentation Congregation could only be secured, according to the bishops, by the amalgamation of autonomous houses within each diocese. In addition, it was also felt amalgamation would benefit new members to the congregation; it would offer 'uniformity in the spiritual [and] secular training of novices'.[68] Bishop O'Sullivan spoke about not only the spiritual training of novices but also their secular training. In his speech he stated that this was imperative, as

> Postulants who entered your convents unqualified for teaching had to remain quite unequipped for the proper work of your Order. Suitable teacher candidates were becoming fewer and fewer; the demands of the educational authorities became daily more exacting, and the number of secular teachers in your schools was increasing, and was likely to increase.[69]

By joining together as one diocesan group, new members could be better equipped for the teaching world. It was pointed out that with amalgamation 'there would then be a common novitiate', which would mean that the amalgamated group would be in 'a fair position to meet certain demands upon their teaching staffs which are imminent in the near future'.[70] It was felt that if change was not introduced immediately 'many of the convents [would] cut a very sorry figure in the educational world'.[71] As a teaching congregation their very existence was at stake. This was a strong argument; the threat of extinction did cause concern among the Sisters, but the response to the prospect of amalgamation was decidedly mixed.

Reaction of the Presentation Sisters to changes

> If we have principles shall we not be true to them? To dig out the old foundation would be to destroy the Order. The matter rests with ourselves: shall we stand or fall?[72]

As early as 1908, the first reaction of the Sisters to the changes was to hold on tenaciously to inherited traditions. From correspondence and internal memoranda, it is evident that the Sisters were aware of changes that would affect their religious life. However, the proposals of the bishops were not received with enthusiasm. On the contrary, a letter of 1908 outlined the status of the congregation from its foundations and papal approval of 1805. In addition it clearly stated their position as 'a religious Order with the free admission of its members to the profession of solemn vows, constituting them real religious'.[73] This letter was written two years prior to the official pronouncement by Rome, in 1910, on the status of the Presentation Congregation, which declared them a congregation with simple vows. It illustrates the importance they attached to their status as a religious institute with solemn vows. This is re-enforced when the writer states,

> Neither in the apostolic brief nor in the rules and constitutions is there mention of 'amalgamation' 'federation' 'branch houses' or 'general noviceship'. Such a system may thrive in simple congregations unenclosed, etc., as is the case in the Presentation in some foreign countries; but it is not for us.[74]

The Mullingar Sisters were definite in what they regarded as suitable for them. They were opposed to a central novitiate and amalgamation in any form, and refer to their Rule and Constitution as evidence of their official position on this subject. However, when they do mention the Synod of Maynooth, it is only to reiterate their status as an institute of solemn vows with papal approval:

> the Decree of the Maynooth Synod has this reminder: '*The Constitutions and Rules of Sisters approved by the Apostolic See may not be altered by any person.*' ... Ours are not only 'approved' but 'confirmed'. A studious reading of the apostolic briefs of the Popes Pius VI and VII shows at once our position in the Church, and in virtue of which we rank distinctly from, may not embrace the observances of simple congregations with simple vows.[75]

Evidently, the Presentation Sisters felt the changes proposed for religious congregations at Maynooth would not, and could not, apply equally to them.

By 1908, the changes in education were a matter of discussion among the Sisters. They were not opposed to some form of training but the idea of a central novitiate was one they implacably opposed.

> A scholasticate we may indeed desire, a college where candidates for the Order may pursue their higher studies, etc.... it has been spoken of for some years past in the Order: perhaps the time for its realisation has come: but, a central novitiate for our Order is not constituted: its subjects are to be trained on the field of their future work, within their own enclosure.[76]

The idea of change was something that was clearly not welcome at this stage. The whole idea of amalgamation or central novitiates was seen as threatening their Rule and Constitution. On the subject of teacher qualifications they were not totally against them but also did not offer any suggestions. What is clear is that preserving tradition was most important to the Sisters: 'if we remain united humbly as one ... we should be the better of the test, the Order shall remain intact'.[77]

In 1910, the declaration by Rome that the Presentation Sisters were a congregation with simple vows jeopardized the hopes to keep the 'Order ... intact'. Juridically they were no longer recognized as a congregation with solemn vows and could hardly insist otherwise when Rome had pronounced so authoritatively. However, what they did have to observe were the bishops' instructions to nuns regarding teacher training, a matter very much to the fore in 1913 when the bishops formed a committee to tackle the problem. The Presentation Sisters were forced to confront the issue that had developed concerning education. Although it was not confronted immediately, evidence suggests this was an issue discussed by many autonomous houses and, most importantly, one that had created a dialogue among houses.

Presentation Sisters and the implementation of change

Ireland experienced great change as the Free State come into effect on 6 December 1922.[78] With the new Free State also came a new Department of Education which came into being in 1923. The new policy on education put emphasis, according to Dermot Keogh, on 'curriculum rather than structural change'.[79] The first ministers for education introduced administrative initiatives: 'systematic investigations were launched into various issues, a new secondary examination and curricular structure was devised'.[80] In this climate, change was inescapable for the Presentation Congregation. The emphasis was on a new curriculum, which needed qualified teachers to teach. By 1922, the stance against change that had been taken by the Sisters in 1908 had weakened somewhat and the issue of teacher training could no longer be avoided. The old system, in which many Sisters were unqualified, was no longer accepted, and it had become imperative that the issue of training be confronted. According to Presentation correspondence there was increased pressure from the bishops: 'You probably have got a copy of the Maynooth circular re amalgamation and the training of Sisters as teachers.'[81] It seems that the Sisters were also advised to hold a conference to discuss the matter. One Sister mentioned that she and her mother superior had to attend 'a conference in Thurles Presentation'.[82] In Dublin the Sisters of various houses in the diocese also held a conference in relation to teacher training.

> 12 representatives of the archdiocese met in conference at the Presentation Convent, George's Hill ... the superioress and a companion from each

house being present. The desire of those present at the meeting to enter fully into the needs of the Sisters in all that regards studies and training was unanimous.[83]

It was finally felt that the 'needs of the Sisters' should be a primary concern for all. However, the solutions did differ in each diocese.

A 'scheme' had been compiled by the Sisters in the Cashel and Emly diocese, which set out various suggestions:

> a general novitiate to be erected in or near Dublin for all Presentation convents in Ireland. This to be presided over by a mother general and her assistants including mistress of novices who would look after the interests of the Order and novices. Novices to be sent there for their spiritual year and then to remain for such training as would qualify them to become primary or secondary teachers.[84]

It was said to be 'far better for us Presentations to erect a general novitiate in or near Dublin with house of studies combined'.[85] It was hoped this suggestion would find favour with other Presentation houses as the writer, although wary of the reaction to the suggestion, concludes, 'You may copy the enclosed if you wish and make use of it among Presentation but as a favour I ask you not to reveal from whom or where it came.'[86] However, the proposals that were made at the Dublin conference differed. 'It was suggested that if permitted the convents situated in the city and Lucan, should send their Sisters who would never number more than three at a time to lectures daily at the National University', and 'to meet the needs of the Sisters from the other country convents it was proposed that provision at Terenure convent should be made for their convenience'.[87] Although there were differences in how training might be implemented, it was evident that the Sisters had become concerned enough about their position in the world of education, and suggestions at both conferences related to rectifying this matter. At one stage it was suggested that, 'most Presentation in the south as also in Dublin would wish to have "an all-Ireland conference"'.[88] This was a rather daring proposal and would require quite a shift in thinking for the Presentation Sisters, who had become isolated within the structure of autonomy since their founding days. However, the suggestion put forward by the Sisters for either a training college or a hostel of some kind was also presented as an alternative to the dreaded notion of forced diocesan amalgamation.

The Presentation Sisters and the question of amalgamation

The idea of diocesan amalgamation was put to the Sisters from the early 1900s but it was not until 1922 that the idea reached its peak. At this period of the Presentation Sisters' history there was an outpouring of letters discussing the move of amalgamation. The idea was greeted with mixed feelings and was a cause of internal divisions. For some groups, especially those familiar with the painful story of the early amalgamation of Cashel and Emly in 1914 (discussed below), it was looked on with disfavour as it threatened the tradition of the congregation. There were also those groups that wanted to avoid the subject altogether or were totally against it. Some groups felt it was the only way to break away from the problems and issues that surrounded the traditions of the congregation. However, it is evident that throughout this period of transition there was increasing dialogue among the Sisters, as they shared ideas and suggestions regarding changes within the congregation as a whole, and there was a change in attitude to the idea of a common link between houses.

The amalgamation of Cashel and Emly was described as 'a trial on diocesan level for the past six years. In charity to the whole Order we must confess it has done more harm than good.'[89] It seems that as it was only on a 'trial basis' there were hopes that it could be revoked: 'all here are now most anxious to break it up and hope and pray that this opportunity may bring a change for the better'.[90] According to one Sister of the Presentation convent in Ballingarry, Tipperary there were many disadvantages to diocesan amalgamation. She felt it meant 'the breaking up of our Holy Order into so many diocesan congregations each with its own rules and fads', and did not allow them 'to take or select any subjects'.[91] The result was that as they could not recruit any new members themselves they had 'lost many postulants for the past six years'.[92] This Sister made this complaint eight years after the amalgamation of the Presentation convents in the diocese of Cashel and Emly. She hoped to warn others about the disadvantages of amalgamation and offered an alternative by encouraging Sisters to favour a central novitiate for the spiritual formation and educational training of Presentation Sisters in Ireland. She felt a move to 'joining up of all the houses would tend to keep up the old spirit of Nano Nagle'.[93] What is interesting about this perspective is that she encouraged the Sisters' views on both topics – amalgamation and a central novitiate – stating 'the more we discuss the matter now the better'.[94]

The issue of amalgamation for many houses was either avoided or ruled out when the topic was first broached. In the case of autonomous houses within the diocese of Dublin, it was suggested by a Sister 'to say nothing about … anything that might open up the question of amalgamation'.[95] There was opposition to entering into any discussion about amalgamation but, although resisting the subject, she stated, 'it is well to be sincere with our own and this is what I wish to be in writing this openly'.[96] The Sisters in Kerry also wrote openly about their views on amalgamation when it was first proposed by the bishop. They clearly stated their position to him, pointing out that:

you will not be surprised to learn, that though ready and willing to carry out your wishes, we are all with the exception of two, most strongly opposed to amalgamation. Of course, if you compel, we must submit but never of our own free will.[97]

The bishop did compel. As discussed earlier, he had stated that until the houses in Kerry amalgamated, no new postulants could enter unless they held a diploma in education. It was the subject of education that led to the eventual amalgamation of the ten houses in Kerry in 1927. According to a Sister in Dingle in relation to the question of education, 'depend upon it, that where education is concerned, even though far removed from your general pressure, we will rise to the occasion and please God'.[98] Although the decision took time, the insistence of the bishop and the good of education were the deciding factors: 'To comply with your wishes and to keep the schools in the hands of the religious (which must be done at any cost) we have decided to make the sacrifice and God knows what a sacrifice it is to us and accept amalgamation.'[99]

Amalgamation in the diocese of Kerry was achieved only under episcopal pressure. The reason for objecting to the amalgamation of the ten houses centred on the area of authority. Following this decision to amalgamate, a general meeting of all reverend mothers of the Kerry Presentation houses was held in January 1922, in Tralee. The agenda was to discuss the final issues around amalgamation. However, it became an arena for objections to amalgamation, even though it had already been accepted. According to the chairperson of the meeting, she feared the meeting would be a failure, as at its opening many of the representatives stated 'We want no amalgamation.'[100] The reasons given related to the area of government; it was felt that 'The mother general will give no show to any convent but her own. She will keep the best of everything.'[101] The Kerry Sisters were not alone in expressing their fears in relation to the abuse of authority within an amalgamated group. Other groups also harboured fears relating to this matter and felt that 'diocesan amalgamation would mean failure. It weakens much the authority of each local superior and this leads more or less to laxity.'[102] This is an interesting point and one that will be discussed further below in relation to what were felt to be the advantages of diocesan amalgamation.

The synods of St Patrick's College, Maynooth in the early-twentieth-century had called for changes in the structure of women's religious institutes. The bishops saw amalgamation as a move that was to the advantage of the Sisters' position within the world of education. In addition, it was also seen as an advantage to the internal position of the congregation. Problems with autonomous structures had come to a head by the early-twentieth-century. The subject of authority was central to this tension and it became a major factor to many in their decision to amalgamate. Unlike those who felt that amalgamation would 'weaken the authority of each local superior' there were those groups who felt this would be of great advantage. When the idea of amalgamation was proposed, certain houses hoped it would solve some of the problems that had developed. Sources reveal that these hopes were shared by Sisters from different houses and were not confined to one.

In their private correspondence with the local bishop, individual Presentation Sisters articulated their views on amalgamation and also offered their full support in this move. One Sister from Presentation Convent Kilcock stated:

> I readily give my vote for whatever form of amalgamation you can put through whether provincial or diocesan ... If I have any preference it is for a diocesan, but you may see a greater benefit to the Order by provincial especially for the education of the novices.[103]

She continued, expressing apprehensions about the existing form of voting:

> We were told at chapel on Saturday that our votes were to be taken next Sunday re amalgamation scheme. Well. My Lord, I trust you will pardon me for writing on my own, but I remember in Dr Foley's time, RIP, votes were taken to be sent to him for the filling of an office and they were tampered with and as one vote often turns the scale I [am] determined to run no risks.[104]

This Sister expressed an urgent appeal to the bishop that amalgamation must be achieved at whatever cost. Her concern over discrepancies in elections was central to her favouring amalgamation. She felt that 'a great deal of the bickering emanates from the one source canvassing for office and those who won't be bought have a bad time for that term'.[105] Amalgamation was felt to be a move that would 'end voting for superiors as it does in all amalgamated Orders'.[106] These problems were not exclusive to just one Presentation convent, as a writer from Mountmellick Presentation declared 'It is a terrible thing that after being in the noviceship, they have no idea of the Canon Law regarding canvassing', suggesting that 'an appointment is degrading, whereas they forget that when it is an appointment it is valid, just and honest'.[107]

The tensions surrounding elections resulted in many favouring amalgamation. It was felt that 'If we have amalgamation ... I fervently hope [it] will be at the very least national for Presentation nuns. The broader the better, to scatter parties, who band together to secure votes and posts in holy religion.'[108] It was hoped that amalgamation would end the practice of the same parties securing positions of power within autonomous houses. This problem was strengthened by the fact that when new members applied to enter a convent, more often than not they were known to those in office. The result was that recruitment of new members who were relatives or friends of existing members was ensured of support. One Sister, a member of Warrenmount Presentation, described the situation:

> I had also intended to try to get my niece, who is coming out of training now ... to enter here. M. Patrick, the present Mistress of Novices, told me they did not want her here. That they would prefer to spend a lot of money in training their own, as they will have votes and will vote for themselves.'[109]

The topic of the training of novices was also commented on, it was believed that 'the Mistress of Novices [avoided] the supervision of nuns'.[110] If amalgamation was achieved, it meant that a central novitiate would also be set up where all new members would enter before they were sent to a particular house. This would prevent Superiors choosing family members and members they knew, which was central to the conflict regarding elections. Unlike the Sister in Cashel and Emly, who felt they were restricted because they could not choose their own subjects, many saw this as an advantage, feeling it was 'in the interest of the Order and religion'.[111]

Early amalgamations

> You are, Sisters, no longer members of independent communities; you are joined by a new bond of interdependence to work for your common interest and progress. The future of your Order is in your own hands to make it a success or a failure. There can be no doubt that you will unite for its success.[112]

Amalgamation was believed to be in the best interest of the Congregation by many of the Sisters, and it is clear that it was not only in relation to their apostolic work in education but also in relation to their religious life. From the period 1914 to 1932, three groups of Sisters formed diocesan amalgamations. As discussed earlier, these included the dioceses of Cashel and Emly in 1914, Kerry in 1927, and a third amalgamation achieved in the diocese of Kildare and Leighlin in 1932. Once these groups amalgamated, the structure changed from independent, autonomous houses to that of a single group of houses within the same diocese. According to the official decree of the amalgamation of the ten Presentation houses of Kildare and Leighlin, 'all the houses of the aforesaid institute shall be fully united so as to form one congregation of papal rite'.[113] Therefore, it was also advised that 'new constitutions are to be drawn up, containing the new form of Institute, the new form of government and whatever else may be deemed necessary'.[114] New Constitutions had to be drawn up by each newly amalgamated group and evidence suggests that these may have differed slightly from each other. However, what is clear is that each group was recognized as a 'new form of Institute', one which now constituted a group of houses governed by a Superior General.

Spiritual and educational training

The new form of government that was introduced into amalgamated groups of the early-twentieth-century was a major transition for the Presentation Congregation. In addition, amalgamation would bring changes to noviceship training. In 1913 the bishops' committee had advised religious institutes to set up a central novitiate where Sisters could carry out both their spiritual and educational training. The bishops recommended this process not only to amalgamated groups but also to those belonging to autonomous houses within the same diocese. In the case of the amalgamated Kerry group, their novitiate had been set up a year prior to the official amalgamation. Bishop Charles O'Sullivan stated that 'an excellent beginning [had] been made by the establishment of a central novitiate ... in Oakpark', although it had been 'only a little more than a year in existence'.[115] He felt that 'amalgamation itself was the necessary consequence of a general noviceship', suggesting that once a central novitiate was set up the next stage for the congregation was amalgamation of the houses.[116] Providing sufficient spiritual training for new members prompted other autonomous houses within the Presentation Congregation to set up central novitiates in the 1930s. This move was seen by Presentation Sisters in the diocese of Cloyne as their 'first move away from isolated autonomous communities' when they set up a central novitiate in September 1933.[117] The bishop of the diocese of Cloyne, Dr Browne, encouraged this move, as amalgamation had not been achieved, when three of the five Presentation convents in Cloyne voted against it. The decision to set up a central novitiate was an alternative, not a preamble to amalgamation, as the five convents remained 'independent, except in so far as the training of the novices is concerned'.[118] A central novitiate was the beginning of common ground for the Sisters within the diocese, yet they still remained autonomous in every other respect.

The suggestion of central noviceships by the bishops in 1913 had centred on the position of women religious in the changing world of education. However, their hope that central novitiates would act as centres of training in both religious and educational aspects did not materialize within the Presentation Congregation. Despite the bishops' suggestion that these central novitiates have a dual purpose, the focus was to be on the spiritual training of novices, an area that had been somewhat neglected to date. Sources suggest that Sisters within the Congregation without teaching qualifications attended colleges either in Dublin or in Galway. According to a questionnaire that was sent to houses in the diocese of Waterford, the bishop enquired in each house, 'the number of nuns to be sent to training and the name of training college to which it is proposed that Nuns will be sent'.[119] However, the number was as low as one or two each year, and the most popular choice of college was Carysfort Park, Blackrock. According to a 1959 memo prepared for the minister for education, 'In the period 1925 to 1958 the number of nuns trained in the two training colleges at Dublin and Limerick was 1,381.'[120] However, there is no breakdown of the number from each individual religious congregation.

Conclusion

From their foundation in 1775, the Presentation Sisters main apostolate was always in education. Although the Rule and Constitution of 1805 introduced enclosure to the order, the Sisters continued to teach. However, the structure of autonomy that evolved after 1805 isolated houses, which created problems both in religious life and in education. In the latter area it prevented the Sisters' progression in the world of education in Ireland.

In 1900, Rome declared the Presentation Sisters to be a congregation with simple vows. Although the Sisters were still to be regarded as 'real religious', the directive from Rome was ignored by the congregation. The Sisters continued to observe a strict Rule of Enclosure and held onto their status of religious with solemn vows, almost like a trophy, which they were very reluctant to let go. The letter of 1908 reflects how strongly they felt about their traditions and how much they objected to change.

However, it was the diocesan bishops who pushed for change. This change came in the form of diocesan amalgamation and central novitiates. Of course, their objective was not only in the interest of the Presentation Sisters but in the bishops' interests as well. By the early-twentieth-century, changes in education meant that teaching congregations needed to meet stringent new requirements to hold their position in the world of education. The question of whether nuns were qualified to teach also arose. Although not officially trained teachers, the Sisters had practised a form of teacher training, with the monitorial system they had introduced in their schools in the nineteenth-century. However, as the bishops' role in education had strengthened somewhat, it was in the Church's interest to encourage the Sisters to acquire teacher qualifications.

The directives from the bishops, coupled with the problems that had arisen within the structure of autonomy, led to the first diocesan amalgamations and central novitiates within the Presentation Congregation in the first half of the twentieth-century. These early amalgamations were the first steps taken by the Presentation Sisters to come together on some level as one group, and would be the beginning of evaluating the future of the congregation in both spiritual life and their role in their main apostolate, education.

Although central novitiates were introduced in the hope of accommodating both spiritual and teacher training, the latter failed to materialize. In this area, it is not fully understood what training the Sisters undertook to become qualified teachers. The questionnaire of 1928 reflects the number of Sisters in the diocese of Waterford, which was quite low. This number, however, does not indicate the numbers of Sisters in other dioceses throughout Ireland. The memo of 1959, prepared for the minister of education, gives an overall number for all religious congregations but again it does not reflect individual congregations. However, what is evident is that schools run by the Presentation Sisters continued, and further changes within the Congregation would not begin until after the conclusion of the Second Vatican Council in 1965.

Notes

1 Charles O'Sullivan, bishop of Kerry, speech given to Presentation Sisters, Kerry, 1927, Kerry Diocesan Archives (hereafter KDA), MS F/C. O'Sullivan.
2 Irene Whelan, 'The Bible Gentry: Evangelical Religion, Aristocracy, and the New Moral Order in the Early Nineteenth Century', in Crawford Gribben and Andrew R. Holmes (eds), *Protestant Millennialism, Evangelicalism and Irish society, 1790–2005* (London: Palgrave Macmillan, 2006), 52–82 (58).
3 Ibid.
4 Ibid., 58.
5 Jacinta Prunty, *Margaret Aylward: Lady of Charity, Sister of Faith* (Dublin: Four Courts Press, 1999), 40.
6 Caitríona Clear, *Nuns in Nineteenth-Century Ireland* (Dublin: Gill and Macmillan,1987), 52.
7 T. J. Walsh, *Nano Nagle and the Presentation Sisters* (Dublin: M. H. Gill and Son, 1959), 182.
8 Deirdre Raftery and Susan Parkes (eds), *Female Education in Ireland, 1700–1900: Minerva or Madonna?* (Dublin: Irish Academic Press, 2007), 34.
9 Royal Commission of Inquiry into Primary Education (Ireland), 1870, 393 [C 6], H.C., 1870, xxviii, Part 1.1.
10 Return of name and loyalty of convent and monastic schools in connection with Commissioners of National Education in Ireland, 1864, 4–30, H.C., 1864 (430).
11 Primary Education (Ireland), 1870, 393.
12 Ibid., 391.
13 Ibid., 211.
14 Ibid.
15 Ibid.
16 Ibid.,102.
17 Ibid.
18 Ibid.
19 John Coolahan, *Irish Education: History and Structure* (Dublin: Institute of Public Administration, 1981), 22.
20 National Education (Ireland) copy of the special reports recently made to the Commissioners of National Education in Ireland on the convent schools in connection with the Board, 1864, 227, H.C., 1864, (405) 225.
21 Gaston Courtois, *The States of Perfection According to the Teaching of the Church: Papal Documents from Leo XIII to Pius XII* (Dublin: M. H. Gill and Son, 1961), 5.

22 Ibid.
23 MS document concerning the 'Holy Rule of the Presentation Sisters', undated, Archives of the Presentation Sisters of New Zealand (no shelfmark).
24 Interview with a PBVM Sister, St Brigid's Presentation Convent Kildare, 15 May 2006.
25 Edward Rogan, *Synods and Catechesis in Ireland, c. 445–1962* (Rome: Pontificia Universitas Gregoriana, Facultas Iuris Canonici, 1987), 93.
26 *Acta et decreta, synodi plenarie episcoporum Hiberniae*, no. 365, 1900 (Dublin: Browne and Nolan, 1906), 116. All English translations from *Acta et decreta* are by Dr Neill Collins.
27 *Acta et decreta*, no. 455, 1900 (Dublin: Browne and Nolan, 1906), 135.
28 *Acta et decreta*, no. 452, 1900 (Dublin: Browne and Nolan, 1906), 134.
29 Rogan, *Synods and Catechesis*, 105.
30 *Acta et decreta concilii plenariae episcoporum Hiberniae*, no. 198, 1927 (Dublin, 1929), 82. English translation by Dr Neill Collins.
31 Ibid., 550.
32 Ibid., 553.
33 Ibid., 553.
34 Seamus O'Buachalla, *Education Policy in Twentieth-Century Ireland* (Dublin: Wolfhound Press, 1988), 38–9.
35 *Irish Magazine and Teachers' Gazette* (1860).
36 O'Buachalla, *Education Policy*, 40.
37 Ibid., 42.
38 *Freeman's Journal* (22 February 1904), 57.
39 Ibid.
40 *Irish Times* (1 January 1904), 5.
41 Ibid.
42 *Freeman's Journal* (9 January 1904), 9.
43 Ibid.
44 *Rules and Regulations of the Commissioners of National Education in Ireland* (Dublin, 1903), 56.
45 Ibid.
46 Ibid.
47 Ibid., 16.
48 Ibid., 50.
49 Ibid., 53.
50 *Irish Independent* (23 June 1904), 176.
51 *Freeman's Journal* (30 August 1904), 211.
52 *Freeman's Journal* (13 October 1904), 247.
53 Richard Alphonsus, bishop of Waterford and Lismore, and Robert [Browne], bishop of Cloyne, secretaries, 'On the Training of Nuns as Teachers in Primary Schools', adopted by the bishops at Maynooth, 24 June 1913, George's Hill Archives Dublin (hereafter GHAD), MS C22/75.
54 Ibid.
55 Ibid.
56 Richard Alphonsus, bishop of Waterford and Lismore, and Patrick [Foley], bishop of Kildare, circular, 29 September 1913, GHAD, MS C22/75.
57 Ibid.
58 Alphonsus and Browne, 'On the Training of Nuns'.
59 Ibid.
60 Alphonsus and Foley, circular.
61 Charles O'Sullivan, bishop of Kerry, promulgation of amalgamation, to all Presentation Convents, Kerry, c. 1927, KDA, MS F/ C. O'Sullivan.

62 Charles O'Sullivan, bishop of Kerry, letter to all reverend mothers, Presentation Convents, Kerry, 20 November 1921, KDA, MS F/ C. O'Sullivan.
63 Ibid.
64 Charles O'Sullivan, bishop of Kerry, speech given to Presentation Sisters, Kerry, 1927, KDA, MS F/C. O'Sullivan.
65 William Codd, bishop of Ferns, memorandum to Sacred Congregation for Religious, Rome, 17 March 1931, Archives of the Sacred Congregation for Religious and Secular Institutes (hereafter ASCRSI), MS C.91/A 2, 2.
66 Ibid., 2.
67 O'Sullivan, speech to Presentation Sisters, Kerry.
68 Ibid.
69 Ibid.
70 Codd, memorandum to Rome.
71 Bishop Michael Cullen, Mounthenry, Portarlington to Bishop Collier, Kilkenny, 9 November 1929, Ossory Diocesan Archive, MS envelope no. 2 (1929–30).
72 'A Reply Letter to a Community of the Presentation and Is Most Respectfully Presented to Reverend Mother and Community', Presentation Convent Mullingar, May 1908, GHAD, MS C22/73.
73 Ibid.
74 Ibid.
75 Ibid.
76 Ibid.
77 Ibid.
78 Dermot Keogh, *Twentieth-Century Ireland: Nation and State* (Dublin: St Martin's Press, 1994), 15.
79 Ibid., 33.
80 Ibid.
81 Sister, Presentation of the Blessed Virgin Mary (PBVM), Presentation Convent Ballingarry, Tipperary, to Presentation Convent Mullingar, 6 January 1922, GHAD, MS C22/73.
82 Ibid.
83 Memorandum of meeting in George's Hill Presentation Convent, 11 Februry 1922, GHAD, MS C53/96-8.
84 'Scheme' attached to letter from Sister, PBVM, Ballingarry, 6 January 1922, GHAD, MS C22/73.
85 Ibid.
86 Ibid.
87 Memorandum, 11 February 1922, GHAD, MS C53/96-8.
88 Sister, PBVM, Ballingarry, correspondence, 6 January 1922, GHAD, MS C22/73.
89 Ibid.
90 Ibid.
91 Ibid.
92 Ibid.
93 Ibid.
94 Ibid.
95 Sister, PBVM, Presentation Convent George's Hill Dublin to Reverend Mother, Presentation Convent Lucan, Co. Dublin, 14 February 1922, GHAD, MS C53/96-8.
96 Ibid.
97 Sister, PBVM, Presentation Convent Dingle to Bishop Charles O'Sullivan, Killarney, Co. Kerry, 29 December 1921, KDA, MS F/ C. O'Sullivan amalgamation of Presentation convents.

98 Ibid.
99 Ibid.
100 Sister, PBVM, Presentation Convent Tralee, to Bishop Charles O'Sullivan, Killarney, Co. Kerry, 12 February 1922, KDA, MS F/C. O'Sullivan amalgamation of Presentation convents.
101 Ibid.
102 Sister, PBVM, Ballingarry, correspondence, 6 January 1922, GHAD, MS C22/73.
103 Sister, PBVM, Presentation Convent Kilcock, to Bishop Michael Cullen, 5 September 1929, Kildare Leighlin Diocesan Archive (KLDA), MS MC/PVM/15, box 33.
104 Ibid.
105 Ibid.
106 Ibid.
107 Presentation Convent Mountmellick to Bishop Michael Cullen, 30 May 1929, KLDA, MS MC/PVM/12, box 33.
108 Sister, PBVM, Presentation Convent Kilcock to Bishop Michael Cullen, 9 July 1930, KLDA, MS MC/PVM/39, box 33.
109 Sister, PBVM, Presentation Covent Warrenmount, Dublin to Bishop Byrne, Dublin, 3 June 1932, Dublin Diocesan Archives (DDA), MS Byrne papers – nuns.
110 Unsigned letter from Presentation Covent Bagenalstown to Bishop Foley, diocese of Kildare and Leighlin, 6 March 1918, KLDA, MS PF/PVM.B/09.
111 Sister, PBVM, Presentation Convent, Kilcock to Bishop Cullen, undated, KDLA, MS MC/PVM/45, box 33.
112 O'Sullivan, speech to Presentation Sisters, Kerry.
113 Alexius H. M. Card. Lipicier, OSM, Praef., SCR, 'Decree', 7 November 1932, in *Constitutions of the Sisters of the Presentation of the Blessed Virgin Mary in the Diocese of Kildare and Leighlin* (Cork: PBVM, 1946), 7.
114 Ibid., 8.
115 O'Sullivan, speech to Presentation Sisters, Kerry.
116 Ibid.
117 Annals of Presentation Convent Midleton, Co. Cork, entry, 1933 (manuscript given to the author by a member of the community).
118 'Statutes for a Central Novitiate for the Sisters of the Presentation of the Blessed Virgin Mary in the Diocese of Cloyne', DDA, MS Byrne papers – nuns.
119 Questionnaire, 'Training of Nuns', 5 March 1928, Presentation Convent Carrick-on-Suir, Waterford Diocesan Archive, MS, box no. JI R/C 1.02.
120 Oifig an Aire Oideachais, document, 11 June 1959, KLDA, MS TK/BP/281 BP/43.

Chapter 9

The situational dimension of the educational apostolate and the configuration of the learner as a cultural and political subject

The case of the Sisters of Our Lady of the Missions in the Canadian Prairies[1]

Rosa Bruno-Jofré

The Sisters of Our Lady of the Missions (the Religieuses de Notre Dame des Missions (RNDM)), a pontifical congregation devoted to foreign missions, were founded in Lyons, France in 1861 and arrived in Manitoba, Canada in 1898.[2] Like many other teaching congregations in English-speaking Canada, the RNDM offered an alternative to the public common school, a powerful component of the modern educational state. The public school had a strong assimilationist thrust with a view to preserving Canadians' heritage as members of the 'great British Empire'.[3] The Prairies (the current provinces of Manitoba, Saskatchewan and Alberta) – with their waves of Catholic immigrants, the Franco-Catholic settlers, struggles to keep their identity and the colonization of the Aboriginal peoples – were a fertile soil for missionary work.[4] The RNDM were invited to further Catholic teaching by the archbishop of Saint-Boniface, Adélard Langevin, after the 1897 elimination of public-funded confessional schools and the ending of the status of French as the language of a founding nation in the province of Manitoba.[5] Their missionary educational work went beyond the parameters of that crisis.

In this Chapter, I examine the RNDM's understanding of education as expressed in the foundress' texts and place them in relation to major positions of the Church on matters of doctrine, truth and modernity. In order to illustrate the situational character of the process of building the Catholic learner as a cultural and political subject, I then move to three distinctive missionary experiences at the turn of the nineteenth-century. They are: the mission in Grande Clairière, Manitoba (Our Lady of the Snows Convent), where the Sisters arrived in 1898 to be in charge of the public school (bilingual, French–English);[6] the mission in Lac Croche (Crooked Lake) (Holy Heart of Mary Convent) with the Aboriginal children of the Cree Reserve, in a residential school in Saskatchewan, also in 1898; and the mission in the city of Brandon, Manitoba (St Augustine Convent), where the Sisters taught boarders and day pupils in the St Augustine Parish School, grades 1–8, and St

Michael's Academy. This last mission was in an English-speaking setting, and the Sisters taught many children from eastern European countries.

Of relevance here, given the religious call to salvation and the creation of a Catholic order, is the 'illocutionary force', or intended force of the linguistic action, a concept of J. L. Austin further developed by Quentin Skinner.[7] This illocutionary force, or intentionality, behind Christian education acquires meaning in relation to the Church's response to modernity and to social and political developments in the nineteenth and twentieth centuries. But this is not enough; it is also necessary to contextualize the apostolate in the cultural and political reality of the missionary field – in this case, the two locations in Manitoba and one in Saskatchewan, Canada.

Here, the process of contextualization is complemented by Charles Taylor's notion of social imaginaries, along with constellations of meanings and nested spaces, to explain the congregation's understanding and practice of education, and the configuration of the learner as a cultural and political subject. Taylor defines the social imaginary as:

> ways in which they [people] imagine their social existence, how they fit together with others, how things go on between them and their fellows, the expectations which are normally met, and the deeper normative notions and images which underlie these expectations.[8]

Occasionally, I will compare this congregation with the Missionary Oblate Sisters of the Sacred Heart and Mary Immaculate, founded in Manitoba by Archbishop Langevin in 1904.[9]

Three main questions are at the centre of the analysis: What were the central concepts, assumptions and principles that informed the Sisters' understanding of education? How did they relate to the framework and directions coming from the ecclesiastical hierarchy? What were the characteristics of the configuration of the learner as a social/cultural and political subject that emerged from the conditions generated by the intersection with the field (the socio-economic environment), in each of the scenarios and within the context of needs of the Church? The 'where' becomes relevant in the construction and reconstruction of meanings and intentionalities. Not less important are the macro-contexts, nested spaces and configurations, be they the Church's doctrine, the needs of the Church in those particular places, the unique socio-economic and political setting, or the social imaginary of the communities where the Sisters developed their educational apostolate.

Education as Christian (Catholic) education within an ecclesiocentric model of mission

The RNDM were founded by Euphrasie Barbier (Marie du Coeur-de-Jésus) in France in 1861. The context was described by Eric Hobsbawm as a new form of colonial empire, developed from the last quarter of the nineteenth-century to the Great War.[10] Religious missionaries found a space for their vocation with a civilizing mission and by providing education to colonial settlements. It was a time of changes of the structures of world capitalism, a global world, as Hobsbawm wrote, with 'two sectors combined together into one global system: the developed and the lagging, the dominant and the dependent, the rich and the poor'.[11] The active apostolate of Sisters in various parts of the world was part of the increasing intercontinental movement of people and communications (including the electric telegraph), and can be inscribed within the Church's condemnation of modernity, and a distrust of the secular world and the development of science. In a general way, and without neglecting the power of the religious call and inspiration, schooling was a means to try to keep a Catholic order. The unpredicted element was the way the missionaries experienced their apostolate in time and space and generated new meanings, new knowledge, and new ways of being Catholic.

Article 2 of the RNDM *First Constitutions* establishes that the Sisters would devote themselves to the instruction and Christian education of children and women, above all in 'infidel' and non-Catholic countries.[12] In practice, the congregation did most of its apostolic educational work among European settlers – as was the case, for example, in western Canada and in New Zealand.[13]

The foundress, Euphrasie Barbier, made clear in the 1870s that 'it is principally in order to teach Christian doctrine that you have become religious missionaries'.[14] In another letter, she wrote "[i]t is to impart Christian education we are Religious Missionaries."[15] This approach was quite dominant in teaching congregations in the second part of the nineteenth-century and well into the twentieth-century. The pupil could be a Catholic or an Aboriginal; the central aim was to build a Catholic self – but the self is constructed in a relational process. This is what makes the historicity of the process relevant in order to explain the relations deriving from the insertion in local social imaginaries and the characteristics of the various social spaces in which those imaginaries are situated.

At the core of the foundress' aim was:

> to impart to our children an education which would be thoroughly religious, and at the same time very practical so as to help the children to acquire those virtues which will make the young Catholic girls hence women, real treasures both in the Church and in the family.

She wanted 'valiant women, worthy of God and of the praise of Holy Writ'.[16] Going deeper, the illocutionary force resides in 'the salvation of the souls of the children or others entrusted to us: "And for them I sanctify myself …"'. The goal would be achieved by 'carrying out faithfully and conscientiously our religious duties, and in practicing the virtues of our state that we shall be able to do any real good to the people who surround us, and help to sanctify and save their souls'.[17] Salvation of others was rooted in the example of piety. This view was nourished by an ultramontane Church that emphasized papal authority, centralization and the vow of holy obedience. Similar ideas appeared in the lectures given to the Missionary Oblate Sisters by the archbishop of St Boniface, Adélard Langevin, in Winnipeg, Manitoba, Canada. Langevin did not neglect to stress that religious teaching could only be done under the authority of the Church, for only the Church could provide the true sense of the sacred texts.[18] Visiting priests gave lectures on education to the Oblate Sisters; one of them was Father Beauregard, parish priest of St Charles in Winnipeg. He told the Oblate Sisters that they should aspire to be catechists, the role of teacher being subordinate, because it was the heart and the soul that they wanted to reach.[19]

The educational aims of the RNDM take their original traits from their spiritual intuition (mission and vision) and the directions from the foundress, who advocated child-centred education, proper teacher training and an integrated formative education. The latter related spiritual, academic and practical aspects, none to the detriment of the other.[20] The centrality of the child is at the core of Christian education, as Pius XI noted in 1929:

> But nothing discloses to us the supernatural beauty and excellence of the work of Christian education better than the sublime expression of love of our Blessed Lord, identifying Himself with children, 'Whosoever shall receive one such child as this in my name, receiveth me.'[21]

It can be also inferred that the RNDM, as other congregations, may have become familiar with ideas from Pestalozzi, Froebel and Herbart, and with the educational ideas of the De La Salle Brothers.[22]

This 1882 paragraph taken from a letter from the RNDM founder, Euphrasie Barbier, is illustrative of the Sisters' early approach to education:

> There is no need to mention the obligation we have of giving the first and most important place to the practical study of the knowledge and love of God and of our holy religion. The education which we endeavor to impart to each one must be eminently Christian, whatever the social standing of the children entrusted to us may be. Furthermore, we must strive to make virtue attractive to the children and form them, with God's help, to a love of duty, in the fear of God certainly, but a fear which comes from love. The children will be trained to perform tasks and make the sacrifices which the service of God and the neighbour require, with joy and devotedness in order to please God.[23]

The paragraph contains concepts such as sacrifice, joy and devotedness, fear of God, obedience as coming from love, and pleasing God with joy. These concepts of religious life conformed to a semantic field that captures the way the Sisters were moved to construe their world, which is present in most documents related to the missions in Canada, in particular in the first decades of the twentieth-century. Thus, the narration of the first missions in Canada made by Sister Mary of the Holy Trinity in 1923 made recurrent references to sacrifices, privations, filial submission and crosses of all sorts – a language that was not alien to the way the Sisters experienced their apostolate at their arrival, as I will show.[24]

However, the Sisters' narrative gains meaning in relation to the doctrine of the Church at the time, and its impact on education in particular, because the congregation's apostolate was based on an ecclesiocentric model of mission – in other words, within the intellectual (theological) boundaries of the Church authority and the notion of Catholic education. Thus, as Susan Smith explained, the Trinitarian inspiration (charism) of the congregation needs to be understood in line with Tridentine Catholicism, which institutionalized the Spirit in the progression from God to Christ to Church, consolidated by neo-scholasticism, thus controlling the radical freedom of the Spirit.[25] The work of the Sisters and their original Trinitarian intuition to sanctify the Church was mediated by obedience to the Church authorities and their interpretations, even as they carved their own spaces and meanings. However, the Church had varying needs in particular spaces, and local churches often had various strands of thought or practical action.

Nonetheless, the authority of the magisterium established by Pius IX with *Syllabus errorum* (1864); the proclamation of papal infallibility, *Pastor aeternus* (1870); and *Dei filius*, insisting that the teaching authority of the Church was the authentic interpreter of the Bible, were high points of ultramontanism. These were positions opposed by prominent Catholic intellectuals of the period.[26] The encyclical letter of Leo XIII in 1879, *Aeterni patris*, embraced neo-scholasticism, which gradually became the highest authority and the only intellectual framework by and large until the 1950s.[27] Pius X condemned modernism in 1907. Meanwhile, neo-Thomism would develop between the 1920s and 1950s. It signalled a return to the writings of Thomas Aquinas himself and to ways of integrating contemporary culture within its theology, as well as an emerging renewed Catholic philosophy of education.[28] However, of relevance to Catholic schools is the encyclical on education, the *Christian Education of Youth*, issued by Pius XI in 1929 and often referenced by the Sisters, which underlies the position of the Church very much in line with the *Aeterni patris* from Leo XIII. Education, as Article 14 reads, 'belongs to all three societies [the family, the civil society and the Church] in due proportion, corresponding according to the disposition of Divine Providence, to the co-ordination of their respecting ends'.[29] Article 15 reads: 'And first of all education belongs preeminently to the Church, by reason of a double title in the supernatural order, conferred exclusively upon her by God Himself; absolutely superior therefore to any other title in the natural order.'[30] The notion that the Church has immunity from error in faith and morals is reiterated.[31]

The RNDM's overall conception of education was, out of necessity, related to an ecclesiocentric model of mission, one that took various meanings depending on the context of each setting and the positioning of the Church there. The Manitoba School Question, which culminated with the elimination of public support for confessional schools and the consolidation of the common school, had placed Archbishop Langevin face-to-face with modernity.[32] He expected the French–English bilingual congregations to sustain the French and Catholic heritage and identity. He understood the latter as a collective identity based on the notion of two founding nations and non-territorial cultural duality, although Quebec was a major point of reference. While the French Canadian identity was a defining component of the Manitoban Missionary Oblate Sisters' mission and identity, for the RNDMs, the French issue was not a congregational matter at the core of their identity.[33] Nonetheless, the French RNDM Sisters working in those communities were fully engaged with the Franco-Manitoban and French Canadian cause, having the support of their congregation.

Langevin organized as many private and parochial schools and hired as many certified teaching Sisters as possible. He wanted Sisters to teach in the public system, particularly in largely Catholic communities, where struggles over values with the Department of Education were waged through the boards of trustees, since schools were under the jurisdiction of these elected boards.[34] One of the RNDM Sisters wrote that he had:

> the noble end of uniting the settlers according to their respective nationalities, to ensure their religious formation and to help them to encourage parish organizations such as churches, Catholic schools, etc., and protecting the faith from the progressive and threatening menace of error which surrounded them from all parts.[35]

Still, he thought that the future of the Church in Canada depended upon French-speaking Catholics; he talked of the French race, its distinctive qualities, and the role of the school in maintaining those qualities and the language: 'If our people lose their language all those treasures are in peril since they will then acquire the English temperament.'[36]

Archbishop Langevin, who closely related Catholic schooling and faith, had a large archdiocese and tried to cover the linguistic and educational demands in his diverse constituency, which included not only French Canadians but Ukrainian, Polish, German and Italian Catholic immigrants, in addition to those of Irish or Scottish descent. The retention of the maternal language was seen as a fundamental countermeasure to Protestant proselytizing. The work of the Sisters in the schools is difficult to reconstruct, given the paucity of the information kept in archives, but the analysis of surviving documents – such as narrations, journal entries and letters – helps to illuminate the nuances of the missionary work and consider the many ways in which the apostolate was configured in its interactions with the local church, the social imaginary of the communities, the actual living experiences of the families and their socio-economic context, and, eventually, the state through the Department of Education.[37]

The three scenarios

Grande Clairière: building a French Canadian identity

The RNDM Sisters initiated work in the Canadian West in 1898 in rural Manitoba, in the village of Grande Clairière, which had been founded ten years earlier when Father Jean Gaire (1853–1925) – a native of France and a diocesan priest – arrived in Manitoba and filed a property claim, which the government made available to 'homesteaders'. As Veronica Dunne asserts, it was this property and this village that invited the Sisters, with the full endorsement of Langevin who wanted the Sisters in his diocese.[38] They stayed there until 1923, when a fire caused by a furnace destroyed the convent.

The RNDM Sisters conducted their educational apostolate in rural areas such as the school in Grande Clairière, as well as in cities such as Brandon in Manitoba. While the emerging labour movement was strong in Brandon at the beginning of the century, in the rural areas independent farmers asserted their interest vis-à-vis the commercial grain companies, and conflicted with commercial, industrial and financial capital at the local and national level. However, the tradition of agrarian activism in the Prairies often displayed anti-immigration/anti-continental European and anti-Catholic prejudices.[39] The political scene in Manitoba was intense, and the ethnic and religious issue was there at the beginning of the twentieth-century, along with the struggle for cultural survival – not only of the Franco-Manitobans, but also of the immigrant communities.[40]

The school in Grande Clairière, Manitoba, run by the RNDM Sisters (Convent of Our Lady of the Snows), was a public bilingual school that served French Canadian and Métis (descendants of First Nations and Europeans, in this case, French)[41] families who formed a village and a community scattered over a stretch of land in hard climatic conditions.[42] The community at large was defined by a social imaginary rooted in their faith, their language and their culture (highly interwoven with the priest and the Sisters), and a strong sense of solidarity. A set of related shared cultural and religious values and feelings of injustice forged their identity as a community of independent producers, in the midst of a provincial population that was overwhelmingly British by national origin with pockets of non-British agricultural settlements. This was a cultural composition that was about to change, since along with French Canadians and Métis, a community of immigrants – many of them Catholics who were not of British origin – began to settle in the Prairies.[43]

The narration from one of the Sisters assigned to this mission is revealing. After a difficult and long trip they arrived 'at the post assigned to us by holy obedience': the dilapidated and poor rectory of Grande Clairière, accompanied by the priest who hosted them. No one was there; the door was open. Four planks nailed to the wall and covered with a rough straw mattress would be their beds, but they found clean sheets. The priest took his fur coat and went to the upper storey of the school to try to sleep. The next day, young ladies had come to help with the house, and a few mothers came to greet the Sisters:

> They [the mothers] were unable to express their happiness at the thought that Sisters had come to devote themselves to the education of their children. Seeing only two or three houses in the neighbourhood, we had the impression that we were living in a place almost uninhabited. What a surprise we had the next Sunday when we saw the church filled with people! They lived in the neighbouring districts; many had come from a long distance as the parish was as large as one of the extensive dioceses of France.[44]

The school in Grande Clairière opened on 28 August with twenty pupils, boys and girls from 6 to 15 years of age, 'all of whom were sincere, docile, respectful, and delighted to see us'.[45] One of the Sisters taught French, and the other English. The Sisters lived in the ruined rectory until the priest, aided by a Métis (as indicated in the narration), built a house near the school – the RNDM's first convent, though free of any comfort. The classroom was no better: 'In the centre were four long shaky tables, seemingly true relics of antiquity, joined to benches no less ancient; a desk for the teacher whose chair was an ordinary packing case, a blackboard almost unusable.'[46] Some girls lived at the convent as boarders and eventually the priest built bunks – that is, four rough boards nailed together, that, unlike the straw mattresses on the floor, allowed the Sister to sweep the room: 'Fortunately, the nine young girls we admitted were not exacting; they considered themselves lucky to be accepted while their companions were refused because of lack of space.'[47] The school was a public one, but the life of the Church was intertwined with the life of the school, so they became one. Even the poverty of the Sisters and the notion of mortification were re-created in the midst of life in the Prairies.

The visits from Archbishop Langevin were important events for the community and for the school, and the pupils were taught a welcome song and an address for the occasion. The tribulations of his visit due to the weather were duly registered. The Sisters appreciated 'his blessing and his paternal encouragement'.[48] The celebration of first communion was a community event for

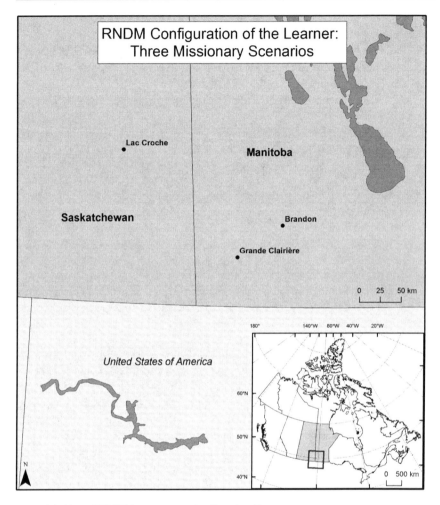

Figure 9.1 Map of RNDM missions in the Canadian Prairies.
Map designed by Graham Pope for the author of the chapter.

which the church and the schools were gracefully decorated. The clergy met the procession at the school. The Sisters registered that:

> [t]he whole parish was in jubilation; we felt that God really dwelt among his people and gave them a taste of the peaceful sweetness of his loving yoke. We were rewarded for our many sacrifices by the mere thought that, by our weak efforts, we had in some way contributed to this triumph of our divine Master.[49]

The language of the Sisters gives insights into their gendered world and their living spirituality.

The four Sisters assigned to the first mission in Canada were French. Mother M. St Paul (prioress) and Sister M. de l'Eucharistie had been the novices of the congregation's foundress, Euphrasie Barbier (Marie du Coeur-de-Jésus), and had made profession in 1894. The former, named Superior, had taught at Armentières and Houplines; the latter, though French, had lived at Deal, England, where she studied English, and spoke it fluently. Sister M. St Valérie had spent the two years of her religious life in Fribourg, Switzerland. Mother M. Madeleine of the Cross, professed for twenty years, was seen as a true daughter of the foundress, and had worked at Armentières and Sturry. She was described as a symbol of self-denial, humility, obedience and eagerness to work. The pioneering Sisters had taught in France, most of them knew English, and they had experience beyond France. At the time, the congregation had missions in England (three towns in Kent), New Zealand (Napier, 1865) and Australia (Sydney, 1867, closed in 1870), the Pacific Islands (Tonga, Apia, Samoa, and Wallis, 1871, from which they withdrew in 1878), India (Chittagong, 1883, and Akiab, 1897) and Switzerland (Fribourg, 1896).[50] The congregation had an international character, contrary to the Missionary Oblate Sisters, who were from French Canadian families, from Quebec or Saskatchewan, or were daughters of people from Quebec who had moved to the USA. The RNDM had known a different world and its conflicts. The Superiors travelled to the missions, and the chapters reunited the Provincial Superiors from different parts of the world. However – although their universe of meanings moved within the parameters of the notion of universal truth contained in the teaching of the Church and a highly centralized governance, as well as arguably colonial 'civilizing' understandings – the missions generated responses to the needs of the Catholics in specific localities.

Thus, the configuration of the learner needs to be analysed in the context in which the various social, political and cultural configurations are nested; it is situational. Then, when the Sisters talked of obedience and docility in referring to their pupils, these qualities applied well to the understanding of the relationship with the Church, not to some directives from the Department of Education. Over time, the schools in Franco-Manitoban areas cultivated an oppositional notion of citizenship, which took shape at the intersection with the curricular demands from the Manitoba Department of Education. Over the years, the congregation established foundations in a number of French Canadian and Métis parishes in Manitoba and Saskatchewan, and its apostolate in the schools, as it happened in Grande Clairière, served as a social integrative force. French Canadian communities had a strong desire for recognition that took the form of a collective challenge in which the Church was fully involved. After 1897, Franco-Manitobans had a strong feeling of being victims of injustice when they lost their status as a founding nation and public funding of Catholic schools ended.[51]

The original inspiration or illocutionary force, the formation of a Catholic self, acquired complex dimensions in the field. The early public school in Grande Clairière – a setting of colonists and Métis, as the Sisters described it – illustrates one of the early steps of Franco-Catholic communities in their pursuit of achieving their educational aims and their cultural and political identity. The relations between the French Métis and the Euro-French members of the Franco-Manitoban community took their own contours in Manitoba, an issue that is beyond the life of the little school and of the scope of this chapter.[52]

The cultural religious rites and stories would set the basis for deployment of various identities following attachments and identifications, creating a different way from the official discourse of becoming Canadian. Meanwhile, the public schools imbued with Anglo-conformity were intended to instil in children – in particular, those of non-British immigrants – a certain view of Canadian citizenship; 'the strangers within our gates' had to be Anglicized.[53] In 1916, the Association d'Education des Canadiens-Français du Manitoba was created, having the mandate of protecting the interests of French Catholics in Manitoba. It was part of a provincial and national institutional network that, as Marcel Martel argued, was instrumental in the process of elaborating the identity of the French Canadian nation (Quebec and communities outside Quebec).[54] The Association would play a role parallel to the Department of Education, while the congregations of teaching Sisters played a central part in public and parish schools.[55]

The mission at Lac Croche: redemption or the silencing of the soul?

A different dimension of the Sisters' understanding of their educational apostolate becomes evident in Lac Croche (Crooked Lake), a Cree Aboriginal reserve in Saskatchewan, where the male Oblates of Mary Immaculate ran the Marieval Indian Residential School for Aboriginal children funded by the federal Department of Indian Affairs, which opened in December 1898.[56] The education of Aboriginal children was under federal jurisdiction, and the state and the Christian Churches – including Catholic, Anglican, Methodist, Presbyterian and Congregationalist – converged in their intentions.[57] While the Christian Churches aimed at conversion to the new religion and the salvation of a self-disciplined child, the state pursued assimilation and a governable Aboriginal subject. In the residential school, the learner is the other with dramatic overtones; redemption and transformation were brought in the name of civilization. Four RNDM Sisters (two French, one Belgian, the other Irish) who came from Deal, England were in charge of the mission to provide these children 'the benefits of a Christian and civilizing education'.[58] The building of a Catholic self by creating a new cultural identity reveals the full scope of the doctrine of the Church, its dualistic theology and the frame of the missions as the true religion (no different from other Christian Churches of the time involved in missionary work). In the narration prepared by Sister Mary of the Holy Trinity, there is a poignant story:

> One day, Father Campeau arrived on horseback, preciously carrying something wrapped in a blanket. 'Quick, a tub of water', he exclaimed as he dismounted.
> 'Is it a fish, Father?', asked Sister, hurriedly complying with his request.
> 'Yes, and a famous fish!' He unrolled his bundle and, to the surprise of his questioner, let fall into the tub a youngster 2 or 3 years old and terribly dirty. It was Moses which in Cree means 'Frog's Leg'. His father, Yellow Calf and his mother, White Cow, had been brought up as pagans, but were later baptized and so was their son. The missionary, anxious to give the latter a Christian education, had taken him, by force, because these good Indians are very much attached to their children and do not want to be separated from them. The mother often came to see dear Moses. Trying to adorn herself, to give herself more importance, she wore, around her neck, a real harness decorated with copper nails. She seemed very proud of this adornment.[59]

What was the force, the intention behind removing and keeping a child from his family? The text tells the reader that the intention was to provide a Christian (Catholic) education – in other words, a way of being saved, but also of being an assimilated Aboriginal child. There were indeed preoccupations with the child, a child-centred approach, a thorough Christian education and feelings of love toward the children, but these were situated in relation to the inculcation of universal truths, the only true faith and a particular way of life. In this case, the notion of child-centredness, dear to the congregation, goes along with the dehistoricization of the Aboriginal child (Moses) and his family. The concept of child-centred education, if de-contextualized, becomes hollow. The editorial page of the first issue of *Les cloches de Saint-Boniface*, a periodical publication of the archdiocese of St Boniface, records:

> As Christopher Columbus raised the cross in the new world, these missionaries raised as well the sign of Redemption and all will come to kneel at the foot of this cross to receive the benefits of the Religion. The savage will hear for the first time the sweet word of the Gospel.[60]

This was the force behind education of the Aboriginal children.

The Christian Churches joined the state policy with different intentions in the process of colonization of the Aboriginal peoples and their culture and, Phillips has argued, in the goal of ending their claims for land, which were not compatible with the settlements and the western economy.[61] The missionaries failed to understand the relationship of the Aboriginal peoples with the natural world and its religious dimension as distinctive of their culture.[62]

The Sisters were employees under the direction of the missionary priests (Missionary Oblates of Mary Immaculate), who acted as official agents. Given the congregation's pontifical character and structure of governance, it had a degree of autonomy in relation to local authorities;[63] the kind of administration to which they had to submit was consistent neither with their customs, nor with the way of life of the congregation. Therefore, the RNDM Sisters left the residential school after seventeen months. Unlike the Missionary Oblate Sisters, a diocesan congregation, the RNDM Sisters did not participate in any other residential school apostolate in Canada.

The mission in Brandon: the quest for social recognition

The mission in the city of Brandon, Manitoba introduces another configuration of the learner as a cultural and political subject in a Protestant and, at moments, even hostile setting – one that was changing with the presence of immigrants from continental Europe.[64] In 1899, the RNDM Sisters occupied the former convent of the Faithful Companions of Jesus, a French congregation founded in 1820 that established foundations in England and Ireland, as well as expanding throughout the world. It was located on Third Street and Lorne Avenue, where they had run very successfully the St Joseph School, which had even attracted Protestant families. The Faithful Companions of Jesus left Brandon in 1892, victimized by attacks initiated by members of two Brandon congregations, Methodist and Presbyterian, combined with the Orange Lodge, at the dawning of the crisis leading to the abolition of the dual confessional system (Protestant/Catholic), and the setting of the common school (the Manitoba Schools Question).

Brandon had grown gradually from 1881 to 1901, when it reached 5,620 inhabitants, and by 1911 it had advanced to 13,893 inhabitants. Most of the new people were men from other homelands, or those driven to the city by employment in the expanding transportation and building industries. The British and Protestant character of the city's population changed rapidly at the beginning of the twentieth-century. While, in 1901, 83 per cent of the population was British, that percentage declined to 74 per cent in 1911. The proportion of the city's population of central and eastern European origin grew from 2 per cent in 1901, to 9 per cent in 1911.[65]

The location of the convent, within Brandon, on Lorne Avenue, south of the commercial district, is also important. The city acquired, as Errol Black and Tom Mitchell point out, a distinctive residential pattern. The most affluent families lived along Princess, Louise, Lorne and Victoria Avenues to the south and west of the central business district. The homes of workers occupied the rest of the city, particularly to the east of First Street. South of Victoria Avenue, in the area known as the English Ward, there was an expanding working-class neighbourhood to the east of First Street; the area north of the Canadian Pacific Railway, the North End, was populated by manufacturing plants and the overcrowded homes of central and eastern European working-class immigrants.

The public schools were construed as Protestant by Catholics, who complained that:

> Catholic children now forced to attend these schools were influenced by the constant association of Protestant teachers and companions .... To the new and zealous pastors, it seemed urgent that they secure religious teachers for their parish, threatened by the enemy, trying to scatter and draw parishioners away from the path of salvation.[66]

The request went to the Mother-House in Lyons, and an Oblate escorted the group of Sisters to their new destinations: Brandon; Manitoba; and Lebret, Saskatchewan. Religion and ethnicity were at the core of the educational mission.

The RNDM opened St Augustine's Parish School, grades 1 to 8, and started with 50 pupils at a time when Brandon had a population of 5,000, mostly British and Protestant.[67] Cultural diversity permeated the classroom where 'English' children (a description used by the Sisters to mean British children) attended the school or were boarders along with the children of recent continental European immigrants. Catholic teaching was at the core, even as Archbishop Langevin wanted the schools to follow the provincial curriculum. One of the Sisters recalled, in a narrative referring to the old convent though not to a particular year,

> I was assigned the girls' large dormitory with pupils of Polish, Ukrainian, German and Russian origin, some 60 in all. These children received religious instruction daily from two Perès Redemptoristes (CSSRs), one Ruthenian Rite, the other, a Polish, both spoke and taught in the language of the pupils.[68]

Until 1916, the Manitoba Public School Act of 1897 allowed religious instruction when there were at least ten pupils of the same faith, and bilingual teaching when at least ten pupils spoke French or any other language.[69] Despite the disparate and scanty character of the information regarding the social composition of the school, it is possible to infer that the St Augustine School, in particular, attracted a large number of children from working-class families, British and central and eastern Europeans.

There was a quest for social recognition in the process of building community identity; here, faith, language and ethnic origin are related in various ways. The school cultivated the worth of the cultural language rooted in the way the group experienced the Catholic faith. It broke with the universality of the common school and its approach to building a cohesive society through Anglo-conformity. The illocutionary force – salvation of the soul and a Catholic way – was inserted in the living experience of the community to which the Church was responsive. There was a powerful dimension in the life of the learner that is in line with the idea that withholding recognition can be a form of oppression. In the words of Charles Taylor:

> On the intimate level, we can see how much an original identity needs and is vulnerable to the recognition given or withheld by significant others. It is not surprising that in the culture of authenticity, relationships are seen as the key loci of self-discovery and self-affirmation .... They [love relationships] are also crucial because they are the crucibles of inwardly generated identity.[70]

The idea of preserving the cultural language, being true to themselves, not conforming to the dominant culture, was heavily framed by the doctrine of the Church and by Church politics. Within this framework, the schools were cultivating a sort of proto-multi-culturalism, a notion of difference.

The Sisters did not charge fees at St Augustine's School, as the narratives tell that Catholic parents were not able to support two school systems. Families gave what they could afford to cover boarding expenses. A Sister recalled that, in those days, the Brandon people were rather fanatical; this is the reason why the Redemptorist Fathers were anxious to keep Catholic children in St Augustine's School. She went on to say:

> We, then, were really doing missionary work such as Mother Foundress would approve. My pupils never had money to give or spend. However, each morning saw my desk growing under the load of donations. Apples, jams, pickles, etc. These were all carefully carried to St Mike's [St Michael's Convent] where they were stored away in the pantry.[71]

The Sisters soon opened St Michael's Academy, a senior day and boarding school for girls, with instruction entirely in English. A new building for St Michael's Convent, where the schools functioned, was built in 1910 and blessed by Archbishop Langevin. Even before this blessing on 29 September 1910, the classrooms were operational. The connections with the parish were strong, as shown in the bazaars organized to defray costs, and the involvement of parents in the activities organized by the school and the parish.

The visits from Archbishop Langevin were occasions to display the musical abilities of the students and their participation in plays, as well as to build ties with the community. The Catholic ethos was at the core, and there were a number of conversions of pupils registered in the journals.[72] No records survive to indicate what and how the Sisters taught in daily classrooms. However, music permeated the various religious festivities in the schools; the Sisters provided music lessons that over time gained a great reputation. There is a record, for example, of an examiner from Trinity College of Music, London coming to St Michael's Academy, and that the examinations were very good,[73] and later on the students went through the music examinations at the University of Manitoba. It is interesting to note that music created a link with the community through the students who took classes. Even St Augustine's Church, pastored by the Redemptorist Fathers, which had acquired a state-of-the-art pipe organ, attracted people of all faiths to a concert by a prestigious artist from Quebec.[74]

The parish school and the Church were powerful forces in the quest for recognition and preservation of cultural values in the midst of a hostile environment where the political struggles often acquired anti-immigrant tones, and the notion of otherness was conveyed in several expressions such as 'strangers within our gates',[75] referring to foreigners and others who needed to be assimilated. The school provided a space with a configuration of alternative meanings in the pursuit of immigrants trying to find their place in Canada. Further exploration beyond what is in the RNDM archives may uncover some information about the pupils' families, in order to understand their social imaginaries beyond the ethnic and religious network.

Conclusion

Education was conflated with Christian education within the teachings of the Church, but it became inserted in specific historical configurations in time and space, and the teaching Sisters saw themselves as religious missionaries, with the central aim to build a Catholic self. The 'illocutionary force' sustaining the Sisters' work was the salvation of souls, and the keeping or re-creation of a Catholic order in the particular setting of the apostolate. The Sisters' understanding of education as child-centred and integrative of the spiritual, academic and practical aspects acquired meanings within the configuration of the Church doctrines and the authority of the magisterium. Consequently, the Sisters' apostolate fell within an ecclesiocentric model of mission beyond the spaces the Sisters could carve. Thus, there were normative boundaries, but also configurations emerging from the needs of the Church in specific settings – as in the three scenarios examined here – that would generate unexpected meanings, and cultural and political practices.

The formation of the Catholic self appears highly relational and situational, not separated from the cultural and political subject. The school in Grande Clairière, a public school located in a Franco-Manitoban area, represents one of the first steps – at the time, within Archbishop Langevin's vision of a dualistic French–English Canada – towards the configuration of a French Canadian (and, in this case, a Franco-Manitoban) cultural and political language rooted in language, faith and Catholic education. The socio-economic context and the social imaginary of the community were present in the life of the parish and the school, which acquired a contested oppositional character in relation to the Department of Education.

In contrast, the mission in Lac Croche exemplified how the illocutionary force and the notions of education become hollow, even cruel, in a setting in which the imaginary of the community is silenced and the pupils are culturally de-contextualized. The Congregation's schools in Brandon were nested in the socio-economic characteristics of the city, its demographic changes and political struggles. St Augustine's school became a space for ethnic Catholic minorities and Catholics to quest for social recognition and develop their place in Canada, in the midst of distrust of their culture and class struggles, and where, at the beginning of the twentieth-century, they found it difficult to situate themselves. The learners and their families brought their struggles to the Church and the school. Grande Clairière and Brandon are two different cases, but both speak to the insertion of the Catholic Church in time and space, while interweaving agendas and religious intentions. On the other hand, Lac Croche embodies the complex process of colonization of the Aboriginal peoples, whose pain and resilience have been a topic of great contention in Canada.

It is noticeable, that in the process of building a Canadian identity on their own terms and circumstances, Catholic educators cultivated in their students the ability to govern themselves and to be governed, qualities fostered by the modern liberal state. In the last instance, morality and good character were the foundations for governance, and were at the foundations of Catholic education and the work of religious congregations.

Notes

1 This chapter is part of a major research project funded by the Social Sciences and Humanities Research Council of Canada. I appreciate the comments made by Eva Krugly-Smolska on an earlier draft of the chapter.
2 Marie Bénédicte Ollivier, *Missionary beyond Boundaries: Euphrasie Barbier, 1829–1893*, trans. Beverley Grounds (Rome: Istituto Salesiano Pío XI, 2007). This is a non-hagiographical biography of the founder.
3 Ken Osborne, 'One Hundred Years of History Teaching in Manitoba Schools, Part 1: 1897–1927', *Manitoba History*, 36 (Autumn/Winter 1998–9), 3–25.
4 Gerald Friesen, *The Canadian Prairies: A History* (Toronto and London: University of Toronto Press, 1987).
5 When the RNDM Sisters came to Manitoba, its public school system was going through a process of reorganization and consolidation that began in 1890 and ended in the 1920s. The crisis that developed between 1890 and 1897 is known as the Manitoba Schools Question. In 1890, the provincial government abolished the dual system (Protestant/Catholic) created under the Manitoba Act; in 1897, a new Manitoba Education Act incorporated the terms of the Laurier–Greenway Compromise (between the federal and provincial governments) that ended the crisis and set the basis for the common school. The Catholic Church could no longer have its own school districts under its jurisdiction supported by public funding. However, the Act read that religious exercises were permitted when there were ten pupils belonging to a faith in any school, and also that, when ten or more pupils spoke French or any language other than English as their native tongue, the teaching could be bilingual. In 1916, the Manitoban government abolished the bilingual (multi-lingual) schools, which had voluntary attendance, and replaced them with a secular, unilingual and universal system of public schooling where private schools were allowed, but had to follow the public school

curriculum. Osborne, 'One Hundred Years of History Teaching'; Robert Perin, *Rome in Canada: The Vatican and Canadian Affairs in the Late Victorian Age* (Toronto: University of Toronto Press, 1990), Chapter 5, 127–57.

6 The impact of the official discourse in the classroom was mediated through the multitude of school districts, each with its locally elected Board of Trustees controlling one- or two-room schools, and by poorly trained and frequently changing teachers. This allowed the Catholic Church to 'take control' of public schools in rural areas where the population was Catholic and homogeneous. The inspectors were the mediators between the Boards and the Department of Education. Rosa Bruno-Jofré, 'Citizenship and Schooling in Manitoba, 1918–1945', *Manitoba History*, 36 (Autumn/Winter 1998–9), 26–37.

7 Quentin Skinner, 'Meaning and Understanding in the History of Ideas', *History and Theory*, 8:1 (1969), 3–53, esp. 45 and 46. James Tully, 'The Pen Is a Mighty Sword: Quentin Skinner's Analysis of Politics', in James Tully (ed.), *Meaning and Context: Quentin Skinner and His Critics* (Cambridge: Polity Press, 1988), 7–25.

8 'I speak of "social imaginary" here, rather than social theory, because there are important differences between the two. There are, in fact, several differences. I speak of "imaginary" (i) because I am talking about the way ordinary people "imagine" their social surroundings, and this is often not expressed in theoretical terms, it is carried in images, stories, legends, etc. But it is also the case that (ii) theory is often the possession of a small minority, whereas what is interesting in the social imaginary is that it is shared by large groups of people, if not the whole society. Which leads to a third difference: (iii) the social imaginary is that common understanding which makes possible common practices, and a widely shared sense of legitimacy.' Charles Taylor, *A Secular Age* (Cambridge, MA and London: Belknap Press, 2007), 171–2. The notion of nested spaces came out of a conversation with James Scott Johnston.

9 Rosa Bruno-Jofré, *The Missionary Oblate Sisters: Vision and Mission* (Montreal and Kingston: McGill-Queen's University Press, 2005); Rosa Bruno-Jofré, 'The Process of Renewal of the Missionary Oblate Sisters, 1963–1989', in Elizabeth M. Smyth (ed.), *Changing Habits: Women Religious Orders in Canada* (Ottawa: Novalis, 2007), 247–73.

10 Eric J. Hobsbawm, *The Age of Empire: 1875–1914* (London: Weidenfeld and Nicolson, 1987), 56–9.

11 Ibid., 16.

12 Cited by Maureen McBride, '"Our Students Must Become Valiant Women!" Approaches to Education of Euphrasie Barbier 1829–1893, Foundress of Sisters of Our Lady of the Missions', paper presented to the RNDM Education Symposium, St Mary's College, Shillong, North East India, 26 January 2006, 3.

13 For a detailed account of educational theory and spirituality, see Rosa Bruno-Jofré, 'The Missionary Oblate Sisters and the Sisters of Our Lady of the Missions (RNDM): The Intersection of Education, Spirituality, the Politics of Life, Faith, and Language, in the Canadian Prairies, 1898–1930', *Paedagogica historica*, 49:4 (2013), 471–93. See also McBride, 'Our Students Must Become Valiant Women!', 3; Colleen Mader, 'Mother Mary of the Heart of Jesus: Her Thoughts and Ideas on Education', box 3, file 4, Centre du Patrimoine, Société Historique de Saint-Boniface, St Boniface, Manitoba (hereafter CPSHSB).

14 Letter of Mother Mary of the Heart of Jesus to Mother Mary of the Angels, prioress of Christchurch, and to the assembled council, 21 May 1870, Translation of the Writings of Mother Mary of the Heart of Jesus, 2/2/419. Archive of the British Isles Province of the Sisters of Our Lady of the Missions, Sturry, UK (hereafter RNDMUK).

15 Letter of Mother Mary of the Heart of Jesus to Mother Mary of the Redemption, 12 October 1873, Translation of the Writings, 2/3/725.
16 Mader, 'Mother Mary of the Heart of Jesus', 2. McBride, 'Our Students Must Become Valiant Women!', 8; original letter consulted. Mother Mary of the Heart of Jesus to Mother Mary St Michael, 2 June 1878, 1/F/2/5/1293, RNDMUK.
17 Letter of Mother Mary of the Heart of Jesus to Mother Mary St Jude, prioress of Napier, 5 March 1873, 2/3/619, RNDMUK. Mader, 'Mother Mary of the Heart of Jesus', 3. Note that in public schools in Manitoba, the Sisters taught both boys and girls.
18 Bruno-Jofré, *The Missionary Oblate Sisters*, 103.
19 Ibid.
20 Mader, 'Mother Mary of the Heart of Jesus'. For a more detailed analysis, see Bruno-Jofré, 'The Missionary Oblate Sisters'.
21 Pope Pius XI, '*Divini illius magistri*: Encyclical of Pope Pius XI on Christian Education to the Patriarchs, Primates, Archbishops, Bishops, and Other Ordinaries in Peace and Communion with the Apostolic See and to All the Faithful of the Catholic World', http://w2.vatican.va/content/pius-xi/en/encyclicals/documents/hf_p-xi_enc_31121929_divini-illius-magistri.html (accessed 1 July 2013), Article 9.
22 Further research is necessary. Often, the concepts they employed insinuate familiarity with these pedagogues.
23 Letter of Mother Mary of the Heart of Jesus to Mother M. St Peter, 15 October 1876, 2/4/962, RNDMUK.
24 The language of citizenship displayed by the Ministry of Education in Manitoba and quite forcefully after the First World War was an amalgam of national identity and patriotism, a sense of tradition and heritage (Canadian and British), and depended on the understanding of the sacrifices of the predecessors. Osborne, 'One Hundred Years of History Teaching', 9.
25 Susan Smith, *Call to Mission: The Story of the Mission Sisters of Aotearoa, New Zealand and Samoa* (Auckland: David Ling Publishing, 2010), 275. Neo-scholasticism refers to the preferred form of speculative theology supported by the magisterium. It became an antidote to modern thought, a conceptual framework that defined the norms of orthodoxy, and was not open to reality and history. Jürgen Mettepenningen, *Nouvelle théologie – New Theology: Inheritor of Modernism, Precursor of Vatican II* (New Zealand: T. & T. Clark, 2010), 11.
26 This was clear among those members of the Free Teaching Institute who espoused an anti-dogmatic Catholicism compatible with freedom of conscience and religious plurality, including that of the institute. Gonzalo Jover, 'Readings of the Pedagogy of John Dewey in Spain in the Early Twentieth Century: Reconciling Pragmatism and Transcendence', in Rosa Bruno-Jofré, James Scott Johnston, Gonzalo Jover and Daniel Tröhler (eds), *Democracy and the Intersection of Religion and Traditions: The Reading of John Dewey's Understanding of Democracy and Education* (Kingston and Montreal: McGill-Queen's University Press, 2010), 79–130.
27 There was indeed the 'modernist crisis' in the 1920s, prompted by intellectuals (theologians) who tried to integrate the historical-critical method. Mettepenningen, *Nouvelle théologie*, 19–27.
28 Ibid., 25–9. John L. Elias, 'Whatever Happened to Catholic Philosophy of Education?', *Religious Education*, 94:1 (Winter 1999), 92–110. See Mettepenningen, *Nouvelle théologie*, 31–40.
29 Pius XI, '*Divini illius magistri*', Article 14.

30 Ibid., Article 15.
31 Ibid., Article 18.
32 See n. 4.
33 Bruno-Jofré, *The Missionary Oblate Sisters*. Veronica Dunne wrote: 'Langevin cherished the prospect that French Canadians would form a "compact corridor of settlement" from Québec to the Rocky Mountains. In his view the survival and expansion of a living Catholic culture in North America depended on language as much as on denominational education. Langevin's vision was of a Canada of ethnic communities, each preserving its language and culture and having the church at the core of its social life. The alternative, he feared, was massive loss of faith resulting from assimilation.' Veronica Dunne, 'The Story of the RNDMs in Canada 1898–2010,', 14 (manuscript provided by the author).
34 Ibid., 4.
35 'Sister Mary of the Holy Trinity, Sisters of Our Lady of the Missions in Canada 1898–1923', manuscript commemorating the Silver Jubilee of the RNDM (undated), provided by the Provincial Superior Sister Veronica Dunne. The author compiled the narrations from the foundresses of the missions. The original quote was not edited for grammar.
36 Bruno-Jofré, *The Missionary Oblate Sisters*, 27.
37 Although the Vatican rejected concepts emerging from New Education (in particular, pragmatism and John Dewey's theory of education, given its negation of duality and its reliance on experimentalism, and especially its notion of warranted assertability), the Sisters had to obtain professional, state-regulated teaching certificates and were exposed to progressive ideas and pedagogical methods that often permeated their practice. Although this is beyond the scope of this chapter, it should be noted that for many years, the Church and Catholic educators reacted against pragmatist philosophies of education, notions of instrumental knowledge and evidentialism. However, in the late 1920s and 1930s, when neo-Thomism at the core of the 'nouvelle théologie' gained some intellectual space (although questioned by the Vatican), Catholic theologians with a strong interest in education, like Frans de Hovre and, in particular, Chilean Jesuit Alberto Hurtado, examined Dewey. They tended to separate pragmatism, as the philosophical foundation of Dewey's educational theory, from his educational theory. See Frans de Hovre, *Essai de philosophie pédagogique* (Brussels: Librairie Albert Dewit, 1927); Alberto Hurtado, *Le système pédagogique de Dewey devant les exigences de la doctrine catholique* (Belgium: Université de Louvain, 1935). See Rosa Bruno-Jofré and Gonzalo Jover, 'The Readings of John Dewey's Work and the Intersection of Catholicism: The Cases of the Institución Libre de Enseñanza and the Thesis of Father Alberto Hurtado, SJ on Dewey', in Rosa Bruno-Jofré and Jürgen Schriewer (eds), *The Global Reception of Dewey's Thought: Multiple Refractions through Time and Space* (New York and London: Routledge, Taylor and Francis Group, 2012), 23–42.It is important to mention innovative directions provided by Jacques Maritain and Etienne Gilson in the 1940s and 1950s. See Elias, 'Whatever Happened to Catholic Philosophy of Education?'.
38 Dunne, 'The Story of the RNDMs', 3.
39 Such was the case of the largely British Canadian Saskatchewan Grain Growers' Association and its successor, the United Farmers of Canada, Saskatchewan section, who complained about Ottawa's failure to restrict immigration as part of the nativist backlash. Furthermore, the Ku Klux Klan entered Ontario from the United States in the mid 1920s and spread to Saskatchewan. Friesen, *The Canadian Prairies*, 404.

40 Land reserves were offered in Manitoba to attract ethnic colonies, and various ethnic groups established informal settlements in Manitoba and North West Territories (Saskatchewan, where the RNDM opened missions very early, was created as a province in 1905). Paul Phillips, 'Manitoba in the Agrarian Period: 1870–1940', in Jim Silver and Jeremy Hull (eds), *The Political Economy of Manitoba* (Regina, Saskatchewan: Canadian Plains Research Center, University of Regina, 1990), 3–24 (6).

41 The congregations in general refer to French populations, having as point of reference the language and related culture and faith; for example, they included *les canadiens* from Quebec, settlers from France, French who had moved from the USA and Acadians. The Métis are one of the recognized Aboriginal peoples in Canada. They are descendants of First Nations and Europeans (in this case, French Métis). They spoke Mitchif, a mixture of mainly French and Cree. See Nicole St-Onge, Carolyn Podruchny and Brenda Macdougall (eds), *Contours of a People: Métis Family, Mobility, and History* (Norman: University of Oklahoma Press, 2012); Ute Lischke and David T. McNab (eds), *Long Journey of a Forgotten People: Métis Identities and Family Histories* (Waterloo, ON: Wilfrid Laurier University Press, 2007).

42 In 1891, Manitoba and North West Territories as a region had 251,500 people, with 151,000 in Manitoba; in 1901, the region had 419,500 inhabitants, of which 255,200 lived in Manitoba. Phillips, 'Manitoba in the Agrarian Period', 8.

43 'Almost half of all prairie residents at the start of the First World War had been born in another country, and the proportion was still 1 in 3 as late as 1931.' Friesen, *The Canadian Prairies*, 244.

44 'Sister Mary of the Holy Trinity', 12.

45 Ibid.

46 Ibid., 13.

47 Ibid., 14.

48 Ibid., 17.

49 Ibid., 18.

50 'Development of the Sisters of Our Lady of the Missions', manuscript provided by Veronica Dunne, Provincial Superior of the Canadian Province, August 2011. See also anon., *The Life of Mother Marie du Saint-Rosaire, Second Superior-General of the Institute Notre Dame des Missions* (Hinckley: Samuel Walker, 1935).

51 See n. 5.

52 Donald A. Bailey, 'The Métis Province and Its Social Tensions', in Silver and Hull, *The Political Economy of Manitoba*, 51–72.

53 See Bruno-Jofré, 'The Missionary Oblate Sisters'.

54 Marcel Martel, *Le deuil d' un pays imaginé: Rêves, luttes et déroute du Canada français. Les rapports entre le Québec et la francophonie canadienne (1867–1975)* (Ottawa, ON: Presses de l'Université d'Ottawa, 1997), 20. Marcel Martel, *French Canada: An Account of Its Creation and Break-Up, 1850–1967* (Ottawa: Canadian Historical Association, 1998), 3–5.Thus, the Association Canadienne-Française d'Education de l'Ontario was formed in 1910, two years ahead of the provincial decision to limit the teaching of French to the first two years of elementary school. The Association Catholique Franco-Canadienne de la Saskatchewan was founded in 1910, and the Association Canadienne-Française de l'Alberta in 1926. The role of the Catholic Church is not a negligible one. The first national Congress of French took place in 1912. The associations for Alberta, Manitoba and Saskatchewan were active in developing French and religious educational programmes, administering French exams, and inspecting the schools.Parish circles,

local parents, the trustees' associations of these schools, the associations of teachers of French language and, very specially, the Catholic Church were involved with the Association. In 1916, in Manitoba, 56.5 per cent of a total of 258 teachers in these schools for francophones were religious, with approximately 8,000 students in 133 schools. The numbers were lower in 1926, but are reliable since they were taken from the list of the Association. The decline is explained by the fact that a number of bilingual schools that were counted in 1916 had a heterogeneous clientele. Jean-Marie Taillefer, 'Les Franco-Manitobains et l'éducation 1870–1970: Une étude quantitative' (Ph.D. thesis, University of Manitoba, 1987), 270–1.
55 Bruno-Jofré, 'The Missionary Oblate Sisters'.
56 'The Sisters of Our Lady of the Missions Receive a Warm Welcome in Crooked Lake Mission, 14 December 1898', brochure celebrating the ninety-fifth anniversary of arriving in Canada and the Sisters' second foundation at Crooked Lake Mission, box 54, file 10, CPSHSB; Revd Théophile Campeau, OMI to SA Grandeur Monseigneur Langevin, Archevêque de St-Boniface, Manitoba, 1 December 1898.
57 See J. R. Miller, *Shingwauk's Vision: A History of Native Residential Schools* (Toronto: University of Toronto Press, 1997).
58 'Sister Mary of the Holy Trinity', 12.
59 Ibid., 33.
60 'Editorial', *Les cloches de Saint-Boniface* 1:1 (1902), 1–2.
61 Phillips, 'Manitoba in the Agrarian Period'.
62 Gerald Friesen, *Citizens and Nation: An Essay on History, Communication, and Canada* (Toronto: University of Toronto Press, 2000), Chapter 2, 'Interpreting Aboriginal Cultures', 31–54.
63 'Sister Mary of the Holy Trinity', 35.
64 Patrick J. O'Sullivan, *By Steps, Not Leaps: St Augustine of Canterbury Parish, Brandon, Manitoba, 1881–1981* (Brandon, Manitoba: P. J. O'Sullivan, 1981).
65 Errol Black and Tom Mitchell, *A Square Deal for All and No Railroading: Historical Essays on Labour in Brandon* (St John's, Newfoundland: Canadian Committee on Labour History, 2000), introduction, 13.
66 'Sister Mary of the Holy Trinity', 37.
67 Journal, St Augustine Convent, Brandon, Manitoba, 1 September 1899, box 54, file 22, CPSHSB. 'Sister Mary of the Holy Trinity', 37–46.
68 'The Convent on Victoria and Lorne, Brandon,' manuscript, box 54, file 17, CPSHSB, 1. There is a note saying that this is by Sr Cecile Jordang, RNDM (name not clear).
69 Ibid., 14.
70 Charles Taylor, *Multiculturalism and 'The Politics of Recognition'*, (Princeton, NJ: Princeton University Press, 1992), 36. Taylor wrote about the concept of authenticity that Herder put forward – the idea that each of us has an original way of being human – a new idea that went deep into modern consciousness. 'It accords moral importance to a kind of contact with myself, with my own inner nature, which it sees as in danger of being lost, partly through the pressures towards outward conformity, but also because in taking an instrumental stance toward myself, I may have lost the capacity to listen to this inner voice' (30).
71 'The Convent on Victoria and Lorne', 1.
72 Journal, St Michael's Convent, May 1903, box 54, file 22, CPSHSB.
73 RNDM, St Michael's Academy, Brandon, Manitoba, June 1921, box 54, file 22, CPSHSB.

74 The RNDM Sisters wrote in their account that the Superior allowed them to attend the concert, something quite extraordinary given their difficult articulation of contemplative life and apostolic work. 'Sister Mary of the Holy Trinity'.
75 Revd James Woodworth wrote *Strangers within Our Gates* in 1909. The Methodist reformist leader, although sympathetic to the plight of immigrants, was concerned with the need to assimilate them.

Chapter 10

A path to perfection

Translations from French by Catholic women religious in nineteenth-century Ireland

Michèle Milan

Introduction

This chapter explores new perspectives on the history of women religious in Ireland, and it does so through the lens of translation history. It draws attention to the significant output of Catholic literature translated from French into English in nineteenth-century Ireland, and to the role played by Ireland's female religious communities in this process. According to a survey of Ireland's library holdings, Catholic writings formed a major area of translation activity from French into English in nineteenth-century Ireland.[1] The socio-historical background is crucial to our understanding of patterns in translation. In this case, the progressive strengthening of Irish Catholicism over the course of the century, following years of social and political restrictions under the Penal Laws, is of critical relevance. Accordingly, the growing array of Catholic publishing outlets offered increased opportunities to translators of Catholic writings. Furthermore, the growth of the conventual movement in nineteenth-century Ireland not only coincided with the re-emergence of Catholics into Irish public life,[2] but may also be correlated with contemporary developments in continental Europe. In particular, despite the French Revolution and the rise of anti-clericalism, female religious congregations witnessed a significant growth in nineteenth-century France.[3] In fact, while France was typically viewed as a 'Godless' nation following the French Revolution and its attack on religion and the Church, the century nonetheless witnessed a religious revival there, particularly between 1830 and 1860.[4] What is more, French Catholic writings were often prevalent in the overall body of contemporary Catholic literature, with key figures such as Chateaubriand, Lacordaire, Lamennais, Montalembert and a myriad of lesser-known writers.[5]

One of the most significant areas of French influence in nineteenth-century Ireland relates to French Catholic religious orders. Besides the Ursulines, who arrived in Ireland in the 1770s, several female religious orders, principally of French origin, came to Ireland in the nineteenth-century. The French congregations were the Sisters of the Sacred Heart (1842), the Faithful

Companions of Jesus (1844), the Sisters of the Good Shepherd (1848), the Sisters of Our Lady of Charity of the Refuge (1853), the Daughters of Charity of St Vincent de Paul (1855), the Sisters of St Louis (1859), the Sisters of St Joseph of Cluny (1860), the Little Sisters of the Poor (*c.* 1860s), the Sainte Union des Sacrés Coeurs (1862), the Sisters of Bon Secours (1865), the Religious of the Sacred Heart of Mary (1870), the Marist Sisters (1873), the Little Sisters of the Assumption (1891) and the Daughters of the Heart of Mary.[6] Additionally, the creation of Irish native congregations such as the Irish Sisters of Charity was often inspired by French traditions.[7] Moreover, as O'Connor puts it,

> While orders such as the Ursulines, Sacred Heart, and the [Faithful Companions of Jesus] displayed the greatest degree of French influence, most convent boarding schools in Ireland were influenced to some degree by various aspects of French culture and traditions during the nineteenth century.[8]

In particular, convent schools often emphasized the learning of French.

For the general population, however, access to French literature largely depended on translation. Advanced levels of French proficiency were acquired mostly among the upper classes or by those who were educated in France.[9] Another crucial element to the production of translations in nineteenth-century Ireland is the dramatic language shift from Irish to English that characterized the period, with a clear increase in English literacy over the course of the century.[10] Accordingly, print culture in that period was principally an English-language culture, and translation from French was, for the most part, performed into English.

Set against this context, this chapter focusses on the remarkable contribution of Irish women religious to nineteenth-century translation of French Catholic writings, highlighting the main areas to which they have contributed and outlining their motives. The most active communities as regards published translation were the Ursulines and the Sisters of Mercy, but there were also translators among other communities, such as the Presentation or the Loreto Sisters. Female religious translators played a significant role in the translation of two main types of French Catholic writings: devotional-spiritual literature, and writings dealing with religious life.

By making use of the translators' own prefaces and comments, this chapter shows their awareness of the necessity of translation in Ireland at the time, and even of the cultural impact of translation. Furthermore, comments on textual 'chastity' or 'simplicity' reflected the moral and spiritual direction of religious translators, as well as more general, both tradition-bound and fashionable, approaches to texts and translation. This chapter also briefly touches on the ideas of (near) anonymity and (semi-) invisibility, and establishes links among translation, women and religious life.

Religious communities and the clergy represented an important part of the target audience, but many translations were also aimed at the wider English-speaking Catholic community. In this regard, the present chapter supports Mary Peckham Magray's argument that, while women religious have often been presented as products of the Catholic cultural revolution in nineteenth-century Ireland, they were in fact at the centre of the creation of a devout Catholic culture.[11] This chapter therefore argues that translation should be included as one of the means by which female religious helped create that change. It seeks to show that Irish women religious played an active part in a growing cross-cultural network of religious and literary exchanges and, ultimately, it underlines the intercultural element that is fundamental to the history of women religious.

Women religious and translation: main contributions[12]

Women religious in nineteenth-century Ireland played a significant role in translation of two main types of writings: devotional and spiritual literature, which was the overall prevailing trend in religious translation, and writings dealing with religious life. There is naturally a great deal of overlap between these areas. Other key topics in translation by women religious relate to religious history, particularly religious biography.

Devotional and spiritual literature

French Catholic literature was an important source for devotion to Jesus, particularly the Sacred Heart, and to the Blessed Virgin. Traced back to the Middle Ages, and strengthened by Sainte Marguerite Marie Alacoque and Saint Jean Eudes in the seventeenth-century,[13] devotions to the Sacred Heart of Jesus and to the Blessed Virgin Mary seem to have gained added strength in nineteenth-century Ireland and France. This is particularly evidenced by several contemporary developments in the Roman Catholic Church. In 1856, the Feast of the Sacred Heart was officially established by Pope Pius IX in the Roman Catholic liturgical calendar.[14] Both Ireland and France were solemnly consecrated to the Sacred Heart in 1873. The foundation stone of the Basilica of the Sacred Heart in Paris was laid on 16 June 1875. Lourdes, where Marian apparitions were reported by Bernadette Soubirous in 1858, became almost instantly one of the most visited sites of pilgrimage, attracting among others a great number of Irish Catholics.[15] Pope Pius IX approved Marian veneration in Lourdes. He is also known for his efforts towards the dogmatization of the Immaculate Conception, which was officially declared a Roman Catholic dogma in 1854.[16] Within this context, translated devotional literature dedicated to the Sacred Heart and to the Blessed Virgin belonged to, as well as supported, a significant transnational Catholic tradition in the period.

Typical examples of religious literature in this area are *Devotions to the Sacred Heart for the First Friday of Every Month* (*c.* 1884), translated from the French of Père Huguet, Marist, by 'a Sister of Mercy', and *Reflections on the Passion of Our Lord Jesus Christ* (1872), which was compiled and translated from various French authors by 'a Religious of Loretto Convent, Navan'. Published by London-based Catholic publishers Burns and Oates and sold by Irish booksellers, the latter work was advertised in nationally circulated newspapers such as *Freeman's Journal* and the *Nation*. For the second edition, the publishers stressed that this compilation was published 'under the auspices, and with the special sanction of his Lordship, Right Rev. Dr Nulty, Lord Bishop of Meath', which undoubtedly lent prestige and authority to the work. The success of the first edition was also stressed and the advertisement reproduced a substantial extract from the translation.

The Interior of Jesus and Mary (1847) was translated by a 'Miss Kennelly', and published by James Duffy, one of Ireland's leading Catholic publishers in the nineteenth-century. This translation from the Jesuit Abbé Grou was included in the list of 'James Duffy's Valuable Catholic Publications Adapted for the Holy Season of Lent' in the *Nation*, and advertised as being from the pen of 'a member of the Ursuline Community, Blackrock, Cork'. Another 'Member of the Ursuline Community, Cork', quite possibly the same person, was the translator of *Mary, the Morning Star* (*c.* 1855) from Abbé Grou. This translation too was advertised several times by Duffy in the *Nation*.

Other than texts specifically aimed at devotion to Jesus and Mary, there were numerous works of piety intending to guide Christians in their spiritual lives. Among these, one of the most popular in nineteenth-century Ireland was *Spiritual Consolation; or, A Treatise on Interior Peace; Interspersed with Various Instructions Necessary for Promoting the Practice of Solid Piety, by the Authoress of the "Ursuline Manual"* (1835, 1840, 1875), whose original author was a Capuchin, Ambroise de Lombez, i.e. Jean de La Peyrie. The copy held at Trinity College Dublin was bought from the Franciscan friars in Killiney. We have here a good example of the role played by Catholic teaching and monastic orders in the dissemination of ascetical works, the author being a Franciscan friar and the translator an Ursuline nun. The 'authoress of the Ursuline manual' was probably Mother Mary Borgia McCarthy of the Ursuline convent at Cork.[17] This translation was issued in 1835 and 1840 by Richard Coyne in Dublin. Coyne was printer and bookseller to the Royal College of St Patrick, Maynooth, as well as publisher to the Roman Catholic Bishops of Ireland. Another title in this category is *Solid virtue; or, A Treatise on the Obstacles to Solid Virtue, the Means of Acquiring, and Motives for Practising It* (1879, 1887), originally written in Latin by Revd Father Bellécius, SJ, translated into French by Abbé Louis Berthon and translated from the French by 'a member of the Ursuline Community, Thurles'. The English-language translation included a preface by Thomas William Croke, archbishop of Cashel.

Religious life

The Ursulines were also actively involved in the area of translation specifically devoted to religious life. For example, *Meditations on the Duties of Religious Especially Those Devoted to the Instruction of Youth* (1901) was translated by 'a member of the Ursuline Community, Sligo' and published by Gill and Son, another major publisher of Catholic literature in nineteenth-century Ireland. Not only does this translation illustrate that the Ursulines imported texts especially relevant to their vocation, but, with the original produced by the 'Superioress of the Ursulines of Montargis', we have here an example of translation which is at once cross-cultural and within the same religious order. Moreover, while much of the translation and publishing activity was increasingly centred in Dublin, as well as in major cities abroad such as London and New York, we can clearly see from the titles mentioned in this chapter that women religious translators were nonetheless based in various towns around the country, writing from Cork, Kerry, Thurles, Sligo or Navan. Cork, in particular, appears to have been a cradle of translation and of congregational activity at the time.

The Path of Perfection in Religious Life: A Work Intended for Persons Consecrated to God (1862) partly provided the inspiration for the title of this chapter. The book was translated from Abbé Alexandre Leguay, 'vicar-general of Perpignan, director of several religious communities'. The translation was entirely anonymous, but the translator's preface, as we shall see shortly, provides us with greater insight into the motives behind translation. *Conferences for Ecclesiastical Students and Religious* (1878) was translated from the French of Louis Tronson by Sister M. F. Clare. Mary Francis Clare was the name taken in religion by Margaret Anne Cusack (1829–99), also known as 'the Nun of Kenmare'. Born in Dublin of Protestant parents, Cusack converted to Catholicism in 1858 and soon after entered the religious community of the Poor Clares.[18] She published numerous works of Irish history, religious biography and religious life. It is worth noting that one of Cusack's writings on religious life, *The Spouse of Christ*, was published in 1878, the same year as her translation from Tronson. Sister Mary Francis Clare is known to have had a strong connection with French Catholicism, particularly with the ultramontane journalist Louis Veuillot.[19]

History and religious biography

As regards more historically oriented texts, special mention must be made of a popular translation titled *The Martyrs of Castelfidardo* (*c*. 1881, *c*. 1883, 1886, 1895), translated from the French of 'A. de Ségur' by 'a member of the Presentation Convent, Lixnaw, Co. Kerry'. It relates the story of those who fought and died to defend the Papal States in 1860, and reflects the then prevalent concern among the Irish Catholic community for the papacy's temporal power.[20] The various editions of this book were published by M. H. Gill and Son. A copy held at the Central Catholic Library, Dublin bears the stamp of the Carmelite Monastery, Stillorgan, and another copy comes from the Pollard Collection at Trinity College Dublin. This suggests that the translation may have had quite a broad readership which included younger readers.

Religious biography and hagiography were popular themes in translation from French at the time. One typical example is the *Life of the Ven. Father Perboyre, Priest of the Congregation of the Mission* (1875), from the French of an unknown author. Apart from their historical or anecdotal interest, such works were often produced and appraised for their edifying potential. This life of Perboyre was translated by 'a Sister of Mercy'. Along with the Ursulines, the Order of Mercy played a considerable role in the area of religious translation. Moreover, thanks to their publications, the Sisters of Mercy provide us with some rare insight into the mindset of women religious translators at the time. It is to them, therefore, that special attention is here called.

A significant contribution to translation: the Sisters of Mercy

Originally intended as a lay charitable institution, the House of Mercy at Baggot Street, Dublin, which was founded by Catherine McAuley in 1828, soon became a religious congregation.[21] Several branches were subsequently created around the country as well as abroad. *A Series of Exhortations on the Nature and Duties of the Religious Life* was translated by 'a member of the Order of Mercy, Cork' and published in 1843 by Belfast and London-based publishers Simms and McIntyre. In *Leaves from the Annals of the Sisters of Mercy*, Sister Mary Teresa Austin Carroll notes that the translator of this work was Sister Mary Vincent Deasy (18??–78), and that she was of 'a highly cultured family' from County Cork.[22] Sister Mary Vincent was a founding member of the Convent of Mercy in Cork in 1837.[23] She was also the translator of *The Perfect Religious: A Work Particularly Conducive to Arouse the Tepid, to Animate the Fervent, and to Attract the More Advanced in the Perfection of Their Holy State* (1845) by Michel-Ange Marin. This translation was 'published and sold at the Depository of St Mary's Asylum, 23, Essex-Quay, Dublin', and the profits of the sales were donated to that institution, then situated in the Drumcondra area.

Translation appears to have been a meaningful activity among the Order of Mercy. According to Carroll, Mother McAuley

> gave much encouragement to the literary tastes of her children, and the amount of translating, transcribing, and composing done by the earlier members was something marvellous when viewed in connection with their other labours. In this way much of the spiritual reading of the first houses was supplied.[24]

Sister Mary Teresa Austin Carroll knew well about the importance of translation in the life of the religious community in nineteenth-century Ireland, as she herself was actively involved in the production of translations. She was born Margaret Anna Carroll in 1835 in County Tipperary. She received the habit of the Sisters of Mercy in 1854, and from 1856 onwards, she was assigned to various convents in North America, where she died in 1909.[25] Lunney notes that Carroll was a prolific writer, editor and translator. Her literary and charitable contributions earned her special recognition in New Orleans, Louisiana.

The titles of Carroll's works are clearly evocative of the main translation trends for women religious at the time. From Revd Jean-Baptiste de Saint Jure, SJ, she translated *A Treatise on the Knowledge and Love of Our Lord Jesus Christ, with an Original Sketch of the Author* (1875), *The Spiritual Man; or, The Spiritual Life Reduced to Its First Principles* (1878) and *The Religious: A Treatise on the Vows and Virtues of the Religious State* (1882).[26] She was also the translator of *History of Blessed Margaret Mary, a Religious of the Visitation of St Mary; and of the Devotion to the Heart of Jesus* (1867) from another Jesuit father, Revd Charles Daniel. Based on various paratextual elements, it is however quite possible that some of these translations were collaborative works, principally based in North American convents.

Women religious and translation: a necessity

In reading the few valuable commentaries on translation left to us by nineteenth-century Irish women religious, one cannot fail to be struck by the importance they accorded to this activity. Often regretting the scarcity of appropriate Catholic works in the English language, they were concerned with providing Irish, as well as British and American, Catholics with a larger and more pertinent choice of writings.

In this regard, the anonymous translator of Leguay's work provides us with the most eloquent commentary. Referring to herself as an Irish *religieuse*, she is concerned that 'The religieuses of Ireland' do not have sufficient leisure to study 'the voluminous treatises that have been written on the subject of religious perfection'.[27] She metaphorically presents translation as a way to free a text, to bring it out of some dark recess, and even to bestow life upon it.

> Most of these productions, too, *locked up* as they are in a foreign tongue, are inaccessible to the greater number of those who, in our country, embrace this state of life. Nor has much been done until recently to place these works within the reach of the many by the medium of translation.... the 'Mystic of God', of Sister Mary of Jesus of Agreda, is still *entombed* in its Spanish original, or has been but partially *revived* the other day in a garbled French version.[28]

'No translation' therefore means death from this perspective. The translator is deeply aware of the necessity of translation, not only for its direct vital and remedial effect, but also for the impact it can have on a literary system:

> The translator deems, accordingly, that in giving an English version of this work to the light, she is conferring a boon upon those who, like herself, have embraced the holy state of religion. It may also lead to the republication amongst us of works of a still higher and more ascetical character.[29]

The translator is hereby stressing the importance of her role ('a boon') and believes in the cultural impact of translation, that is, its potential for stimulating further literary and publishing activity.

Similarly, Sister Austin Carroll highlights the crucial role played by translation in the development of a spiritual literature in the English language in the nineteenth-century:

> There were few spiritual books in English fifty years ago, and if they had not been supplemented by translations the Sisters who could read only one language would have had but little variety of spiritual reading for the instruction and recreation of their minds.[30]

She notes that in this way the Sisters of Mercy supplied the community with numerous works, 'chiefly educational, catechetical, ascetic, and biographical', including:

> translations of several useful works from the French, German, Spanish, and Italian languages; lives of saints and other holy persons; story-books for children, etc; historical dramas for schools etc; simple dialogues for little girls, etc. – almost all of which are found invaluable in convents and schools, as well as in many pious families. In French-speaking districts the Sisters of Mercy have published some useful works in French, and translated several from English, etc., into that language.[31]

The Sisters' impact through translation was therefore not confined to Ireland. Owing to the transnational nature of many congregations, women religious played an active part in a growing cross-cultural network of religious and literary exchanges. Translation was an essential part of their lives.

Women religious in translation: anonymity, chastity, simplicity (near) anonymity and (near) invisibility

This survey of translation titles clearly illustrates that female religious were often anonymous – and perhaps more accurately 'near anonymous' – on the title-page. In other words, they often signed their works not as distinctively named individuals, but as members of their groups. This was not necessarily exclusive to female religious. Indeed, similar patterns are noticeable in writings by the Irish Christian Brothers and other male religious. Only very occasionally, religious translators such as Margaret Cusack were fully identified. Overall, translation by women religious provides us with the most consistent pattern of near anonymity, that is, translation by 'a member of' a religious order. The group is clearly named but not the person herself. Her work reflects the aspirations of her community. Mutual interdependence within a community, religious selflessness and forgoing of private ownership meant that women religious were inclined to write and translate as members of that community because that is exactly what they aspired to be, rather than sign as the individuals they were before making their profession. It is therefore not necessarily a question of concealment, mask or prudence, as it may be in other areas of translation such as politics, poetry or fiction, but rather a question of vocation.

Yet, anonymity or near anonymity may also be considered as a contributing factor to, or a sign of, translators' invisibility. Although the complex notion of translators' invisibility cannot be discussed here owing to space constraints, a correlation may be established between translation and women by invoking the position of female translators and of women religious in the nineteenth-century.[32] While the invisible status of translators, male and female, has often been highlighted by translation scholars, women translators in the nineteenth-century were often in a situation of double invisibility. One way of looking at this pattern is by referring to the historical association between 'women' and 'translation', namely, the idea that women and translations were traditionally seen as subordinate and derivative.[33] Women were not allowed to access academic realms, nor any religious or political hierarchy.[34] With regard to the position of women in the world of letters, translation generally appears to have been one of the few areas where women's participation was more socially approved.[35] Similarly, outside marriage, convent life was one of the few situations deemed respectable for a woman in nineteenth-century Ireland, at least amongst the middle classes.[36] In effect, women translators were largely excluded from classical translation, and generally underrepresented in scientific, scholarly and political areas. Nuns, as Clear argues, were kept in a subordinate position within the Catholic Church,[37] and ultimately, women religious have often been overlooked in historical narratives and discussions of cultural and social change.[38]

Chastity and simplicity

Commentaries left by Irish women religious on their approach to texts and translation are unfortunately rare, but judging from what is extant, there appears to be an emphasis on ideas of simplicity, sobriety and chastity. Issues of 'fidelity' form another interesting thread, which cannot, however, be addressed here. It is not necessarily unrelated either.

According to Sister Austin Carroll, 'the elegant French of Monsieur Asselin' is rendered by Sister Mary Vincent Deasy into 'clear, concise, and vigorous English', and her translation displays a certain 'chaste beauty'.[39] In her preface to *The Religious: A Treatise on the Vows and Virtues of the Religious State*, Carroll observes that 'florid expressions and beautifully rounded periods have not been our aim, but simply the earnest, matter-of-fact, and even quaint diction of the author'.[40] Accordingly, she 'curtailed redundancy' and omitted 'what was exuberant'.[41] An introduction by the editor of the translation, who signs himself 'D. S. Phelan', provides the following motive for textual simplicity: 'simplicity of diction best comports with the dignity of the truths discussed'.[42] Contemporary reviews developed a similar type of discourse, pointing to the possibility of a dynamic interaction between the production and reception of translations. For example, the Catholic journal the *Irish Monthly* stressed that the incidents recorded in the *Life of the Ven. Father Perboyre* were set forth 'with a clearness and simplicity that lose nothing in the English version'.[43]

Notions of textual chastity and sobriety naturally fit in with the general religious observance and the vows of poverty and chastity. The modesty of the translation can be seen as a reflection of the simplicity and sobriety of the religious habit. Moreover, such an approach to translation seems to belong to a long Irish tradition of translating religious texts. Cronin notes that post-Reformation translation already promoted a plainness of 'dress', which was the true expression of 'a direct and honest relationship with God and the Word'.[44] In nineteenth-century translation, the text, in form and content, reflected the moral and religious aims of authors and translators, whose purpose was to foster piety and virtue, indeed religious renewal. Furthermore, in an era of evangelization,[45] and with a growing readership in English, it seemed important that the message should be simple and clear to reach a wider audience.

The democratic factor and the appeal to the masses on the one hand, and the introvert and spiritual factors on the other, were crucial to the Romantic period. The Romantic emphasis on 'plainness' and 'chastity' reflects a desire for the 'pure', the 'natural'. As Cronin observes, it refers to the essential meaning of a text, that which is 'immanent in the text itself'.[46] This, we argue, can be correlated, not only to much of the spiritual literature found in translation, but also to the increasingly powerful attachment to the concept of the Sacred Heart in nineteenth-century Ireland and France. Indeed, the Sacred Heart – the core element of Jesus, the unadorned heart of love, compassion and suffering – may be another expression of a Romantic move inwards towards the 'essential'. It is therefore no coincidence that in the preface to Miss Kennelly's translation from Grou, the editor includes the following quotation from her translation: 'Let the heart alone speak and let it express what it feels.'[47]

In her preface to *The Religious*, Carroll's greatest hope is that the instructions hereby translated 'would cause a greater diligence and assiduity in the care of religious perfection'.[48] Furthermore, we are told in the introduction that 'Prayer is the practice of perfection; spiritual reading is its theory.'[49] In religious translation, texts were therefore committed to the 'care' and 'cure' of souls. In the same above-cited passage, Revd David S. Phelan sums up eloquently the motives behind translation, and for what concerns us here: the mindset of women religious translators at the time. Referring to 'the wonderful and majestic pictures of spiritual grandeur' found in the original French text, he notes: 'We felt that to remove the veil of language that shut them off from the view of the English-speaking world were a service most acceptable to God and incalculably profitable to souls.'[50] By fostering personal and public piety through devotional and spiritual literature, devotions to the Sacred Heart and emulation of the Blessed Virgin, the practice of translation was used as a means to salvation and perfection.

Conclusion

This chapter has sought to present the untold story of Irish Catholic women religious who engaged in translation from French into English in the nineteenth-century. The topic naturally raises further questions, for which there may be no definite answers because those answers depend to a great extent on the existence and availability of relevant archival material. What were the conditions under which translations were produced in nineteenth-century convents? How was the entire translation process managed? Additionally, we may wonder what the interactions were between translation and composition in the life of religious writers such as Cusack or Carroll. Moreover, while the present study looks at published translation, another possible area of enquiry could involve non-published translations. We have thus far shed light on the prominent role played by the Ursulines and the Sisters of Mercy, and on the type of works they translated, but we still need to determine if translation was as popular an activity among the numerous congregations of French origin mentioned at the beginning of this chapter.

To conclude on the impact of Catholic women religious through translation, we should first pay brief attention to their direct legacy amongst children educated at convent schools. In other words, in addition to the dissemination of texts and ideas through translation, it may be suggested that women religious also passed on the tradition of translating texts to a number of their pupils. As French was one of the subjects taught in convent schools, it is very likely that the students practised translation as well. There were indeed past convent school students who in turn played a role in the production of translations. For instance, one Irish translator who emerged in nineteenth-century religious translation was a Mary Hackett, 'late a pupil of the Ursulines, St Mary's Convent, Waterford'. She translated several works from French, notably the popular *Life of St Elizabeth of Hungary, Duchess of Thuringia* (*c.* 1849, 1852, 1873) from Charles Forbes de Montalembert, one of the key figures of French liberal Catholicism in the nineteenth-century.

Furthermore, the publication of her translation offered Hackett a means of advocating religious freedom in Ireland, as she dedicated her work 'To the count de Montalembert, the illustrious champion of religion and liberty throughout the world', on 'behalf of the Irish People'.[51] James Duffy advertised it several times in the Irish nationalist organ the *Nation*, notably in February 1853 as part of his 'Valuable Catholic Publications Adapted for the Holy Season of Lent'. It was then reissued in North America by a leading Irish-American Catholic publishing house, D. and J. Sadlier. There were two other translations of Montalembert's *Elizabeth*, but for most of the nineteenth-century, Mary Hackett's version appears to have been the most common. There is a handwritten dedication on the copy held at the National Library of Ireland. Although it is barely legible today, it is suggested that the book was given to a Mary Elizabeth Archbold by a person called O'Brien, in the hope that the dedicatee would 'imitate the great St Elizabeth'.

Like most of the translations mentioned above, Hackett's *Elizabeth* received its own share of reviews, notably a very sympathetic one in the *Dublin Review* (1849). This leads us to the next point. While the issue of invisibility is crucial to our understanding of translation and of women religious translators, we should however note that translation and translators were not always invisible. If translations were discussed in the public sphere, they must have carried significance for critics and readers. By their very existence, commentaries and reviews brought translation to the fore and recognized its importance, even in cases where little attention was paid to the person of the translator. While on the one hand we needed to draw attention to the self-effacing nature of translators – particularly women religious translators – on the other hand, and to use Clear's words when she pointed to the selfless commitment of nineteenth-century nuns, we may argue that we should not 'dismiss as valueless the "invisible" ' work which they performed.[52] Furthermore, as a result of their close connection with European languages, principally French, religious women translators in nineteenth-century Ireland were thereby able to develop a translation tradition of close contact with wider European trends and spiritualities.

Trends in religious translation indicate that from the 1840s onwards, a religious impulse was being felt in Ireland, illustrated by an increase in the translation and publication of Catholic works in the second half of the century.[53] Translation served as a means to disseminate religious writings, notably Catholic devotional literature and spiritualities, as well as texts specifically intended for religious communities. Translation was therefore viewed as a means to increase piety and enhance spiritual life. Moreover, in the area of Catholic literature, we can safely suggest that the most effectual trends in translation from French were those which promoted devotions and dogmatic statements that were, above all, in direct line with Roman practices and post-Tridentine doctrine. The rising tide of devotional literature helped strengthen the link with Rome and contributed to the 'Irish counter-reformation' and the Catholic 'devotional revolution'.[54] The link with the Holy See was carefully nurtured by the promotion of dogmas and devotions along Roman lines. For example, on the devotional side, there was an increasingly lively interest in Marian and Sacred Heart devotions over the course of the nineteenth-century. For a great part of the century, French-language literature was the main source for translation of this type of devotional writing, and many of these devotional texts were engagingly translated and published in Ireland. In addition, Irish translators and publishers based outside Ireland, particularly in England and North America, played a crucial role. There was a lively trade in books between these various locations, and religious orders often maintained cross-national contact. Irish women religious such as Sister Austin Carroll, who were based in Britain and America, contributed to the spread and strengthening of that network.

These members of religious communities, anonymous or not, have been a driving force in translation and beyond. We need to acknowledge the role played by female religious in nineteenth-century Ireland, because, as Magray argues, they may have been considered as less influential than the clergy, and presented as products of the Catholic cultural revolution in Ireland rather than as agents in that process.[55] For Magray, women's religious orders were at the centre of the creation of a devout Catholic culture in nineteenth-century Ireland. This was not an isolated endeavour, and their role has to be viewed within a network of various activities, people and institutions: 'Together with reform-minded friends and relatives – among them priests, bishops, and laypeople alike – they developed a new form of women's religious activism that proved to be a very effective method of bringing post-Tridentine Catholicism to Ireland.'[56] It is accordingly significant that some of the translations mentioned above were endorsed by the Catholic hierarchy, bearing letters of approval or prefaces from such eminent figures as Archbishop Croke. They were also published by the best-established Catholic publishers in Ireland and abroad, and advertised in well known periodicals.

Women religious were therefore instrumental in strengthening the link between Ireland and Roman Catholicism. As they became more numerous and engaged in social activity in nineteenth-century Ireland, women religious succeeded in reaching out into Irish society in various ways. Indeed, Clear points out that 'with their schools, hospitals, workhouses, sick-visiting and many other projects female religious were, without doubt, the most effective arm of the Catholic church in nineteenth-century Ireland'.[57] Translators' prefatory remarks often stress that translation into English was a way of widening the readership of Roman Catholic writings. Seen in this light, translation and other literary endeavours should be included as one of the means by which female religious helped bring post-Tridentine Catholicism to Ireland.

As the work done by women religious needed to be placed within the wider religious and cultural changes occurring in Irish society, so does translation need to be situated within this same context. Moreover, as we have seen with some of the aforementioned titles and quotes, women religious were instrumental in providing their communities with a literature that was relevant to their vocation.

It is hoped that this chapter has now added another dimension to the term 'transforming power', which Magray used in the title of her study of Irish nuns. From both a historical and socio-cultural point of view, women religious have had a special relationship with translation. The intercultural element is fundamental to the history of women religious in general. The in-betweenness, and connective and transformative nature of translation form an integral part of their cultural and spiritual makeup. In the nineteenth-century, Irish women religious contributed to the growth of a Catholic literature in English by translating French-language texts, thereby constructing intercultural bridges. Translation, it appears, was also crucial in pursuing their path to perfection.

Notes

1 See Michèle Milan, 'Found in Translation: Franco-Irish Translation Relationships in Nineteenth-Century Ireland' (Ph.D. thesis, Dublin City University, 2013), http://doras.dcu.ie/17753/. The body of data used for the survey includes books as well as nineteenth-century periodicals and catalogues.
2 Caitríona Clear, *Nuns in Nineteenth-Century Ireland* (Dublin: Gill and Macmillan, 1987), 53.
3 Tony Fahey, 'Nuns in the Catholic Church in Ireland in the Nineteenth Century', in Mary Cullen (ed.), *Girls Don't Do Honours: Irish Women in Education in the Nineteenth and Twentieth Centuries* (Dublin: WEB Press, 1987), 7–30 (7–8).
4 Robert Tombs, *France 1814–1914* (London and New York: Longman, 1996), 135, 241–8.
5 As regards translation of contemporary Catholic writers, the Bavarian author Christoph von Schmid (1768–1854) merits a mention here for the popularity of his stories in translation from German.
6 These details were gathered from various works, such as Clear, *Nuns in Nineteenth-Century Ireland*; and Anne V. O'Connor, 'The Revolution in Girls' Secondary Education in Ireland 1860–1910', in Cullen, *Girls Don't Do Honours*, 31–54. There is no existing study focussing on that particular aspect of Franco-Irish history. It still needs to be written.
7 Clear, *Nuns in Nineteenth-Century Ireland*, 102.
8 O'Connor, 'The Revolution in Girls' Secondary Education', 38.
9 Máire Kennedy, *French Books in Eighteenth-Century Ireland* (Oxford: Voltaire Foundation, 2001), 23–35.
10 Michael Cronin, *Translating Ireland: Translation, Languages, Cultures* (Cork: Cork University Press, 1996); Niall Ó Ciosáin, *Print and Popular Culture in Ireland, 1750–1850* (New York: St Martin's Press, 1997), 6, 41, 154, 190.
11 Mary P. Magray, *The Transforming Power of the Nuns: Women, Religion, and Cultural Change in Ireland, 1750–1900* (New York and Oxford: Oxford University Press, 1998).

12 The dates shown beside translation titles in this chapter are those of the copies consulted for this study, either in the library holdings or from online repositories. They may not correspond to the first date of publication.
13 Charles J. Moell, 'Sacred Heart, Devotion to', in *New Catholic Encyclopedia* (New York: McGraw-Hill, 1967), 818–20.
14 Catherine Lawless, 'Devotion and Representation in Nineteenth-Century Ireland', in Ciara Breathnach and Catherine Lawless (eds),*Visual, Material and Print Culture in Nineteenth-Century Ireland* (Dublin: Four Courts Press, 2010), 95.
15 Ibid., 93.
16 Ibid., 92.
17 Sinéad Sturgeon, 'Young, Mary Ursula', in James McGuire and James Quinn (eds), in *Dictionary of Irish Biography: From the Earliest Times to the Year 2002*, 9 vols (Cambridge: Cambridge University Press, 2009), Vol. IX, 1109.
18 Patrick Maume, 'Cusack, Margaret Anna ("The Nun of Kenmare")', in McGuire and Quinn, *Dictionary of Irish Biography*, Vol. II, 1131–4.
19 Ibid., 1133.
20 On pro-papal sentiment among Irish Catholics at the time, see for example Danilo Raponi, *Religion and Politics in the Risorgimento: Britain and the New Italy, 1861–1875* (New York: Palgrave Macmillan, 2014), 115.
21 Caitríona Clear, 'The Re-Emergence of Nuns and Convents, 1800–1962', in Angela Bourke, Seamus Deane and Andrew Carpenter (eds), *The Field Day Anthology of Irish Writing*, 5 vols, Vol. IV, *Irish Women's Writing and Traditions* (Cork: Cork University Press, 2002), 523.
22 Margaret A. Carroll, *Leaves from the Annals of the Sisters of Mercy* (New York: Catholic Publication Society, 1881), 240.
23 Mary C. Sullivan, *The Correspondence of Catherine McAuley, 1818–1841* (Dublin: Four Courts Press, 2004), 85n.
24 Carroll, *Leaves from the Annals*, 241.
25 Sheila Lunney, 'Carroll, Margaret Anna (Sister Mary Teresa Austin)', in McGuire and Quinn, *Dictionary of Irish Biography*, Vol. II, 373–4.
26 She may also have been the translator of the above-mentioned *Devotions to the Sacred Heart*.
27 Anon. (trans.), *The Path of Perfection in Religious Life: A Work Intended for Persons Consecrated to God* (Dublin: James Duffy, 1862), vii.
28 Ibid. (my emphases).
29 Ibid., viii.
30 Carroll, *Leaves from the Annals*, 241.
31 Ibid., 241n–242n.
32 See for instance Lawrence Venuti, *The Translator's Invisibility: A History of Translation* (London and New York: Routledge, 1995); Rosemary Arrojo, 'The "Death" of the Author and the Limits of the Translator's Visibility', in Mary Snell-Hornby, Zuzana Jettmarová and Klaus Kaindl (eds), *Translation as Intercultural Communication* (Amsterdam and Philadelphia: John Benjamins, 1995), 21–32.
33 Sherry Simon, *Gender in Translation: Cultural Identity and the Politics of Transmission* (London and New York: Routledge, 1996), 1, 39.
34 Mary Cullen, 'Introduction', in *Girls Don't Do Honours*, 1–2.
35 Sherry Simon, 'Gender in Translation', in Peter France (ed.), *The Oxford Guide to Literature in English Translation* (Oxford: Oxford University Press, 2001), 27.
36 Clear, *Nuns in Nineteenth-Century Ireland*, 155; Fahey, 'Nuns', 15.
37 Clear, *Nuns in Nineteenth-Century Ireland*, 154.

38 It is worth noting here that while attending the conference from which these proceedings derive, it struck me how widespread the discourse on the 'invisibility' of women religious was. Coming from the field of translation history, this sounded like a very familiar discourse indeed.
39 Carroll, *Leaves from the Annals*, 240.
40 Jean-Baptiste Saint-Jure, *The Religious: A Treatise on the Vows and Virtues of the Religious State*, trans. Margaret A. Carroll (New York: P. O'Shea, 1882), ix. The translation is sometimes presented as the result of teamwork. Although Carroll is here credited for writing these words, we should bear in mind that there may have been several hands on the pen.
41 Ibid., ix.
42 Revd David S. Phelan, 'Introduction', in Saint-Jure, *The Religious*, xiii.
43 'New Books', *Irish Monthly*, 3 (1875), 177, http://www.jstor.org/stable/20501592 (accessed 12 February 2015).
44 Cronin, *Translating Ireland*, 72. In the nineteenth century, the 'dress' metaphor was commonly used in reference to language and translation.
45 Clear, *Nuns in Nineteenth-Century Ireland*, 53, 103.
46 Cronin, *Translating Ireland*, 74.
47 Jean-Nicolas Grou, quoted in Samuel H. Frisbee, 'The Editor to the Reader', in Jean-Nicolas Grou, *The Interior of Jesus and Mary*, trans. 'Miss Kennelly' (New York, Cincinnati and Chicago: Benziger Brothers, 1893), x.
48 Carroll, in Saint-Jure, *The Religious*, ix.
49 David S. Phelan, 'Introduction', xii.
50 Ibid., xi.
51 Mary Hackett 'Dedication', in Charles Forbes de Montalembert, *Life of St Elizabeth of Hungary, Duchess of Thuringia*, trans. Mary Hackett (Dublin: James Duffy, 1848), iv.
52 Clear, *Nuns in Nineteenth-Century Ireland*, 166.
53 See also Milan, 'Found in Translation'.
54 On these topics, see for example James H. Murphy, 'The Role of Vincentian Parish Missions in the "Irish Counter-Reformation" of the Mid Nineteenth Century', *Irish Historical Studies*, 94 (1984): 152–71; Emmet Larkin, *The Historical Dimensions of Irish Catholicism* (Dublin: Four Courts Press, 1997).
55 Magray, *The Transforming Power of the Nuns*, vii–viii.
56 Ibid., vii.
57 Clear, *Nuns in Nineteenth-Century Ireland*, 517.

Chapter 11

Loreto education in Australia
The pioneering influence of Mother Gonzaga Barry

Jane Kelly

Introduction

In December 1914, several Mothers Superior of Loreto[1] houses gathered in Loreto Abbey Mary's Mount in Ballarat. They gathered in the spirit of farewell to their Provincial Superior, Mother Gonzaga Barry, in whom they had placed their trust for over forty years and who was now edging closer to death. Gonzaga Barry was too weak for lengthy speech, so she wrote them a letter. It ranged over many things, dwelling on what was most significant to the writer at least:

> I take this opportunity, my dear Mothers, of expressing to you my heartfelt gratitude and affection for all your loyal and loving co-operation with me in any work I set before you to do for the good of our dear Institute; it is very little I could have done, only for your prompt, unhesitating obedience, and zealous efforts in the cause of God.[2]

In a few words we have a pen portrait of a remarkable religious leader, who had inspired confidence in her followers but who did not presume on that confidence. Barry knew from long experience that if any undertaking was to thrive it could best do so in the spirit of collaboration and trust; that alone, even with the best intent and motivation in God, the achievement of any one individual could not match what might be achieved by the group. Not insignificantly, though 81 years old and knowing she was dying, Barry took the time to put into writing her gratitude. Who was Gonzaga Barry, and what was this 'success' of which she wrote? This chapter examines Barry's achievements in Australia, on behalf of the Loreto Order.

Chosen to lead: Gonzaga Barry and Ireland

Gonzaga Barry was the leader of the first group of Loreto Sisters (Institute of the Blessed Virgin Mary, hereafter IBVM) to come to Australia in 1875.[3] Over a period of forty years, she would oversee the establishment of twenty-one foundations, communities and schools; two kindergartens; and two teachers' colleges, fanning out over the southern reaches of the continent. In a land in its early stages of European development and bearing with it still the ambiguities of its settlement from convict origin to land of opportunity, Barry emerges as a woman with a vision, and the educational achievement of her lifetime was underpinned at every level by her faith and religious commitment.

The Loreto Sisters came to Australia from Ireland in response to a request from the newly appointed bishop of Ballarat, Dr Michael O'Connor, whose invitation focussed clearly on the needs of the fledgling Ballarat diocese.[4] The order, though inspired by the late-seventeenth-century foundation in York (the Bar Convent), was barely 50 years old in Ireland,[5] yet it managed to respond to O'Connor's request. Michael O'Connor had arrived in Melbourne on 18 December 1874, a passenger of a ship named the *Ceylon*. It was to this same vessel twelve days later, on its departure from the port of Melbourne, that he entrusted a letter addressed to Mother Scholastica Somers, the Superior of Loreto Rathfarnham, Dublin, in which he made a request for Sisters to be sent to Australia to establish a convent which 'would in every way be a great success ... I would say that eight sisters in all would be required'.[6] O'Connor acknowledged that the order was well known 'as the nuns that educate the higher classes', and he expected that a Loreto school in Ballarat would thrive. Mother Scholastica Somers agreed to the request, and selected Mother Gonzaga Barry to lead the group, plucking her from a Loreto community in Enniscorthy, County Wexford.

Mother Gonzaga Barry had been born Mary Barry, on 24 July 1834. She was always called 'Mamie' by her family and was the eldest of seven children. Her father's appointment as the first manager of the Enniscorthy branch of the National Bank in Ireland afforded opportunities for his family's home schooling in the early years. Mary's formal education began as a boarder at Loreto in Gorey in 1846, followed by a comparatively brief time at Loreto Rathfarnham. Although she suffered a period of ill health, in August 1853 she joined the novitiate of Loreto Gorey and was given the name Aloysius Gonzaga. Within a short period the newly professed Gonzaga Barry held various positions of responsibility. At twenty-five, she was given charge of novices and then became Superior of the Gorey community. A few years later, she was sent as founding Superior of a new foundation in Enniscorthy, thirty miles from the Gorey house. It was there she received the invitation from Mother Scholastica Somers to consider seriously a call to lead the Ballarat mission. While she had been briefly in school as a child in Rathfarnham – at a time when the founding Superior, Teresa Ball, was still in charge – and would have witnessed the missioning of nuns to foreign parts, Barry's origins were grounded in Wexford, and in all probability it was the area in which she imagined living out her religious life. At 40 years of age, tiny in stature, of indifferent health and with her hearing failing, Barry hadn't volunteered to go anywhere. Subsequent correspondence with Thomas Furlong, bishop of Ferns and trusted mentor, suggests her disinclination for the role, while her retreat notes indicate her reluctance for the task:

> I feel that in going to this mission in Australia as if God gave me the grace to die, as it were, TWICE. For I am, as it seems to me, passing away out of this world into another. I think it will be Purgatory ...[7]

However, Barry acceded to her Superior's request, and within a month eight professed Sisters and three companions – two intended for the Ballarat novitiate and one other for whom the bishop had made provision – left Rathfarnham. Mother Gonzaga Barry's travel journal poignantly records the start of the journey, as the group departed the convent at daybreak on 20 May 1875.[8] Her companions wept, but Barry resolved: 'My hands are in God's hands. He can lead me where He wills.'[9]

The pioneering community accompanying her included Gertrude Quinn, aged 57, the eldest of the group, a musician and in very poor health. The next in age was Barry; then Aloysius (Mary) Macken, born near Dublin and 35 years old. Sister Bruno (Ellen) McCabe, a lay Sister from County Longford, was 31; Boniface (Antonia) Volker, born in Münster, who, having trained as a teacher in Cologne, had entered the Rathfarnham novitiate in 1866 aged 18, was 28 when she left for Ballarat. Xavier (Brigid) Yourell, born in Dublin, had entered Rathfarnham in 1865 at age 16 and was 26 when embarking for Ballarat. Dorothea (Katherine) Frizelle was 23 years old, and Berchmans (Anna) Stafford was 24. The two aspiring to enter the novitiate, Helen Hughes (later to become Sister Margaret Mary Hughes) and her companion, Margaret O'Brien (Sister Joseph O'Brien – a lay Sister) were 18 and 19 respectively. The only one with any formal teacher training was Boniface Volker. If they faced a formidable task they did so, from the beginning, as a community, each one aware of the trust placed in her personally for the success of the enterprise.

Loreto in Australia: the beginnings

Nineteenth-century Australia was a colonial society with burgeoning cities and centres of population at vast distances one from another, lit by gaslight and served by rudimentary sanitation; while local transport was by horse and cab, distances relied on locally constructed railways, in most cases and according to colonial rescript on gauges differing one from another across the country. For the more distant colonies the only alternative was a ship's voyage. Wherever the community were asked to go, it fell to their leader to make the necessary negotiations with local authorities, ecclesiastical and secular: with land agents in matters of buying and selling; with builders, architects and banks.

As an institute that did not formally come under the jurisdiction of the bishops, ties with Ireland were also important, and just as no presumption would be made about moving either in or out of a diocese without the courtesy of maintaining personal and professional communications with bishops and parish priests, it was also incumbent upon the leader to ensure Superiors in Ireland remained informed, updated and in accord with decisions made. All communication was by letter, and early letters home were full of news. Descriptions of train journeys and Ballarat with its fine main thoroughfares and buildings; of gold diggings, the sounds of quartz grinding, day and night; of fruit trees, black swans and blue gums; of crowds of visitors who would travel up to ten miles to the presbytery of St Alipius where the community were staying, 'just to see a nun'; of orchards and laughing jackasses; of meals and champagne; centipedes, snakes and domestic pets.[10]

The nuns took possession of their own property in Ballarat, later to be called 'Loreto Abbey Mary's Mount', on 23 September 1875. On 29 September, the school opened with seven pupils and seven nuns on the staff: the first Catholic convent school in the city. On the same day the novitiate opened with the formal admission of the two young women who had travelled with the community. Before year's end more pupils arrived. By the end of 1875 there was, in Loreto Abbey, a day and boarding school, the eight members of community now being accompanied by two novices and there was a day school a mile or so distant, in Dawson Street, for local Ballarat children. In 1877, Barry took over the administration of the local parish primary school, St Joseph's. Gonzaga Barry had a clearly expressed wish that wherever there was a Loreto fee-paying school, there should always be a school entirely free of charge.[11]

Matters domestic and educational

A letter to Rathfarnham on 28 December 1875 offers a glimpse of the first Christmas:

> Our first Mass was 6.30 a.m. The day was remarkably cool, almost cold in the morning; we had our little Crib, a very pretty one, and made up our minds not to read our letters until the next day lest the remembrance of our loved ones so far away might be too much for us individually and collectively. I gave all the dear Sisters their letters, amounting to 74 ... and they spent a happy Xmas thank God. The Bishop sent us some wine and champagne to make us merry ...[12]

Now housed and 'on mission' by early 1876, practicalities of schooling started to emerge. A fragment of correspondence illustrates a situation where help might be needed:

> The children here are wonderful at Arithmetic & Morell's Analysis both of which subjects sorely puzzle our poor Srs M. Berchmans and

Dorothea (who) study for hours at sums & often cannot make them out. Sr M. Gertrude who was thought so clever at Arithmetic is not as good as either of them and can give them no help.[13]

Early requests for assistance were on a domestic scale. Educational needs were immediate and Barry was not slow to make a direct approach – whatever the cost to the mother-house. The bishop seemed also to be having his say, indicating a desire that Mother Hilda Benson should come out to manage the school. Mother Hilda Benson was English, from Yorkshire and a convert of Catholicism. She was also a graduate of one of the only teacher training colleges in England – the Notre Dame Teaching College in Liverpool. In 1876 she had charge of the school in Rathfarnham. This was a tall order. Not knowing her well personally, Barry was guided not only by the bishop, but by the judgement of her community on the matter: 'the sisters all say Sr Hilda would get on with all in the Community here, and it would be a sad mistake for anyone who would not, or could not, to come to Australia'. From the beginning there was a sense of the balancing act: professional needs to be considered, but always within the context of the well-being of the community.

In the same letter she put in a request for another – this time, from her own community experience in Gorey and Enniscorthy:

> The Second Sister I would beg of you to Consider about sending is Sr de Sales Field ... she is strong, a good head, particularly for Arithmetic and Grammar, hands that can turn almost to anything, her friends are thinking she should come & the Srs here are nearly all anxious she should come and I know from seven years' experience of her that she will never wish for anything but constant HARD WORK.[14]

Both Sisters Hilda and de Sales were sent from Rathfarnham, arriving in November 1876 with one or two others. This trend of requesting assistance through the kind offices of the Mother-House was one that continued and was actively pursued by Barry throughout her life. By August 1876 she noted that vocations were already 'springing up amongst the Boarders';[15] the first Australian-born novice was admitted to the Novitiate in May 1878.[16]

In May 1879 another letter rendered quite an account:

> Music, Singing, Sacred & Secular, Drawing, Painting, Printing. There is a splendid staff here D.G. & you all! of [sic] Arithmeticians, Geographers, Historians, Grammarians, but not very well up on Analysis of difficult Poetry, here all the rage, General Knowledge, Literature etc. very good. Languages ditto. S. M. de Sales is our best at Globes or Astronomy, she has not time for the Boarders & this is also a weak point with us, but the Music & Singing wd be more for AMDG than anything. It was wretched to be depending on one & that one not too amiable. Mgt Mary is a

second self in this department. It is not good for the child & she is so weakly she can seldom play our Harmonium. M. Kilian (recent arrival from Ireland) was a great God send to divide the Music Pupils, but she only gets beginners. Dear M. Xavier's voice is grand in the choir, but she is so wanting in courage or self-confidence even to play an accompaniment on the Piano for her Pupils that all the good singers, concert songs etc. are taught by S. M. Gertrude, who with little or no voice has so much energy that she gets them on well, when once wound up to it herself ... M. M. Aloysius' voice is beautifully sweet but she is no Musician.

I often feel inclined to say with dear Dr Furlong R.I.P. 'Ah Plague on it for Music'! It causes more trouble than all the other branches of Education put together.[17]

Within the first ten years of their arrival in Victoria three communities within the diocese of Ballarat served seven foundations: the boarding school at Loreto Abbey, a day school at Loreto Dawson Street and two parish schools within reasonably close proximity, a boarding school at Portland approximately 200 miles distant but within the diocese, and a parish school in Portland. A more daring initiative in Ballarat itself had been to establish a 'Catholic Teachers' Training College', the aim of which, as stated in its prospectus, was 'to supply efficient Teachers for Catholic Schools by training young girls who intend to adopt teaching as a profession'.[18] Its director was Mother Hilda Benson. Years later in a talk given at the college, Mother Hilda was to comment on this initiative. She quotes a prominent educationist of the day:

'What is the highest, the most profound, the most general, the most simple conception of education? It is this. To cultivate, to train, to develop, to strengthen and to polish all the physical, intellectual, moral and religious faculties which constitute nature and human dignity in the child. Education is culture and exercise, instruction and study. The teacher cultivates, instructs and labours outwardly, but it is essentially necessary that there should be exercise, application and labour within. In education what the teacher does himself is a trifling matter. What he causes to be done is everything. Whoever does not understand this understands nothing of the worth of human education.'[19]

Mother Hilda continued:

These words might have been those of Rev. Mother Gonzaga Barry, so often did she refer to them, so unvaryingly act according to their teaching. 'We will train our own teachers and make them at the same time thorough, conscientious and valiant women.'[20]

The training college commenced in January 1884. One month earlier, in December 1883, a most significant event had taken place at the University of Melbourne, significant enough to have been reported in a number of newspapers.

> The ceremonies of conferring University degrees were performed at the University by the Vice-Chancellor. Amongst those who received degrees of Bachelor of Arts was Bella Guerin of Ballarat, the first lady in the colony who has attained the honor. She was heartily cheered by the undergraduates and congratulated by the Vice-Chancellor.[21]

The following day there was another report:

> Smart Girl Graduates (Intercolonial Telegrams from one of our own Correspondents) Melbourne, Monday. Miss Bella Guerin, who has taken the first Ladies' Bachelor of Arts degree in the Melbourne University, has been appointed to one of the leading Ladies' Colleges.[22]

The 'leading Ladies' College' is believed to have been Loreto Abbey in Ballarat. To many observers this appointment of the first female graduate from any Australian university might have appeared a risk. And this one was not backward in positioning herself in the public arena even as a young graduand, posting articles and letters in the press, becoming more prolific over time in supporting socialist and feminist causes. In the context of Loreto Ballarat, however, she appeared as the inaugural editor of the school magazine publication, *Eucalyptus Blossoms*. She put her name to the first editorial, offering her critique of 'Loreto education' as well as her own take on her employer:

> Both mind and heart can be thoroughly cultivated only by our own cooperation with the means so generously placed at our disposal by the religious of Loreto. We may be well educated, gracefully accomplished, and altogether very nice girls, but we will never realise the ideal of a Catholic heroine unless we cultivate abstract thought and thoroughness. Much is being done at present by the gentle lady who rules the fast-increasing commonwealth of Loreto to develop and encourage amongst those committed to her care that true mental culture to which we have before alluded. Owing to her liberal and energetic action, Loreto has the means of enabling her children to shew what Catholic girls in a Catholic Convent can do .... We must earnestly trust that many years will be added to the holy, useful life of the dearly-loved foundress of the Institute of the Blessed Virgin in Australia. We are debarred, by her own special desire, from saying all that we could truthfully express respecting our dear Reverend Mother, but we leave her with proud confidence for future times to appreciate and praise.[23]

Eucalyptus Blossoms became a feature of Loreto Mary's Mount for forty years. It offered a forum for students and teaching members of the community, while providing a vehicle whereby the philosophy of a Loreto education in Australia could be expounded as the publication itself started to reach an ever-widening audience of schools Australia-wide, and most importantly of former students and nuns, wherever they might have been sent, as well as a growing circle of families and friends. From the beginning it was printed on the school printing press. For Gonzaga Barry herself, from the mid 1880s until her death in early 1915, it offered a unique opportunity, first expressed in the second edition of the paper.

> Now, Deo Gratias, every six months as long as the power to wield a pen is given me, the Eucalyptus Blossoms will bring a letter to Loreto children from their old Mother: a 'talk' like those in days gone by, of things we were wont to prize, interests we had in common, ideas and sentiment we shared.[24]

The 'Mother's Letter' was given prominence in every edition. Within the paper itself children wrote, visitors wrote, as did former students. In December 1886, Bella Guerin made a second appearance with a long essay on 'Higher Education of Women' among other articles on topics as diverse as art, cooking classes, philology and views of Frankston bay. Three years on, in 1889, students reported on the introduction of an educational initiative within the Abbey, the 'Sloyd Room', its high educational purpose promulgated with pride:

> to implant a respect for work in general, even the coarser forms of manual labour and develop activity, order, cleanliness, neatness and accuracy. Our Sloyd room already contains a printing press, which has turned out some exceedingly good work, a washing machine, a cooking range, where our Domestic Economy class prepare all kinds of delicacies, a sewing machine etc.; and in the near future we are to have a class for wood carving, and another in fine art house painting and decoration under the supervision of competent artists, or should we rather say artisans?[25]

In 1890, the magazine provided a forum for Barry to expand on a philosophy of education that was to become a touchstone for Loreto schooling with her essay on 'A Sensible School for Girls', in which she argues for the education of the child 'according to the capabilities, talents, tastes and position in life which God has given her …. A school for all grades and classes, beginning its work in the infant school and ending in the university or domestic college'.[26] Two years later, in 1892, the professor of English at the University of Melbourne was invited to Mary's Mount to offer a series of university extension lectures. These initiatives are indicative of the philosophy of Loreto education envisaged by Barry. During her lifetime Loreto Abbey Mary's

Mount offered the blue-print for other foundations to copy, adapting to their circumstances.

Lucy Mooney, a student, also wrote for the December 1886 issue of *Eucalyptus Blossoms*. Hers was a theme that was to become familiar to readers as the magazine developed – that of internationality. Her letter, addressed to 'Children of Loreto all over the world' was full of ideas.

> This little paper 'Eucalyptus Blossoms', is edited by Loreto children in Australia. We would gladly leave a place in it for any descriptions of those of far off lands where you live, if you would kindly send us some. You, our European sisters, could tell us about England and other countries ... of Gibraltar. The children in German convents could practice English composition by writing essays for us, and we could improve our German by translating German letters ... descriptions of India ... America .... We have heard one of the Convents is situated near Niagara Falls ... Praetorians ... Loreto children .... It will be grand if this little Journal may help us to know each other and may become a bond of affectionate union between us, for Loreto children, or pupils of the Institute of the Blessed Virgin Mary, all over the world, are sisters.[27]

The first community of Loreto Sisters came from Ireland carrying with them a much broader heritage of which, at the time, they knew little. The first life of Mary Ward by Catherine Chambers was published in the early 1880s and, by her own admission, until this time Gonzaga Barry had little or no knowledge of the intimacy of connection between the foundation made in Rathfarnham in 1821 and the seventeenth-century Englishwoman, Mary Ward. The copy of the Mary Ward life was circulated within the growing number of Loreto houses in Australia. It was a measure of Barry's leadership that her enthusiasm for the book was caught by the Sisters, and passed on to the children. By the mid 1880s, inspired by Chambers' biography, Barry was ready to build on connections among those who shared Mary Ward's legacy. Lucy Mooney was asking for international stories. Able to appreciate the German connection and referring to the common ground of their foundations, Barry was much more daring. As a letter from Bavaria attests, she was asking for nuns. Whilst her original letter has not survived, the reply she received in mid 1886 reveals that it was written on her behalf by her German-born friend and first companion, Boniface Volker. In Nymphenburg, Gonzaga's request for nuns had struck a chord:

> Venerable & Venerated Superioress,
> Do not believe or imagine that any kind of indifference, is the cause of the long delay in answering the welcome letter of Mrs Volker, O No! I was very touched & edified by all that I heard of your blessed & zealous

labours in the Mission & rejoiced at the idea of a Closer Connection of your dear Convents with our houses. O how gladly wd I undertake an interchange of Subjects of the Institute for the advantage of both branches if it were possible for me to make it in anyway useful to you. But I think that Australia is a more fruitful soil for Religious Houses than our own which is becoming more & more barren. I am even obliged to close Schools for want of teaching members, therefore I can offer you nothing.[28]

Barry's personal correspondence was fired by her growing awareness of the importance of international networks, and this also found its way into the pages of *Eucalyptus Blossoms*. Successive editions mapped the expansion of Loreto convents and schools during Barry's forty years of leadership in the Australian province. By 1901, the last four pages offered brief accounts of Loreto Abbey Mary's Mount and the Convent of Our Lady of Loreto Dawson Street, incorporating the Catholic College for Teachers. They also listed the Melbourne Loreto Convent in Albert Park, while in Sydney there was the 'Boarding School for Young Ladies' at Hornsby, and 'Loreto Ladies' College & Preparatory School'. A further 2,000 miles away to the west, another two establishments had been founded: the Convent of Our Lady of Loreto Perth, and Loreto Convent Osborne, in Claremont. In each case, a courtesy note indicated that further information and terms were available by personal application 'to the Lady Superior'.

In 1905, *Eucalyptus Blossoms* included a page-long list of Loreto convents and schools including all of the above, to which Norwood in South Australia has been added. By 1906, there were two more convents: St Michael's in Hamilton (again in the Ballarat diocese) and, in Melbourne, the 'Central Catholic Teachers' Training College' in Albert Park, which Loreto had been asked to administer for the diocese and which was envisaged to include participants from all Australian states and New Zealand.

The extent of this movement across the Australian Continent was impressive. Public advertising through the agency of a school magazine with its increasing readership offered a public statement telling a successful story. With the dispersal of the community across such distances, challenges were faced by Barry, including the difficulties of communication and the dangers of demanding too much from her Sisters. The greater the distance between communities, the greater the challenge to preserve a sense of the whole.[29] There were also costs involved in expansion projects. Visitation books offer glimpses of what was involved in business and professional terms. In Portland, for instance, in 1908, there was concern over the 'considerable outlay' and a necessity to borrow 'from the Bank of Victoria £2,300', an overdraft at 5 percent.[30] The same year, nearly 800 miles away in the boarding school at Normanhurst, there was 'want of sleeping accommodation for the sisters, so few [had] cells'.[31]

Interactions with hierarchies and communities

By commitment, training and faith, Gonzaga Barry was a true daughter of the Church and loyal to its leadership. But from time to time her loyalty, even to the archbishop of Sydney, was tested. Patrick Moran, the Irish-born archbishop, was well acquainted with the Loreto Sisters in Rathfarnham. In 1885 he had written to the Superior of the Rathfarnham convent, to comment on his own Australian mission and how admirably suitable were the various orders of nuns in his diocese. Without making any request for nuns, he referred to Loreto in the colonies:

> From all the accounts which I have recd. it is certain that your good Community at Ballarat has proved a great success. It is a flourishing Diocese, the Sisters have the field clear to themselves in the matter of higher Education & the Bishop is quite in earnest in helping the devoted community. This is just as it should be, and I trust that the Sisters will every day become more flourishing in all their distributions.[32]

Two years later, in 1887, he was visiting Ireland, as was Barry at the time. In the full hearing of two communities, Archbishop Moran said that 'he would only take Nuns direct from Rathfarnham as central government did not answer in the colonies'. 'Just for that', commented Barry, 'he will never get them ....'.[33]

In 1889, Moran made a direct approach to Barry for nuns. In 1892, she obliged him by establishing a convent and school in Randwick, in the Sydney diocese. Uncharacteristically for Barry, she did not make the foundation in a property owned by the Loreto order; rather she established the convent in Aston Hall, a property owned by the archbishop. In early 1901, while in Perth, Barry received an unexpected letter from the Superior at Randwick, advising her that Moran had sold the property. Gonzaga's letter to Moran offers insight into the challenges of balancing personnel and resources, while honouring the Loreto mission:

> My dear Lord,
> Today I got a letter, or rather two letters from Mother Mary Kilian of Randwick telling me that the Little Sisters of the Poor had bought 'Aston Hall' and want to get possession as soon as possible. She asks me what she is to do under the circumstances .... If the Convent the Sisters are in is taken from them & there is no other place for them to go – it would seem as if God wished them to work for Him elsewhere, and certainly there is work for them to do in the other Loreto Convents whose members are at present overworked; and Rev. Mother of Rathfarnham cannot give us any more help .... She tells me so in a letter I got from her today ....We are all praying very earnestly to know what is best to do.

Whatever Your Eminence tells me to do, that I will do – if possible believing it to be the Will of God in our regard. I have just sent a Telegram to Mother Mary Kilian, telling her to continue the school. I will write to her this mail and tell her I have left the issue in Your Eminence's hands ...[34]

Broadening horizons

Gonzaga Barry's initiatives in the 1890s suggest that somehow she was undeterred by interference from the hierarchy, or from the challenges posed by constant expansion. She was vocal in her support of the kindergarten movement at the turn of the century, and is numbered among the pioneers of the kindergarten education in Australia.[35] She also turned her attention to higher education for women. In 1895, Leo XIII had given permission to Catholics to attend the Universities of Oxford and Cambridge, 'provided the regular courses of lectures be established by Catholic Professors of philosophy, history and religion'.[36] That same year, Barry wrote to Sir Anthony Brownless, chancellor of the University of Melbourne, who was a regular visitor to Mary's Mount. Her letter indicated her appetite for higher education for women, and for their professional training as teachers:

> Dear Sir Anthony Brownless
> I do not know if you remember my writing to you some time ago about a Catholic Hostel in connection with the University. His Grace the Archbishop [Archbishop Dr Carr] was spoken to regarding it by the Superior of the Loreto Convent, Albert Park, and I understand from her that His Grace was very favourably inclined towards it, but in a letter I received from him later, he says he fears 'it would excite adverse criticism', and be a failure. He rather recommends the young ladies to lodge wherever they like and attend the University or our schools. They will not do this I feel quite certain ...

The letter continued with her sketch of her own plans to establish a house under the care of her own sister, Miss Barry, and a Mrs Murtagh, sister of the late Bishop O'Connor, in East Melbourne, where two or three young lady students might stay whilst in pursuit of university studies. She continued:

> Whether it comes to anything or not, we intend this year, D.V. to take a new step in advance for the good of our young people here, both Nuns and Pupils, and we have invited Miss Bell from Cambridge to come here and assist us to establish the newest and best methods in our High and Primary Schools.... I also send a copy of Miss Bell's last letter to me. She entertains very large ideas of our future Catholic Ladies College ...[37]

Barbara Bell arrived in Melbourne late in 1895 to work alongside the Loreto Sisters, and later was also to lecture at the Central Catholic Teachers College, established in Melbourne in 1906. In that year the state of Victoria introduced compulsory registration for teachers. Barbara Bell was seconded to the first Board of Examiners. Archbishop Carr of Melbourne, fearful of any initiative that would encourage Catholic women to study at the university, did not hesitate to ask Barry for nuns to administer the college. She agreed to this, albeit reluctantly, given the difficulties in providing personnel for her own schools. The Central Catholic Teachers' College was placed under the leadership of Mother Hilda Benson and Miss Bell. Their task was to establish a diploma course in education and prepare student teachers, and nuns, for registration qualifications. An innovation in its time, the training college enjoyed an excellent reputation until its demise in 1924 when other religious orders made the decision to establish their own.

In the matter of the provision of university accommodation for women, it fell to Barry's successor, Mother Stanislaus Mulhall, to respond to the request of the Melbourne archdiocese in 1917 that Loreto administer the first residence for Catholic women at the University of Melbourne. St Mary's Hall was in Parkville, a mile from the university campus. It was opened officially in March 1918 as an affiliation of Newman College, the Jesuit college for young Catholic gentlemen. It was to take another fifty years for St Mary's to receive permission from the archbishop and his fellow bishops to move to the site directly adjacent to the university and Newman College. In March 1966, St Mary's became a college in its own right, affiliated by statute to the university.

In a letter to a Loreto friend thirty years after Barry's death, Barbara Bell reflected on her legacy:

> [Mother Gonzaga's] life was full of incidents which were history-making .... She was outstandingly progressive in many ways. It was through her initiative that a big impetus was given to (1) Victorian & (2) Tasmanian Catholic education in the opening years of our twentieth century ... Mother Barry with her usual foresight saw the advantages of [teacher] training [for women and nuns]. She secured one of the Catholic Diplomée [from the University of Cambridge] for Mary's Mount, for 1896, 1897, and set aside six of her young Nuns for a two-year'[*sic*] course of Training. Archbishop Delaney, during a visit to Ballarat, realized what such a Course would mean to the Nuns in his Archdiocese and obtained for them a three-year' course. The good results of this latter induced Archbishop Carr to do the same thing for his Nuns. This widespread impetus to Education was really due to M. M. Gonzaga's initiative – a fact unknown to many ...[38]

Gonzaga Barry remembered

Over the final months of 1914 and into the beginnings of 1915, Barry's life was fading. Letters came from all over the world; to many she made reply but many she had to leave for others. One letter that she insisted on writing was her final 'Mother's Letter' for the 1915 *Eucalyptus Blossoms* which went to press in February, immediately prior to her death:

> Dearest Children,
> It is now twenty-nine years since the Blossoms began its career. Seeing, even at that time, that it was impossible to keep up regular individual correspondence, owing to your numbers having so much increased, I made a promise that as long as I was able I would write in the Eucalyptus Blossoms a yearly letter addressed in general to all. That promise I have kept, whether in the Old Country or the New, whether on sea or land. At the same time, I reminded you that if you were in any personal trouble or distress I would do my best to help you; that promise I think I have fulfilled also. The time has now come when I must say farewell ...[39]

Today the Chapel at Loreto Mary's Mount, built under the vigilant eye of the school's founder, continues to be used by the school for special liturgies. Weddings are celebrated there, as are jubilees and funerals. To the right of the front entrance, around a path and across the garden, there is an enclosure: within it a gravestone and the grave of Gonzaga Barry, founding Superior of Loreto in Australia. On a stone opposite are inscribed the names of the pioneering Sisters who accompanied her on that first journey from Ireland. Annually the gardens are opened to the public. Visitors who enter the front gates and walk up the driveway will see near the front door a plaque inscribed with the words of Gonzaga Barry:

> *Cultivate large-mindedness; let there be nothing petty and narrow in your views, judgments and opinions.*[40]

Notes

1. The Abbey and the Institute were originally known as 'Loretto', but by the end of the nineteenth century the name was spelled 'Loreto'. Only in North America, for legal reasons, was the spelling 'Loretto' retained. Throughout this chapter, 'Loreto' has been used.
2. Mother Gonzaga Barry to Loreto Superiors, December 1914, in Mother M. Francis Tobin, *Mother M. Gonzaga Barry IBVM: Her Life and Letters*, MS in 4 vols (1923), Vol. I, 448.
3. For a study of the IBVM in Australia, see Mary Ryllis Clark, *Loreto in Australia* (Sydney: University of New South Wales Press, 2010).
4. See Ronald Fogarty, *Catholic Education in Australia, 1806–1950* (Melbourne: Melbourne University Press, 1959), 264. See also Clark, *Loreto in Australia*, 6.

5 For a history of the founding of the Loreto order in Ireland, see anon., *Joyful Mother of Children: Mother Frances Mary Teresa Ball, by a Loreto Sister* (Dublin: Gill and Macmillan, 1961). The first Loreto convent in Ireland was at Loreto Abbey, Rathfarnham, Dublin. It is referred to, in this chapter, as Loreto Rathfarnham.
6 Bishop Michael O'Connor to Mother Scholastica Somers, 29 December 1874, Loreto Central and Irish Province Archives, Dublin; IBVM Archives Dublin, item 2/55/C2/22 (see also Loreto Province Archives Ballarat, series 344, item 2-002).
7 Mother Gonzaga Barry, MS retreat notes, Rathfarnham, 24 April 1875, Loreto Province Archives Ballarat, series 17, item 36.
8 Mother Gonzaga Barry, MS diary of the voyage to Australia, 1875, IBVM Archives Dublin, item GB/DI/1.
9 Tobin, *Mother M. Gonzaga Barry*, Vol. I, 58.
10 For a vivid account of the experiences of the Loreto community as they settled in Ballarat, see Clark, *Loreto in Australia*.
11 In numerous letters negotiating initiatives as requested by bishops, Gonzaga reiterates the desire that where there are fee-paying schools, there should be free schools subsidized by them: in her terms, 'schools for the poor'. A clear expression of this desire is in a letter to the archbishop of Sydney, Cardinal Moran, in response to his request for nuns and his idea of his wishes in their regard: 'I never like to see a Loreto Convent without a school for the Poor'; Mother Gonzaga Barry, letter to Cardinal Moran, 21 May 1891, Loreto Province Archives Ballarat, series 210, item 252.
12 Mother Gonzaga Barry, Mary's Mount, Ballarat, to Mother Scholastica Somers, 27 December 1875, IBVM Archives Dublin (also Loreto Province Archives Ballarat, series 344, item 2-008).
13 Mother Gonzaga Barry to Mother Scholastica Somers, c. 1876, IBVM Archives Dublin (also Loreto Province Archives Ballarat, series 344, item 2-012).
14 Ibid.
15 Mother Gonzaga Barry, Loreto Convent Mary's Mount, to Mother Scholastica Somers, 6 August 1876, IBVM Archives Dublin (also Loreto Province Archives Ballarat, series 344, item 2-020).
16 Mother Gonzaga Barry, Loreto Convent [Mary's Mount], Ballarat, to Mother Scholastica Somers, 19 March 1878, IBVM Archives Dublin (also Loreto Province Archives, series 344, item 2-028).
17 Mother Gonzaga Barry, Loreto Convent Mary's Mount, to Mother Angela, 14 May 1879, IBVM Archives Dublin (also Loreto Province Archives Ballarat, series 344, item 2-030).
18 Prospectus for Catholic Training College for Teachers, Loreto Province Archives Ballarat, series 127, item 8.
19 Talk given by Mother Hilda Benson recorded in the Annals of Loreto Convent Dawson Street, Loreto Province Archives, series 33, item 15, in which she quotes from Félix Dupanloup, *The Child* (1875), trans. Kate Anderson [Boston, MA: Thomas B. Noonan, 1875], 16.) Monseigneur Dupanloup (1802–78) was a French cleric and bishop: a polemicist of the day with views on education, among many other matters, believing successful education should be a matter for mental activity rather than the 'injection' of knowledge.
20 Benson, Annals of Loreto Convent Dawson Street.
21 *Geelong Advertiser* (3 December 1883), 3.
22 *Newcastle Morning Herald and Miners Advocate* (4 December 1883), 4.
23 Bella Guerin, editorial, *Eucalyptus Blossoms*, 1 (1886), 4.

24 Mother Gonzaga Barry, 'Mother's Letter', *Eucalyptus Blossoms* (June 1886), 3.
25 *Eucalyptus Blossoms* (June 1889), 46. Sloyd was a hand-craft based system of education originating in Sweden in the 1860s. Gonzaga Barry was amongst the first to introduce it to Australia.
26 *Eucalyptus Blossoms* (December 1890), 27–8.
27 Lucy Mooney, letter to 'Children of Loreto all over the world', *Eucalyptus Blossoms* (December 1886), 38.
28 Marie Paur, IBVM, Superioress of the English Institute in Bavaria, to Gonzaga Barry, courtesy of Mother Boniface Volker, 20 July 1886. Translated from original German for the recipient by Mother Boniface Volker, Loreto Province Archives Ballarat, series 16, item 2.
29 In the forty years of Barry's leadership, Sisters of the First Degree – those capable of both teaching and community leadership – numbered, at most, a little under 200, and lay Sisters (Second Degree) 55. Loreto Province Archives Ballarat, statistical sources. From the mid 1890s Gonzaga urges her communities everywhere to write letters, one to another: to be 'united by correspondence'. On 31 December 1896: 'It is not good to get out of SIGHT and out of MIND'; letter to 'The Mothers and Sisters' in Randwick, Loreto Province Archives Ballarat, series 210, item 234.
30 Visitation book, Loreto Convent Portland, 6 May 1908. Loreto Province Archives Ballarat, series 37, item 085.
31 Visitation book, Loreto Convent Normanhurst, 28 October 1908. Loreto Province Archives Ballarat, series 289, item 002.
32 Patrick Moran, archbishop of Sydney, to Xaviera Fallon, Presbytery, 25 March 1885. Loreto Province Archives Ballarat, series 344, item 2-031C.
33 Gonzaga Barry to Mothers, 29 June 1887, Loreto Province Archives Ballarat, series 210, item 219.
34 Gonzaga Barry, Loreto Convent Adelaide Terrace, to Patrick Moran, archbishop of Sydney, 23 July 1901. Sydney Archdiocesan Archives (also Loreto Province Archives Ballarat, series 210, item 315).
35 Letter to Dr Graber, Inspector of Catholic Schools in Melbourne, quoted in Tobin, *Mother M. Gonzaga Barry*, Vol. III, 203–4. For further reference, see Clark, *Loreto in Australia*, 64–6.
36 Benedict Neenan, *Thomas Verner Moore: Psychiatrist, Educator and Monk* (New York: Paulist Press, 2000), 84.
37 Gonzaga Barry to Sir Anthony Brownless, 22 July 1895, Loreto Province Archives Ballarat, series 210, item 278.
38 Barbara Bell to Mother Antonia Good, 23 September 1947, Loreto Province Archives Ballarat, series 126, item 11.
39 *Eucalyptus Blossoms* (February 1915).
40 Inscription on the plaque taken from 'Mother's Letter', *Eucalyptus Blossoms* (December 1897).

Index

Page numbers in *italics* are figures; with 'n' are notes; with 't' are tables.

Abélard, Pierre 16
Aboriginal people, education of 4, 46, 160, 162, 170–1, 176
abuse, and women religious 25
Africa, and Sister-physicians 68, 69, 70
Aikenhead, Mary 79
amalgamation, and Presentation Order 145–55
America *see* United States
Angela de Merici 17
Anglo-Saxon foundations 14
anonymity, and translation of French texts 184, 187, 190–1
Apostolic Visitations, United States 24–5
Aquinas, Thomas 9, 164
Arnaud, M. Angelique 19
Austin, J. L. 161
Australia: Loreto Sisters 199–212; Sisters of Joseph of the Sacred Heart 25
authenticity 174
authority: of the Church 21, 163, 164, 175; conflict with Church 20, 21, 139, 151; in the convent 66; and Sisters in medicine 64, 66, 70–1; of teacher training 127, 130; and women in early Christianity 7, 11, 15
autonomy 4, 10, 106, 108, 155
Aylward, Margaret 79, 136–7

Bailly, M. Cecilia 104
Ball, M. Teresa (Frances) 48, 79, 200
Barat, St Madeleine Sophie 1, 20
Barbier, Euphrasie (Marie du Coeur-de-Jésus) 161, 162–3
Barré, Nicolas 33–4

Barry, M. Gonzaga 4–5, 199–202, 206–12
Beauregard, Father 163
Beckert, Sven 45
Beguines 16–17
Bell, Barbara 210–11
Benedictines 14
Benson, M. Hilda 203, 204, 211
Berta of Avenay 14
'Bible war' 136
biography 6; translation of religious 187–8
birth control 63
bishops, and women religious 11–12
Black, Errol 172
Blauvelt congregation 102, 106; and the Dominican Sisters 117, 130, 131; and the Presentation Sisters 135–6, 139, 149, *see also* amalgamation
bodies, women's 8–9, 13
Brandon (Manitoba) (St Augustine Convent) 160–1, 172–5, 176
Brigid of Kildare, St 14–15
Brónach of Kilbroney 14
Bruno-Jofré, Rosa 4

Canada *see* Loretto Sisters; Sisters of Our Lady of the Missions (RNDM); Sisters of St Joseph
Carolingian foundations 14
Carroll, M. Teresa Austin 188–9, 190, 192, 193, 195
Catechism 19, 84, 91, 92
Catholic culture 52, 79, 111, 179n33, 185, 195
central novitiates 144, 145, 149, 156

Chambers, Catherine 207
Chapter of Faults 33, 122
Charitable Mistresses 34
chastity 62–3, 72, 184, 191–2
Children of Mary sodality 36
Christian Education of Youth (Pius XI) 164–5
Chrysostom, John 7
Cistercians 14
Clare, M. Francis (Margaret Anne Cusack) 187, 191
Clare, Sister (from Loreto Hall) 129–30
Clavin, Patricia 45
Clear, Caitríona 78, 191, 194, 195
Clement V 17
Clondalkin, Presentation Convent (PCC) 92
clubs, Catholic 52–3
Codd, Bishop William 145–6
Code of Canon Law 21, 63
colleges for women: Irish Presentation Sisters 138–44; New Zealand Dominican 3, 119, 129–30; Toronto 44, 50–7; Woman's Medical College (WMC) (Pennsylvania) 3, 60, 65–7, 69, 69t
College Yearbook, The 52
Collins, Jenny 3
Come Follow Me and Forsake Temptation (O'Donoghue) 33
community organization 10–11
conflict: with clergy 4, 5, 11–12, 14–15, 18–20, 25–6; with doctors 70, 71
Congregation of the Sisters of St Joseph (CSJ) 2, 43–4; in America 103; Canadian convent schools/colleges 50, 52; and education in Canada 49–50
Conrad of Marchtal, Abbot 8
Constitutions 10, 21; and Presentation amalgamations 153–4
Convent of Our Lady of the Snows 166–7
convent schools 2, 31, 32, 39, 50–1, 80–1; and history of translation 184, 193; Loreto in Australia 202–6, 208–11; Ontario 49; Presentation Order in Ireland 85, 86, 135, 137, 138, 140, 142–3; Sisters of the Infant Jesus at Drishane 36–8, *see also* colleges for women
Cormack, M. Francis 86

Corneille, Anne 34
Council of Trent 12
Cronin, Michael 192
Cross, Maurice 81
cultural chauvinism 106–8
cultural eclecticism 104–6
cultural transfer/exchange 42n28
culture, Catholic 185
curricula: music in St Michael's Academy (Brandon) 174–5; Presentation Order 89–90; Toronto convent academies 50
Cusack, Margaret Anne (M. Francis Clare) 187, 191, 193
Cuthburga 45

Daughters of Charity 18, 63, 79, 184
Dean, M. Pauline 69; *Primary Health Care Links* 71–2
Dease, M. Teresa 48, 57
Deasy, M. Vincent 188, 192
De Charbonnel, Armand 48–9, 51
De La Salle Brothers 34, 163
Dengel, M. Anna 60, 63–4, 65, 72
Deschamp, Marie 34
devotional literature, translation of 185–6, 195
Dewey, John 179n37
Dillon, Ann Eliza 103
Directory, Presentation 84, 85, 88–9, 90–1
discipline in schools 125
Dobbins, Mary 105
Dolan, Jay P. 68–9
Dominican (OP) order 3, 78, 79; oral histories of teachers 124–7; teacher training 117–32
Dries, Angelyn 61
Drishane (Ireland) convent 2, 31–40, 35
Duggan, Cornelius 35
Dunne, Veronica 166
Duval, Françoise 34

Ebba 14
Eck, Diana, *New Religious America, A* 111–12
enclosure: Presentation Order 84, 136, 137–8, 139, 145, 155; and the Ursulines 83
England 14–15, 34, 48, 169, 170, 172
Etheldreda 14

ethnicity 5; and America 100–4, 106–8, 111–12; and Canada 173, 176
Eucalyptus Blossoms 205–8, 212
Eve 2, 7–8

Fahey, Tony 78
Faithful Companions of Jesus 82, 172, 184
families of women religious 11–12
Fara of Brie 14
Faudoas, M. de 34
feminism 5, 23–5, 54–5
Fidei donum (Pius XII) 68
fidelity 192
Field, M. de Sales 203
First Vatican Council 20–1
Fogarty, M. Patricia 38
Fontbonne, M. Delphine 49
Fontbonne, M. St John 49
Foreign Mission Sisters of St Dominic *see* Maryknoll Sisters
France, and the Sisters of the Infant Jesus 33–4
Franciscan Missionaries of the Sacred Heart 105
Franciscan Sisters 106–7
Franciscans of Perpetual Adoration 105
Francis I 23
Free Teaching Institute 178n26
Frideswide 45
Fulbert of Chartes 16
Furlong, Bishop Thomas 201

Gates, Sister Jane 68
gender, in Christianity 2, 6–9
Gertrud of Nivelles 14
Gillespie, Eliza (M. Angela) 104
Gill, M. Gabriel 120
Good Shepherd Sisters 34
Goodson, Ivor 32
graduates, of Canadian women's colleges 54–6
Grand Clairière (Manitoba) (Our Lady of the Snows Convent) 160, 166–70, *168*, 175
Grogan, M. Karen 36–7, 38
'growing vocations' 32
Guerin, Bella 205, 206
Guérin, St Théodore 104
Guyart, M. de l'Incarnation 46

habit, religious 13, 22, 37, 70, 121, 123

Hackett, Mary 193–4
hedge schools 80, 136
Héloïse 16
Henni, Bishop John Martin 110–11
heresy 17, 119
Hilda 14
Hildegard of Bingen 14–16
history, translation from French 187–8
Hobsbawm, Eric 161–2
Holy Heart of the Mary Convent (Saskatchewan) 160, *168*, 170–2, 175–6
Hoy, Suellen 78
Humanae vitae (Paul VI) 23

IBVM (Institute of the Blessed Virgin Mary) *see* Loreto/Loretto Sisters
identity 72–3, 122, 130–1; American Catholic 3, 99–112, 101t; French Catholic 165–6, 170, 173–4, 175
Ignatiev, Noel, *How the Irish Became White* 105
illocutionary force 161, 162, 169, 173, 175
India, and Sister-doctors 66–7
indigenous population, education of 4, 46, 160, 162, 170–1, 176
Inquisition 18
Institute of the Blessed Virgin Mary (IBVM) *see* Loreto/Loretto Sisters
Intermediate Education (Ireland) Act (1878) 82
invisibility 184, 191, 194
Ireland; Celtic foundations 14; Dominican sisters 78, 79, 81, 117; education in 77–82, 135, 136–7, 142–3; Loreto Sisters 2, 184, 186; training for Sister-physicians 64, 71; translations from French 183–96, *see also* Presentation Order
Irish poem 7–8
Iriye, Akira 15
Ita of Killeedy 45

Jansenism 19
Jerome 13
Jesuits (Society of Jesus) 34, 46
John XXIII 21
Juana de la Cruz 19

Kealy, Máire 36, 78
Kelly, James 77
Kelly, Jane 4

Keogh, Dermot 148
Kilroy, Phil 1–2
King, M. Catherine Maria 85

Lac Croche (Crooked Lake) (Holy Heart of Mary Convent) 160, *168*, 170–2, 175–6
Lalinsky, M. Helen 60, 64–7
Langevin, Adélard 160, 161, 163, 165, 167–8, 174
language: in Canadian schools 160, 173; and identity 100–4, *see also* translations from French
Larkin, Emmet 36
LaVerdier, Claudette 111
Leadership Conference of Women Religious (LCWR) 24
Leo XIII 21, 139, 210
Lestocq, Catherine 34
Life of St Elizabeth of Hungary (Montalembert) 194
Lilies, The 52
Loreto Abbey Mary's Mount (Ballarat) 202, 204, 205–6, 208
Loreto Hall (Auckland) 3, 129–30
Loreto/Loretto Sisters 17–18, 44, 45, 47–9; Australia (Loreto) 199–212; Canadian convent schools/colleges (Loretto) 51–7; Ireland (Loreto) 184, 186; USA (Loretto) 101
Luddy, Maria 78, 97n61
Lunney, Sheila 189
Lynch, M. Rose 110

McAuley, Catherine 79, 188
McCarthy, M. Borgia 186
McCarthy, M. Vincent 127
MacCurtain, Margaret 64
McDonald, M. Maria 128
MacDonald, Simon, 'Transnational History' 45
McGroarty, Susan (M. Julia) 104
MacKillop, Mary 25
Mackle, M. Patricia 129
McLoughlin, M. Isabella 85
magisterium 164, 175, 178n25
Magray, Mary Peckham 78, 185, 195, 196
Malaysia (Malaya), and the Infant Jesus Sisters 34–5
Manitoba School Question 165, 176n5
Marguerite de Porete 17

Marieval Indian Residential School 170
Martin, M. 61
Maryknoll Sisters (Foreign Mission Sisters of St Dominic) 61, 68, 70, 111
Mary Magdalene 9–10, 23
Mary of the Holy Trinity 164, 170–1
Mary, Virgin 9–10, 23
Mayo Clinic 109
Médaille, Jean Pierre 49
Medical Missionaries of Mary (MMM) 61, 64, 70, 72
Medical Mission Sisters (MMS) 60–1, 64–7, 68–9, 70
memory, institutional 121
Mercy Sisters *see* Sisters of Mercy
Milan, Michèle 4
misogyny, historical 10–13, 16
missionaries 2; and the IBVM 48; and Sister-physicians 60–73; and the Sisters of the Infant Jesus 31–40
Missionary Oblate Sisters of the Sacred Heart and Mary Immaculate 161, 171–2, 173
Mistresses of Schools 120, 125
Mitchell, Tom 172
MMM *see* Medical Missionaries of Mary (MMM)
MMS *see* Medical Mission Sisters (MMS)
modernism 160, 162, 164–5, 178n27
monitors, Presentation schools 138, 141t
Monnina of Killeavy 14
Montalembert, Charles Forbes de, Comte de 194
Montessori teaching 123–4, 126
Mooney, Lucy 207
Moran, Archbishop Patrick 209
Morris, M. Winefride 128–9
motherhood 9
'Mother's Letter' (Barry) 206
Mulally, M. Teresa 86
Mullingar Sisters 147

Nagle, Nano 79, 82–3, 86, 93
Nain, Père Charles 35
National Education Board (Ireland) 135, 136–7, 142–3
National Teacher's Organisation (Ireland) 141–2
neo-scholasticism 164
neo-Thomism 164

New Education 179n37
New Religious America, A (Eck) 111–12
New Zealand, and the Dominican Sisters 117–32
Noelle, M. St Marie 40
Nolan, M. Estelle 53–4
Normae 63
novitiate training 154–5; Drishane 37, *see also* central novitiates
Nun of Kenmare 187
nuns, defined 42n9
'Nun Study' 44
nursing 46, 71

Oblate Sisters of Providence 102–3
O'Connor, Anne V. 184
O'Connor, Bishop Dr Michael 200
O'Donoghue, M. St Teresa 39
O'Donoghue, Tom 77–8; *Come Follow Me and Forsake Temptation* 33
O'Flynn, M. Nancy 37, 38–9
oral histories 2, 32–3, 117; of Dominican Sisters 124–9
Order of St Francis 45–6
Order of St Ursula *see* Ursulines
O'Reilly, Louise 4
Osterhammel, Jürgen 45
O'Sullivan, Bishop Charles 145, 146, 154
Our Lady of the Snows Convent (Manitoba) 160, 166–70, *168*, 175

Pastor aeternus 20
patriarchy 10–13
Paul, Apostle 7
Paul VI 23
PBVM *see* Presentation Order
Peter the Venerable 16
Phelan, D. S. 192, 193
Phillips, Paul 171
Pius IX 20
Pius XI 163, 164–5
Pius XII, *Fidei donnum* 68
Poor Clares 18, 187
postulancy 37, 122–3
Power, Bishop Michael 48
Power, M. Augustine 86
prejudice 109, 110
Presentation Order (PBVM) 77–8, 81, 82–5, 93–4, 135–6; and amalgamation 146–55; curriculum 89–90; enclosure 137–8; and episcopal decrees 139–44; and legislation from Rome 139; management 83–4; religious instruction 90–3; schoolhouses 86–7; school organization 87–9; teacher training 138, 139–44; and translation 184, 187–8
professions, and women graduates 55–6
Province of the Felicians 107

qualification of teachers 123; and the Presentation Order 81, 88, 93, 142–4, 155; Teacher's Certificate 123, 125, 131

Radegund of Poitiers 14
Raftery, Deirdre 2, 31, 78
Rainbow, The 51, 53, 54
Raughter, Rosemary 78
Reception 37
recruitment to religious life, Drishane convent 36–8
Religious Hospitallers of St Augustine (Hospitallers of Dieppe) 46
religious life texts, translation from French 187
Religious of the Sacred Heart 107
restrictions on Sister-physicians 62–4
RNDM *see* Sisters of Our Lady of the Missions (Religieuses de Notre Dame des Missions (RNDM))
Robert, Dana L. 61
Rogers, M. Joseph (Mollie) 61, 111
Rule of Enclosure: and the Presentation Order 84, 136, 137–8, 139, 145, 155; and the Ursulines 83
Rule of Life 10, 21

St Augustine's Parish school (Brandon) 173–4
St Michael's Academy (Brandon) 174
St Michael's College 51
St Michael's Hospital 50
Salaberga of Laon 14
Samthann of Clonbroney 45
School Sisters of Notre Dame 105
School Sisters of St Francis 105–6, 107
Second Vatican Council 2, 21–2, 26, 132, 156; and feminism 23; and women as clergy 27n20
Servants of the Immaculate Heart of Mary (IHM) 102–3
Sikes, Pat 32

Silver, Harold 31
simple vows 42n9, 133n15, 139, 144, 147–8, 155
simplicity 191–3
Singapore 34
Sister Formation Movement 68
Sister-physicians 3, 60–1; and the Church 62–4; historiography 61–2; medical education 64–7; medical missions 67–72
Sister-professors 53–4, 57
Sisters, defined 42n9
Sisters of Charity 101, 184
Sisters of the Holy Cross 104
Sisters of the Infant Jesus 2, 31–40
Sisters of Joseph of the Sacred Heart 25
Sisters of Mercy 81, 101, 109, 138, 184, 188–9, 190, 193
Sisters of Notre Dame de Namur (SND) 103–4
Sisters of Our Lady of the Missions (Religieuses de Notre Dame des Missions (RNDM)) 160–1; founding 161–6
Sisters of the Presentation of the Blessed Virgin Mary *see* Presentation Order
Sisters of St Joseph *see* Congregation of the Sisters of St Joseph (CSJ)
Sisters of St Joseph nof the Third Order of St Francis (SSJ-TOSF) 106
Sister-teachers 50, *see also* Dominican (OP) Order; Presentation Order
Skinner, Quentin 161
Slevin, M. Hannah 36, 37–8
Smith, Susan 164
Smyth, Elizabeth M. 2, 4, 121
Smyth, M. Paula 37
SND *see* Sisters of Notre Dame de Namur (SND)
Snowdon, David 44
sobriety 191–3
social imaginaries 161
society, and women 7
Society of Jesus (Jesuits) 34, 46
Society of Mary 118
Society of the Sacred Heart (RSCJ) 1, 20
solemn vows 42n9, 84, 135, 139, 147, 155, 171
Somers, M. Scholastica 200
Spouse of Christ, The (Clare) 187
Stanley Letter 79–80
Stella Niagara Franciscans 107

synods: Maynooth 140, 147, 151; of St Patrick's College 139–40, 151; of Thurles 36

Taylor, Charles 161, 174
teacher education/training: Australian Loreto Sisters 204–5, 208, 211; Irish Presentation Order 139–44; New Zealand Dominican Sisters 117–32; Toronto 50–1
Teacher's Certificate ('Teacher's C') 123, 125, 131
Teresa of Avila 18
Terry, M. Joan 126
Tertullian 7
Tetta 45
Thompson, Margaret Susan 3, 122
Timpany, M. Clare 125–6
'transforming power' 196
translations from French 183–5, 189; devotional/spiritual literature 185–7; history/religious biography 187–8; importance of 189–90; religious life 187; and the Sisters of Mercy 188–9
'Transnational History' (MacDonald) 45
transnationalism 2, 5, 32, 45; Sisters of the Infant Jesus 31–40; Toronto Convent Academies 43–57; and translation of spiritual literature 185, 190
Tridentine Catholicism 164
Trinitarianism 164

ultramontanism 164
United States: Apostolic Visitations 24–5; and Catholic identity 99–112; and Sister-physicians 61, 62, 63
Ursulines (Order of St Ursula) 17, 19, 46, 83; languages 102; translation from French 183, 184, 186, 187, 193

Vatican II *see* Second Vatican Council
Vaughan, Megan, *Curing Their Ills* 61–2
veiling 13
Veuillot, Louis 187
Vincent de Paul, St 63
virginity 13
virgin/whore dichotomy 2, 9–10, 23
Volker, Boniface 207
vows: simple 42n9, 133n15, 139, 144, 147–8, 155;
solemn 42n9, 84, 135, 139, 147, 155, 171

Wall, Barbra Mann 3
Walter, M. Salesia 106–7
Ward, Mary 17, 18, 47–8, 207
Whelan, Irene 136
Windle, M. Imelda 126
witchcraft 17

Women's Medical College (WMC) 3, 60, 65–7, 69, 69t

Xavier, Francis 34

Young, Florence (M. Benedict) 67–8

eBooks
from Taylor & Francis

Helping you to choose the right eBooks for your Library

Add to your library's digital collection today with Taylor & Francis eBooks. We have over 50,000 eBooks in the Humanities, Social Sciences, Behavioural Sciences, Built Environment and Law, from leading imprints, including Routledge, Focal Press and Psychology Press.

Choose from a range of subject packages or create your own!

Benefits for you
- Free MARC records
- COUNTER-compliant usage statistics
- Flexible purchase and pricing options
- All titles DRM-free.

Benefits for your user
- Off-site, anytime access via Athens or referring URL
- Print or copy pages or chapters
- Full content search
- Bookmark, highlight and annotate text
- Access to thousands of pages of quality research at the click of a button.

Free Trials Available
We offer free trials to qualifying academic, corporate and government customers.

eCollections

Choose from over 30 subject eCollections, including:

Archaeology	Language Learning
Architecture	Law
Asian Studies	Literature
Business & Management	Media & Communication
Classical Studies	Middle East Studies
Construction	Music
Creative & Media Arts	Philosophy
Criminology & Criminal Justice	Planning
Economics	Politics
Education	Psychology & Mental Health
Energy	Religion
Engineering	Security
English Language & Linguistics	Social Work
Environment & Sustainability	Sociology
Geography	Sport
Health Studies	Theatre & Performance
History	Tourism, Hospitality & Events

For more information, pricing enquiries or to order a free trial, please contact your local sales team: www.tandfebooks.com/page/sales

www.tandfebooks.com